The Arbitrator's Discretion in Conflict of Laws Matters

Article 1(1) of the CISG in International Arbitration

Inaugural-Dissertation
zur Erlangung des akademischen Grades eines
Doktors der Rechte durch die Juristische Fakultät der
Westfälischen Wilhelms-Universität Münster

vorgelegt von:

Anna M. Lohmann

Dekan:	Prof. Dr. Matthias Casper
Erstberichterstatter:	Prof. Dr. Gerald Mäsch
Zweitberichterstatter:	Prof. Dr. Bettina Heiderhoff
Tag der mündlichen Prüfung:	13. Juli 2021

Streitbeilegung und Streitvermeidung im Zivilrecht –
Schriftenreihe des Munich Center for Dispute Resolution

Edited by Beate Gsell, Wolfgang Hau and
Caroline Meller-Hannich

Volume 10

Anna M. Lohmann

The Arbitrator's Discretion in Conflict of Laws Matters

Article 1(1) of the CISG in International Arbitration

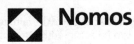

The Deutsche Nationalbibliothek lists this publication in the
Deutsche Nationalbibliografie; detailed bibliographic data
are available on the Internet at http://dnb.d-nb.de

a.t.: Münster, Univ., Diss., 2021

ISBN   978-3-8487-8476-9 (Print)
        978-3-7489-2856-0 (ePDF)

British Library Cataloguing-in-Publication Data
A catalogue record for this book is available from the British Library.

ISBN   978-3-8487-8476-9 (Print)
        978-3-7489-2856-0 (ePDF)

Library of Congress Cataloging-in-Publication Data
Lohmann, Anna M.
The Arbitrator's Discretion in Conflict of Laws Matters
Article 1(1) of the CISG in International Arbitration
Anna M. Lohmann
196 pp.
Includes bibliographic references.

ISBN   978-3-8487-8476-9 (Print)
        978-3-7489-2856-0 (ePDF)

Onlineversion
Nomos eLibrary

D 6

1st Edition 2022
© Nomos Verlagsgesellschaft, Baden-Baden, Germany 2022. Overall responsibility
for manufacturing (printing and production) lies with Nomos Verlagsgesellschaft mbH
& Co. KG.

This work is subject to copyright. All rights reserved. No part of this publication may be
reproduced or transmitted in any form or by any means, electronic or mechanical,
including photocopying, recording, or any information storage or retrieval system,
without prior permission in writing from the publishers. Under § 54 of the German
Copyright Law where copies are made for other than private use a fee is payable to
"Verwertungsgesellschaft Wort", Munich.

No responsibility for loss caused to any individual or organization acting on or refraining
from action as a result of the material in this publication can be accepted by Nomos
or the author.

I want to thank Prof. Dr. Gerald Mäsch and Prof. Dr. Bettina Heiderhoff, not only for being my supervisor and reviewers, but for planting a seed and encouraging me to tackle this project in the first place.
My wonderful parents Lynn and Ulrich, who I can always lean on and who provided endless supplies of love and counsel while I was working on this thesis. My mother, for elevating my writing through her patient proofreading.
Hugh Spitzer, who generously took the time to read a draft and gave valuable and kind feedback.
And finally, Johannes, who went above and beyond, gradually becoming an expert on the subject through countless late-night discussions, bringing structure into my thoughts and prodding me to think further and dig deeper.

Abbreviations

ABA J.	American Bar Association Journal
AEDIP	Anuario Español de Derecho internacional privado
Am. J. Comp. L.	American Journal of Comparative Law
Arb. Int.	Arbitration International
Asian Int'l Arb. J.	Asian International Arbitration Journal
B.U. Int'l L.	Boston University International Law Journal
BB	Betriebs-Berater
BTWR	Beiträge zum Transnationalen Wirtschaftsrecht
Chi. J. Int'l L.	Chicago Journal of International Law
Colum. J. Transnat'l L.	Columbia Journal of Transnational Law
Cornell Int'l L.J.	Cornell International Law Journal
ed.	edition, editor
ERCL	European Review of Contract Law
Eur. J. L. Reform	European Journal of Law Reform
FS	Festschrift
Int'l & Comp.L.Q.	International & Comparative Law Quarterly
IPRax	Praxis des Internationalen Privat- und Verfahrensrechts
J. Int'l Arb.	Journal of International Arbitration
J.I.D.S.	Journal of International Dispute Settlement
J. Priv. Int.	Journal of Private International Law
JZ	JuristenZeitung
Law & Pol'y Int'l Bus.	Law and Policy in International Business
Mich. J. Int'l L.	Michigan Journal of International Law
NYC	New York Convention
p.	page
para.	paragraph
RabelsZ	Rabels Zeitschrift für ausländisches und internationales Privatrecht
RdC	Recueil des Cours
RHDI	Revue Hellenique de Droit International
RIW	Recht der Internationalen Wirtschaft

Abbreviations

Savigny-Zeitschrift	Zeitschrift der Savigny-Stiftung für Rechtsgeschichte
SchiedsVZ	Zeitschrift für Schiedsverfahren
Sec.	Section
U. Toronto L.J.	University of Toronto Law Journal
Unif. L. Rev.	Uniform Law Review
WAMR	World Arbitration & Mediation Review
Yale L.J.	Yale Law Journal

Table of Contents

Introduction   15
    I. Object of Inquiry   16
    II. Steps of Inquiry   19

§ 1. The CISG and International Commercial Arbitration   20

A. The CISG   20
    I. History   20
        1. ULF and ULIS   21
        2. CISG   23
    II. Nature   25
        a) Part of Domestic Legal Systems   26
        b) Independence from Domestic Legal System   27

B. The CISG in International Commercial Arbitration   29
    I. Compatibility of the CISG and International Commercial Arbitration   29
    II. Application by International Arbitration Tribunals   30

§ 2. Article 1(1) CISG – Rules of Application   33

A. Overview over the Provision   33
    I. Connections with Contracting States   34
    II. Further Requirements of Applicability   35
        1. Internationality   35
        2. Sale of Goods   36

B. Legal Nature   37
    I. Structure and Function of Conflict of Laws Rules   38
        1. Function   38
        2. Structure   40
    II. Article 1(1)(a) of the CISG   43
        1. Structure   43
        2. Function   45
            a) Conflict of Laws Analysis Not Superfluous   45
            b) Alternatives Test   47

Table of Contents

  III. Article 1(1)(b) of the CISG   49
    1. Ambiguous Wording   50
    2. Systematic Interpretation   52
      a) *Renvois* Within "the Rules of Private International Law"   52
      b) Effect of Article 95 Reservation   54
      c) Law Applicable to Opt-Out   58
        aa) Choice of Law   58
        bb) Applicable Law   61
      d) CISG Applicable as Domestic Law   64
    3. Conclusion   66
  IV. Consequences for Article 1(1) of the CISG as a Whole   67
    1. Structure   67
      a) Alternative Connecting Factors   67
      b) Unilaterality   68
    2. Effect   71

C. Conclusion   72

§ 3. Binding Effect of Article 1(1) in International Commercial Arbitration   73

A. Legal Framework of Arbitration Proceedings   75
  I. Overview over Potentially Applicable Laws and Rules   75
    1. Institutional Rules   75
    2. The Arbitral Seat and the *Lex Loci Arbitri*   76
    3. Recognition and Enforcement of Arbitration Awards   78
  II. The Localization Debate   79
    1. Localization   80
    2. Delocalization   81
    3. Discussion   83

B. Competence to Make Conflict Rules Applicable in International Commercial Arbitration   85
  I. Legislative Jurisdiction   86
    1. The Lotus Decision   86
    2. Genuine Link   87
    3. Treaty or Customary Law   89
  II. Arbitral Tribunals as "Quasi-Courts" of a State   91
    1. Theories Regarding the Nature of Arbitration   92
    2. Discussion   93
      a) Source of Power   94

b) Application of Law	98
aa) No Maintenance of the Law	98
bb) Application of Non-State Law or No Law	101
c) The Arbitral Award	103
3. Conclusion	106
III. Seat of Arbitration as Genuine Link	107
1. Territoriality	107
2. Party Choice	109
3. Conclusion	113
IV. Customary Law Basis for Arbitration-Specific Conflict Rule	113
1. State Practice	113
2. Opinio Iuris	116
a) New York Convention	117
b) *Travaux Préparatoires* of the UNCITRAL Model Law	119
3. Conclusion	121
V. Conclusion	121
C. Inapplicability of the Rome I Regulation in International Commercial Arbitration	122
I. No Intention of Application by Drafters	123
1. Exception Regarding "Arbitration Agreements"	123
2. Reference to "Court or Tribunal"	125
3. *Travaux Préparatoires* of the Rome Convention	127
II. Incompatibility with International Arbitration	128
1. Party Autonomy: Limitations to the Choice of Law	129
a) Choice of Conflict Rule	131
b) Choice of Non-State Law	131
c) Decisions *Ex Aequo et Bono*	133
2. Superfluous Protections for Weaker Parties	134
a) Consumer Protection	134
aa) ECJ Decisions	135
bb) Specialized Arbitration Procedures	137
b) Employee Protection	139
3. Incongruent System of Public Policy and Overriding Mandatory Rules	140
a) Public Policy	141
b) Overriding Mandatory Provisions	143
4. Forum Shopping	147
III. Conclusion	148

Table of Contents

D. Practical Freedom of Arbitrators to Determine Substantive Law	148
I. Methods Applied in Arbitral Practice	148
1. Voie Indirecte	149
a) Choice of Conflict of Laws Rules of a State	149
b) Cumulative Method	150
c) General Principles of Private International Law	151
2. Voie Directe	151
II. No Reviewability of Application of Private International Law	153
1. Review of Arbitral Awards	153
2. Individual Grounds for Annulment and Refusal of Recognition and Enforcement	155
a) Excess of Authority	155
b) Procedure	156
c) Public Policy	158
3. Conclusion	161
E. Application of the CISG as Non-State Law	161
F. Conclusion	164
§ 4. Application of Substantive Provisions of the CISG in International Commercial Arbitration	166
A. Binding Effect of Substantive Law Dependent on Party Choice	167
I. Historical Application of Law in Arbitration	167
II. Arbitration-Specific Modes of Decision	169
1. *Ex Aequo et Bono* and *Amiables Compositeurs*	170
2. Application of Non-State Law	171
3. Influence of Trade Usages	172
III. Decisions Based on Law	173
B. Reviewability	174
I. Reviewability of Substantive Law Application	175
1. Public Policy Violation	175
2. *Effet Utile* of European Law	176
II. Reviewability of Type of Decision	179
1. Procedural Mistake	179
2. Excess of Authority	181
3. Public Policy	182
III. Conclusion	183
C. Consequences for the Application of the CISG	183

Conclusion 185

Bibliography 187

Introduction

The world is becoming more connected, as evidenced by the constant growth in cross-border trade. In 2017, global trade was at its highest growth rate in six years regarding both volume and value.[1] But international trade has also become more diverse: domination of the top ten trading countries is being challenged by developing economies.[2] The share of world merchandise trade of developing economies has increased to 41 % and trade among them has grown, amounting to up to 50 % of their exports.[3]

Trading partners make agreements that are governed by laws and possibly give rise to disputes. The more States participate in international trade, the more diverse the legal cultural backgrounds of the participating parties and their expectations in regard to contractual agreements. This may constitute a barrier to parties wishing to enter into trade agreements with partners from unfamiliar corners of the world. There is the risk of ending up litigating a contract in a foreign court that applies foreign laws in a foreign language. The cost of preparing for such an eventuality can be prohibitively high for smaller market participants.

International trade without such a risk is possible, and the solution lies in neutral dispute resolution mechanisms and neutral laws. Neutral dispute resolution mechanisms can be found in international commercial arbitration, while an example for a neutral law is the United Nations Convention on Contracts for the International Sale of Goods ("CISG" or "Convention").

International commercial arbitration enables parties to agree to arbitrate their dispute instead of entering into proceedings before a domestic court. The parties can choose their arbitrator or arbitrators and also, to a great extent, the procedure. There are arbitral institutions all around the world, offering arbitration rules and often also infrastructure for arbitration pro-

---

1 World Trade Statistical Review 2018, p. 28, accessible at https://www.wto.org/english/res_e/statis_e/wts2018_e/wts2018_e.pdf.
2 World Trade Statistical Review 2016, p. 5, accessible at https://www.wto.org/english/res_e/statis_e/wts2016_e/wts2016_e.pdf.
3 Ibid.

Introduction

ceedings. Added benefits of arbitration are privacy, since the awards are not published, and a reduction in costs and time.

The CISG is one of the most successful international commercial law treaties ever devised. It provides for a neutral body of international sales law and is the result of decades of effort on the part of international and intergovernmental organizations.[4] It contains a set of rules that covers the formation of sales contracts and the rights and obligations following from them. The Convention is based on a combination of civil and common law principles and it is self-sufficient, to be interpreted independently from domestic legal notions. A rich tapestry of court decisions and arbitral awards applying the Convention has developed since it came into force in the late eighties; these decisions and scholarly writing are accessible in various online databases, globally and free of charge.[5]

International commercial arbitration and the CISG thus both serve as neutral sparring ground for parties from different cultural and legal backgrounds; the first from a procedural perspective and the second from a substantive law perspective. The question remains as to how they interact: Are arbitrators free to either apply or disregard the CISG in arbitration proceedings as they see fit, or are they perhaps even obligated to do apply it under certain circumstances?

I. Object of Inquiry

The object of inquiry of this thesis is whether arbitrators are bound by the rules of application of the CISG or whether they have discretion to apply the Convention. Law plays a contentious role in international commercial arbitration. This is complicated by the fact that there are distinct issues in every arbitral procedure that in turn can potentially each be governed by different legal systems. The laws that need to be determined are:
- the law governing the arbitration agreement and the performance of that agreement,
- the law governing the existence and proceedings of the arbitral tribunal (*lex arbitri*),

---

4 See *infra*, pp. 8 et seqq.
5 Such databases include the CISG Database by Pace University, available at https://www.iicl.law.pace.edu/cisg/cisg, Unilex, available at http://unilex.info/, CLOUT, which is the database by UNICTRAL (http://www.uncitral.org/uncitral/en/case_law.html) and the Global Sales Law Project, available at CISG-online.ch.

- the law or relevant rules governing the substantive issues (substantive law or *lex contractus*) and
- the law or laws governing the recognition and enforcement of the arbitration award.[6]

There is disagreement regarding the determination and application of nearly every one of these laws. Whether arbitrators may or must apply the CISG in an arbitration is a matter of the determination of the law applicable to the substantive issue because the CISG contains a set of substantive rules, specifically governing the formation of international sales contracts and rights and obligations arising out of such contracts.

The CISG determines its own applicability through rules of application, i.e. Article 1(1)(a) and (b) of the CISG. As is generally the case with uniform laws, the drafters of the CISG wanted to maximize the effect of the law and avoid leaving the circumstances of applicability up to each Contracting State. By attaching rules of application, the modalities of application are inserted into the legal system of the Contracting States along with the core provisions of the uniform law. The courts of the Contracting States are then obligated to apply the rules of application. They have to apply the CISG when the requirements are met and are barred from applying it when they are not met.[7] Within the scope of the Convention courts must measure a choice of law by the parties – whether in favor of the CISG or another law – by the provisions of the CISG.[8]

But how do these rules affect international commercial arbitration tribunals? This depends on the legal nature of the rules. Rules that determine the applicability of a body of law are categorized as either conflict of laws rules, determining one legal system applicable over another, or as internal rules of distribution, meaning internal to one legal system, because they determine the applicability of one part of a legal system over another. If the CISG's rules of application are conflict of laws rules, then their applicability in international arbitration depends on whether arbitrators are generally bound by conflict of laws rules. If they are internal rules of distribution, then their applicability depends on the party mandate and which law is determined as applicable to the dispute in general. Once the legal system of a Contracting State is deemed applicable, the internal rules of distribution within that legal system will generally have to be applied

---

6 *Blackaby et al.*, International Commercial Arbitration, ed. 6 2015, p. 157.
7 This is discussed in § 2.
8 The effect of a party choice of law within the scope of the CISG is discussed within § 3, see pp. 58 et seq.

Introduction

by the arbitrator as well.⁹ Thus, the legal nature of the rules makes a difference regarding their application in international commercial arbitration.

While there is relative clarity on the fact that Article 1(1)(a) of the CISG constitutes a conflict rule, Article 1(1)(b) poses a conundrum with its unique structure: Relying on the outcome of a conflict of laws analysis, it stipulates the applicability of the Convention if the forum's private international law leads to the law of a Contracting State. This certainly sounds like an internal rule of distribution, selecting one part of a legal system over another, and consequently, the majority of scholars appears to categorize it as such. However, the wording can be interpreted differently. The legal nature of Article 1(1), in particular in combination with lit. b, has very practical implications for several contentious issues that regularly cause a headache for scholars and judges alike, but this connection is rarely noticed. A systematic analysis of the provision within the context of the treatment of *renvois*, the effect of reservations under Article 95 and the law applicable to opt-out agreements pursuant to Article 6 shows that simply categorizing Article 1(1)(b) as a conflict of laws rule could give a sound explanation for the desired outcome.

If it is categorized as a conflict of laws rule, the binding nature of Article 1(1) of the CISG in international arbitration depends on whether arbitrators are bound by conflict of laws rules in general.¹⁰ In order for rules of private international law, including those stemming from international treaties such as the CISG, to bind international arbitrators, States would have to be competent to make conflict rules applicable in international arbitration proceedings. Such competence is generally believed to lie with the State in which the seat of arbitration is located, just as that State is competent to regulate the arbitral procedure. Whether this is true will be examined in § 3.

The Rome I Regulation constitutes the private international law for contractual obligations in nearly all EU Member States and its advent in 2008 has triggered a fresh discussion of the effect of private international law in international arbitration. As it has led some to the result that arbitrators must surely apply it – and thus also all other private international law, such as Article 1(1) of the CISG –, it deserves a closer look. The text, history and content of the Rome I Regulation will be examined regarding its compatibility with international arbitration proceedings.

---

9 This is discussed in § 4.
10 This is the subject of § 3.

Any legal freedom of arbitrators is complemented by great practical freedom. Unless arbitrators disregard a choice of law by the parties, how and why they select certain rules to apply to the merits of a dispute cannot be reviewed by domestic courts. Even if they are bound by conflict of laws rules such as Article 1(1) of the CISG, their misapplication cannot be penalized. This has led to the development of methods for determining the applicable substantive law in arbitral practice. These methods generally justify the leeway granted to the arbitrators as they are better suited to help select an appropriate applicable law than domestic private international law would be.

In the last chapter, the consequences of any potential freedom of international commercial arbitrators from the rules of application of the CISG on the application of the rest of the Convention's substantive in international commercial arbitration.[11] Would arbitrators be free to apply the substantive rules as they see fit, as well?

II. Steps of Inquiry

In order to show that arbitrators are not bound by the rules of application of the CISG, several different steps are taken in this paper. The first section will introduce the CISG and illustrate its unique position alongside domestic legal systems (§ 1). From this vantage point follows a demonstration that Article 1(1)(a) and (b) of the CISG constitute two parts of one conflict rule: Article 1(1) of the CISG, which establishes the autonomous application of the Convention (§ 2).

Next, the relationship between private international law and international commercial arbitration will be analyzed (§ 3). This section argues that States are competent to set forth broad conflict rules specifically for commercial international arbitration proceedings with arbitral seats in their territory. This is due to a rule of customary international law. Traditional conflict of laws rules, including the rules of application of the CISG, are not binding on them, but can serve as guidance.

Finally, the consequences of such extensive freedom are inspected: If arbitrators are not bound by general rules of private international law, which are laws like any other, are they also free to apply or disregard the substantive rules of the CISG as they wish? This question will be analyzed in the final chapter (§ 4).

---

11 This is the subject of chapter § 4.

§ 1. The CISG and International Commercial Arbitration

This chapter will introduce the CISG (**A.**) and then speak of the use of the CISG in international commercial arbitration (**B.**).

A. *The CISG*

The United Nations Convention on Contracts for the International Sale of Goods – or the CISG – forms part of a small set of uniform law conventions containing substantive law,[12] and is by far the most successful. It has a long history and a unique legal nature.

I. History

What is known today as the CISG began with a suggestion made in 1922 by Ernst Rabel to Vittorio Scialoja, president of the newly founded International Institute for the Unification of Private Law (UNIDROIT)[13], that the Institute should concern itself with the unification of international sales law.[14] The idea was that a uniform sales law would enhance cross-border business and promote international trade through a "secure, fair and

---

12 Other uniform law conventions with substantive law are the Convention on the Contract for the International Carriage of Goods by Road (CMR), Geneva, 19 May 1956, the Uniform Rules concerning the Contract of International Carriage of Passengers by Rail (CIV) and the Uniform Rules concerning the Contract of International Carriage of Goods by Rail (CIM), each contained in Annex A and B, respectively, of the Convention Concerning International Carriage by Rail, 9 May 1980, as amended on 3 June 1999.
13 The International Institute for the Unification of Private Law, UNIDROIT for short, is an independent international organisation set up in 1926 as an auxiliary organ of the League of Nations and re-established in 1940 through an international agreement. It is based in Rome. According to http://www.unidroit.org/, "(i)ts purpose is to study needs and methods for modernising, harmonising and co-ordinating private and in particular commercial law as between States and groups of States and to formulate uniform law instruments, principles and rules to achieve those objectives." It has 63 Member States.
14 Schlechtriem/Schwenzer/*Ferrari*, ed. 4 2016, p. 1.

culturally-neutral international regime for sales contracts"[15]. After Rabel presented a report to the Institute's council, UNIDROIT set up a committee of representatives of the Common law, French, Scandinavian and German legal systems.[16] An initial draft was issued in 1935. The process was interrupted by the beginning of World War II, and was not resumed until 1950.

1. ULF and ULIS

The sales law committee of UNIDROIT resumed its meetings in 1950. By then, the Hague Conference on International Private Law[17] had started its own process to produce a uniform sales law. Combined efforts by both institutions finally culminated in two international conventions, drawn up at the Hague Conference in 1964. One convention dealt with the formation of international sales contracts – the Uniform Law on the Formation of Contracts for the International Sale of Goods ("ULF")[18] – while the other convention dealt with obligations and remedies in connection with international sales contracts – the Uniform Law on the International Sale of Goods ("ULIS")[19]. Together, they were referred to as the Hague Conventions, and they came into force in 1972.[20] Each consisted of an introductory convention, with the actual uniform law attached as an annex.

However, the ULF and the ULIS failed to meet expectations. This was due in large part to the lack of representation of Eastern European countries – only Hungary and Yugoslavia were asked to participate – and of developing countries, of which there were no representatives at all. Twen-

---

15 Kröll/Mistelis/Perales Viscasillas/*Mistelis*, 2018, Introduction to the CISG, para. 3.
16 Schlechtriem/Schwenzer/*Ferrari*, ed. 4 2016, Introduction, p. 1.
17 The Hague Conference on Private International Law is an intergovernmental organization that works for the progressive unification of the rules of private international law (Statute, Art. 1). It had its first session in 1893, convened by the Netherlands Government and become a permanent intergovernmental organisation in 1955 when its statute came into force. It currently has 90 members; plenary sessions are held every 4 years. See https://www.hcch.net/de/home.
18 Convention relating to a Uniform Law on the Formation of Contracts for the International Sale of Goods, The Hague, 1 July 1964, https://www.unidroit.org/instruments/international-sales/ulfc-1964/..
19 Convention relating to a Uniform Law on the International Sale of Goods, The Hague, 1 July 1964, available at https://www.unidroit.org/instruments/international-sales/ ulis-1964/.
20 *Winship*, Cornell Int'l L.J. 1988, 487, 490.

ty-two out of the 28 countries involved were Western European and highly developed;[21] San Marino and the Vatican had full voting rights.[22] The process was also faulted for its purportedly rushed nature, which, to make matters worse, was controlled by mostly civil law countries.[23]

In addition to these general points of criticism of the UNIDROIT's process, the two conventions' rules of application were ill-received. They set forth a universal application of the ULF and the ULIS, to be applied whenever two parties had their places of business in the territory of different States (the so-called subjective element), along with three alternative requirements regarding the internationality of the transaction (the objective element).[24] However, there was no requirement of any type of connection to any of the States that had ratified the conventions ("Contracting States").[25] Only *de facto* was a connection required in that the forum of the court applying the conventions had to be a Contracting State, since courts in Non-Contracting States were not bound by the convention. Thus, merely requirements regarding the jurisdiction of domestic courts in Contracting States under international procedural law indirectly limited the application of the conventions. Additionally, there was a host of reservations that Contracting States could make, two of which affected the scope of application: one reservation in Article III of the introductory conventions enabled Contracting States to apply the conventions only if both parties had their seats of business in the territory of Contracting States. The other reservation, in Article IV, made the application dependent on private international law conventions determining the Hague Conventions as applicable.

---

21 Kröll/Mistelis/Perales Viscasillas/*Mistelis*, 2018, Introduction to the CISG, para. 6.
22 Staudinger-BGB/*Magnus*, 2018, Einl CISG, para. 22.
23 Kröll/Mistelis/Perales Viscasillas/*Mistelis*, 2018, Introduction to the CISG, para. 6.
24 Article 1 of the ULIS and the ULF: "The present Law shall apply to contracts of sale of goods entered into by parties whose places of business are in the territories of different States, in each of the following cases:
(a) where the contract involves the sale of goods which are at the time of the conclusion of the contract in the course of carriage or will be carried from the territory of one State to the territory of another;
(b) where the acts constituting the offer and the acceptance have been effected in the territories of different States;
(c) where delivery of the goods is to be made in the territory of a State other than that within whose territory the acts constituting the offer and the acceptance have been effected."
25 Staudinger-BGB/*Magnus*, 2018, Einl CISG, para. 8.

This scope of application, which was described as "aggressive", combined with the potential inconsistencies produced by different reservations made by different States lead to heavy criticism.[26] In total, only nine States ratified both conventions[27] – too few for the laws to have the lasting global impact that had been strived for.

2. CISG

Even before the ULF and ULIS came into force as a joint effort of UNIDROIT and the Hague Conference, the United Nations General Assembly established UNCITRAL in 1966.[28] UNCITRAL, which was in charge of commercial law reform, conducted a survey of its Member States and UN observers regarding the ULF and ULIS. Due to a lack of enthusiasm, the organization decided not to take on the conventions.[29] Instead, it opted for creating a new uniform law that would be able to garner more support. A Working Group was formed with representatives from 15 States in all regions of the world.[30] A draft that included rules both regarding the formation of contracts and regarding obligations and remedies was circulated among Member States and observers.[31] In 1980, 62 States, one State observer and eight international organizations participated in the Diplomatic Conference in Vienna to work on the 1978 Draft Convention, and the Convention was adopted by the Conference on 10 April 1980. It entered into force on 1 January 1988, after ratification by 10 States as per Article 99(1) of the CISG.[32]

---

26 Ibid., Einl CISG, para. 9.
27 Schlechtriem/Schwenzer/Schroeter/*Schwenzer*, ed. 7 2019, Einleitung, I.
28 UNCITRAL stands for United Nations Commission on International Trade Law, which is a legal body of the United Nations that has universal membership and specializes in commercial law reform. Its aim is to facilitate international trade "by preparing and promoting the use and adoption of legislative and non-legislative instruments in a number of key areas of commercial law"; see https://uncitral.un.org/sites/uncitral.un.org/files/media-documents/uncitral/en/12-57491-guide-to-uncitral-e.pdf. Their website is https://uncitral.un.org/.
29 Kröll/Mistelis/Perales Viscasillas/*Mistelis*, 2018, Introduction to the CISG, para. 8.
30 Staudinger-BGB/*Magnus*, 2018, Einl CISG, para. 24.
31 Kröll/Mistelis/Perales Viscasillas/*Mistelis*, 2018, Introduction to the CISG, para. 8.
32 These 10 Contracting States were Lesotho (1981); France, Syrian Arab Republic and Egypt (1982); Hungary and Argentina (1983); and Zambia, China, Italy and the United States of America (1986).

The highly contested scope of application received a comprehensive makeover, as it was simplified and the reservations that States could make were reduced. The universalist approach of the UFL and ULIS was abolished. Under the CISG, a connection with one or two Contracting States is a requirement of its application, either due to the parties' seats of business or through private international law. The latter alternative can be excluded through a reservation. This mechanism fairly drastically reduces the number of cases in which a court in a Member State can apply the CISG in contrast to the ULF and the ULIS, but in exchange, the scope of application of the CISG was never a barrier to its acceptance.

Today, the CISG has 94 Contracting States from every part of the world and with fundamentally different legal systems.[33] It is estimated that more than 80 % of global trade could potentially be governed by the Convention.[34] It has served as a model for national and international laws[35] and has been described as "the most significant piece of substantive contract legislation in effect at the international level".[36] UNCITRAL has taken steps to ensure the proliferation and uniform application of the CISG. It has published a Digest, in which court decisions from the Contracting States are presented in order to determine the predominant understanding of each provision.[37] There is a network of National Correspondents in all Contracting States who catalogue pertinent court decisions, for which they write English abstracts and add them to an online collection named CLOUT.[38] These actions have served to mollify critics who worry that a lack of a supreme court in charge of interpreting the CISG in a final manner would lead to legal insecurity and counter the purpose of having a uniform sales law in the first place.

---

33 https://uncitral.un.org/en/texts/salegoods/conventions/sale_of_goods/cisg/status.
34 Schlechtriem/Schwenzer/*Ferrari*, ed. 4 2016, Introduction, p. 1.
35 *Schlechtriem*, JURIDICA INTERNATIONAL X/2005, 27, available at http://www.juridicainternational.eu/public/pdf/ji_2005_1_27.pdf.
36 Lookofsky, The 1980 United Nations Convention on Contracts for the International Sale of Goods, in: Blanpain (ed.), International Encyclopaedia of Law (1993), p. 18, as cited by Kröll/Mistelis/Perales Viscasillas/*Mistelis*, 2018, Introduction to the CISG, para. 1.
37 The third edition of the Digest was published in 2016 and is available at https://uncitral.un.org/sites/uncitral.un.org/files/media-documents/uncitral/en/cisg_digest_2016.pdf. .
38 CLOUT is short for Case Law on UNCITRAL Texts and is available at http://www.uncitral.org/clout/.

II. Nature

As a uniform law convention, the CISG occupies a unique position in the legal systems of the Contracting States. The States have a duty to incorporate the Convention in whatever manner their constitutions set forth, making it part of their legal systems. Yet in order to fulfil its purpose as a uniform law it functions differently than non-unified substantive laws. Regardless of who is applying it, it has to provide the same language, methodology and common understanding to the basic issues of international sales contracts.

Uniform laws are defined as laws that are identical in two or more countries and are intended to be that way.[39] Law that is uniform can be established by conventions or identical domestic legislation.[40] The CISG is a convention. To be more precise, it is an integrated convention, which means that the substantive provisions are incorporated in the text of the convention itself rather than in an annex, as had been the case with the ULF and ULIS.[41] The CISG predecessors consisted of framework conventions containing the public international law framework for the uniform laws, including reservations that the Contracting States could make, and the actual uniform laws as an annex to the convention. Ostensibly, the benefit of this approach is that a body of uniform law that is separate from the convention can be integrated into domestic legal systems more easily.[42] However, the supranational source of the law is obscured when it is incorporated into a domestic law, leading to disagreement about whether it is to be applied as domestic or foreign law.[43] Also, the incorporation as a separate law can take time, which can cause confusion for foreign courts regarding the status of the uniform law and whether it has entered

---

39 *Kropholler*, Internationales Einheitsrecht, 1975, p. 1.
40 Kropholler identifies further vessels for uniform laws, such as supra- and international legal instruments, standard contracts, case law and general principles of law, see ibid., p. 93. In particular, the secondary law of the European Union, i.e. regulations, directives and decisions as set forth in Article 288 of the TFEU, can also be considered supranational uniform law.
41 *Sono*, The Vienna Sales Convention: History and Perspective, p. 3.
42 *Kropholler*, Internationales Einheitsrecht, 1975, p. 102.
43 In some legal systems, the application of a law domestic versus foreign is decisive for whether a court decision by a lower court is reviewable in regard to the application of the law by a higher court. Uniform laws should always be applied as domestic law by Contracting States' courts; see ibid., pp. 132 et seq. In regard to the CISG specifically, see *infra*, pp. 62 et seq.

into force yet. Integrating the uniform law into the actual convention can alleviate some of these problems.

a) Part of Domestic Legal Systems

Conventions, also referred to as treaties[44], that are ratified by a State become a part of its legal system. The exact procedure that gives conventions effect within the territory of the individual States depends on the constitution of the respective State, which might adopt a monist or dualist approach to international law, or some form in between.[45] Under the monist approach, treaties become part of the national legal system with no need of further legislation as long as they have been concluded in accordance with the constitution.[46] Some self-executing treaties may be regarded as supreme law, overriding contradicting domestic legislation. The dualist approach, on the other hand, requires domestic legislation to give effect to rights and obligations created by treaties.[47] Such specific legislation is said to incorporate the rights and obligations into domestic law, which can be amended or repealed by later domestic legislation.[48] Which approach is ultimately followed is a matter of interpretation of the individual constitutions of each State, and a clear categorization is not always possible. The result, however, is invariably that the convention becomes part of the domestic legal system, one way or another.

Such is the case of the CISG: once the necessary steps have been taken to give effect to its substantive provisions according to the law of each Contracting State, the provisions are part of the States' national legal

---

44 According to Black's Law Dictionary (2014), ed. 10, "convention" is defined as "[a]n agreement or compact, esp. one among countries; a multilateral treaty", while "treaty" is defined as "[a]n agreement formally signed, ratified, or adhered to between two countries or sovereigns; an international agreement concluded between two or more states in written form and governed by international law". The terms are used synonymously here.
45 *Aust*, Modern Treaty Law and Practice, ed. 3 2013, p. 162.
46 Ibid., pp. 163 et seq.
47 Ibid., pp. 167 et seq. The dualist approach is followed by the UK and almost all other Commonwealth countries, see ibid., p. 163. A more monist approach is followed in France, Germany, the Netherlands and Switzerland, see National Treaty Law and Practice, 2005, chapters 8, 9, 14, 17. The USA follows a mixed monist-dualist approach.
48 *Aust*, Modern Treaty Law and Practice, ed. 3 2013, p. 167.

systems.[49] The law's rank in the hierarchy in the legal system depends on the States' constitutional law, but in principle it will be at least at the same level as other bodies of civil law originating from national legislation and can grant rights to and place obligations on individuals. As such, the CISG can be considered State law. Due to the opt-out mechanism implemented by the drafters, the CISG is applicable if parties choose the law of a Contracting State to govern their contract and do not explicitly or implicitly exclude the application of the Convention.[50]

b) Independence from Domestic Legal System

Despite being formally introduced into the domestic legal systems of the Contracting States, the CISG remains distinct from ordinary domestic law. It may bear similarities to the non-unified sales law of some Contracting States, using familiar terms and mechanisms. In other jurisdictions, the CISG's peculiarities may stand in jarring contrast to existing autonomous law in wording or method. Herein lies the strength of the uniform law: Regardless of whether it resembles domestic law of each Contracting State, it remains the same. This is due in large part to Article 7 of the CISG, which enshrines the principle of autonomous interpretation of ambiguous terms and autonomous gap-filling.

To ensure that the Convention is interpreted independently from the legal system in which the adjudicatory body is based, Article 7(1) of the CISG states that in the interpretation of the text,

> regard is to be had to its international character and to the need to promote uniformity in its application and the observance of good faith in international trade.

This is vital for the broad terms used in the Convention, such as "fundamental breach" in Article 25 or "specific performance" in Article 28, which must be interpreted the same way by any court, regardless of their location, through the use of these autonomous interpretive criteria.[51] The

---

49 Kröll/Mistelis/Perales Viscasillas/*Mistelis*, 2018, Intro to the CISG, para. 12.
50 See only Kröll/Mistelis/Perales Viscasillas/*Mistelis*, 2018, CISG Art. 6 para. 3. Further, see *infra*, pp. 53 et seq.
51 See only *Schwenzer/Hachem*, Am. J. Comp. L. 2009, 457.

CISG thereby creates an "almost self-sufficient system detached from the usual interpretation of domestic laws"[52].

The international character of the CISG becomes even more apparent in Article 7(2), which regulates how gaps in the Convention are to be filled. It states:

> Questions concerning matters governed by this Convention which are not expressly settled in it are to be settled in conformity with the general principles on which it is based or, in the absence of such principles, in conformity with the law applicable by virtue of the rules of private international law.

This provision deals with so-called internal gaps (*lacunae praeter legem*), meaning that the matter is generally covered by the CISG, but the specific question is not answered by its rules.[53] If the solution cannot be found by relying on the general principles of the CISG – such as the reasonability principle, freedom of form and evidence, party autonomy and others – the parties must consult the national law that private international law rules determine to be applicable.[54] This sets the uniform law apart from national laws: even if the latter are *leges speciales* for a specific type of transaction, gaps are filled with the *leges generales* of the legal system of which they form part, or at least with general principles found within them. Regarding uniform laws, recourse to national law is the *ultima ratio* if a gap in the Convention arises[55], and the national law has to be determined through a new conflict of laws analysis.

Through these mechanisms, Article 7 of the CISG ensures the independence of the Convention from domestic legal systems. It has been called the most important article of the Convention for this precise reason.[56] Without it, the whole concept of a uniform law would be jeopardized. Because of Article 7, the CISG is formally part of the Contracting State's national legal system but behaves in a distinctly international manner that sets it apart from ordinary national legislation. The resulting independence of the CISG from domestic legal systems affects the role of the rules of application of the CISG, since these rules do not merely select one out of

---

52 Kröll/Mistelis/Perales Viscasillas/*Mistelis*, 2018, CISG Art. 7 para. 7.
53 Ibid., CISG Art. 7 para.1. For external gaps, i.e. *lacunae intra legem*, the applicable law must be found through private international law.
54 Staudinger-BGB/*Kaiser*, 2018, CISG Art. 7, paras. 41 et seqq.
55 Kröll/Mistelis/Perales Viscasillas/*Mistelis*, 2018, CISG Art. 7 para. 1.
56 Ibid., CISG Art. 7 para. 2.

several potentially applicable domestic sales laws. This will be discussed in detail in the next chapter.

B. The CISG in International Commercial Arbitration

The international nature of the CISG makes it a perfect candidate to govern sales contracts in international commercial arbitration proceedings, which parties choose in order to maintain a distance from domestic legal systems and their courts. In fact, arbitration proceedings constitute a large volume of proceedings in which the Convention is applied.

I. Compatibility of the CISG and International Commercial Arbitration

Both the CISG and international commercial arbitration are neutral, especially in comparison to their alternatives, domestic sales laws and domestic court proceedings. A big motivation for parties to select international commercial arbitration is to stay out of foreign courts, especially out of the domestic courts of the other party's home State, in which that party would have a home advantage.[57] The risks are a lack of familiarity with the national court procedures in comparison to the other party and potential language barriers that might not be satisfactorily bridged with translators and other aids, or even so-called "home town justice"[58], which describes a preferential treatment of a party because they come from the court's forum State. In international arbitration the parties can choose their own procedure – either through individual agreement or by choosing the rules of an arbitral institution – and their own arbitrators. The parties can further agree that the proceedings be conducted in a language shared by both parties. Due to these aspects, international arbitration offers a compromise and an often-superior alternative for parties hesitant to submit their dispute to a foreign court.

The CISG plays the same role on a substantive law level – its rules are not based on any one domestic legal system. They are the product of an international consensus, balancing common law and civil law principles, and its rules are to be interpreted free from domestic notions.[59] It

---

57 *Schroeder*, Die lex mercatoria arbitralis, 2007, p. 27.
58 Ibid.
59 See Art. 7 of the CISG and *supra*, pp. 16 et seq.

also boasts no less than 6 authentic languages: Arabic, Chinese, English, French, Russian and Spanish.[60] This creates common ground for parties with different cultures, legal and otherwise, from around the globe, and it makes the application of the Convention predictable, regardless of where the dispute is decided. It is also hailed for its substantive neutrality: neither the buyer nor the seller has a particular advantage under the uniform law.[61]

The Convention is also fine-tuned to the specific needs of international transactions, for example by providing for flexible deadlines – using terms such as "reasonable"[62] – for actions and notifications, instead of strict and potentially too short deadlines as can be the case in domestic sales laws.[63] Most importantly, however, it gives wide birth to party autonomy. Nearly all provisions can be replaced by party-agreed clauses.[64] Contracts governing international transactions often contain intricate detail, leaving little to be substituted by statute. Domestic laws, which invariably have mandatory provisions that cannot be derogated from, may impede the enforcement of the will of the parties, unlike the CISG. In case the parties do leave an issue open, however, the CISG rules will provide for generally adequate solutions, so that the parties are not faced with an eccentric domestic rule that could impact the case in unexpected ways.

For these reasons, the CISG is well-suited to be applied in international commercial arbitration proceedings.

II. Application by International Arbitration Tribunals

Studies in the past have shown that about a quarter of all published cases in which the CISG was applied were decided by arbitral tribunals.[65] Seeing as most arbitral awards are never published, this number is potentially

---

60 The authentic texts are available at https://www.cisg.law.pace.edu/cisg/text/text.html.
61 *Fountoulakis*, Eur. J. L. Reform 2005, 303, 319.
62 E.g. Artt. 46(3), 49(2), 63(1), 65(2), 72(1), 73(2), 75, 77, 79(1), 85, 86(1), (2), 87, 88(1), (2), (3) of the CISG.
63 *Schlechtriem/Schroeter*, Internationales UN-Kaufrecht, ed. 6 2016, p. 6 para 12.
64 See Art. 6 of the CISG. The exception is Art. 12 of the CISG, which prohibits parties from agreeing on a different form than the written form under certain circumstances.
65 *Mistelis*, CISG and Arbitration, pp. 386 et seq. The numbers were confirmed for the following years by *Janssen/Spilker*, RabelsZ 2013, 131, 133 et seq.

B. The CISG in International Commercial Arbitration

much higher. It has even been suggested that up to four out of five of such cases could stem from arbitration proceedings.[66]

The reasons given by the arbitrators for the application of the Convention – if any reasons are given at all – vary widely and betray starkly differing attitudes regarding the binding force of the CISG's rules of application. According to a study by Mistelis, the Convention was applied because it was chosen by the parties in 11 % of the cases and following an application of domestic conflict of laws rules in 22 %. In 57 % of the cases, the arbitral tribunal applied it as its own choice of law. Finally, in 2 % of the cases it was applied as general principles of law and in the remaining 8 % of the cases there was no explanation for the application of the Convention at all.[67] Statistics published by the ICC suggest that the CISG was applied as non-State law in 1 % and 2 % of cases in 2015 and 2016, respectively.[68]

As international trade continues to grow and arbitration becomes ever more popular as a mechanism for dispute resolution, the opportunities to apply the CISG will also expand. German associations that had initially advised opting out of the CISG no longer do so.[69] Lao, Guatemala, Liechtenstein and Portugal, to name a few, have joined the ranks of Contracting States to the Convention in the past couple of years, resulting in a total of 94 Contracting States at the time of writing.[70] This sends a signal to the citizens of these countries that the Convention is not to be considered foreign law, potentially encouraging more parties to choose it as applicable law in their contracts. It also increases the cases in which the requirements of either Article 1(1)(a) or (b) of the CISG are met.

Parties can choose the CISG directly, as part of domestic law or arguably as non-State law.[71] Often, however, parties make no choice of law at all. Upwards of 12 percent, at times even up to a quarter of contracts subject to ICC arbitration proceedings in the last years did not contain a choice of law clause, leaving it up to the arbitral tribunal to determine the applicable

---

66 *Janssen/Spilker*, RabelsZ 2013, 131, 134.
67 *Mistelis*, CISG and Arbitration, pp. 388, 389.
68 2015 ICC Dispute Resolution Bulletin, p. 15; 2016 ICC Dispute Resolution Bulletin, p. 17.
69 Staudinger-BGB/*Magnus*, 2018, Einl CISG, para. 5.
70 See fn. 33.
71 This is discussed in detail below, in § 3 E.

law.[72] This can happen due to any number of reasons, be it because the parties simply forget to address the matter, or because they cannot agree and decide not to endanger an otherwise promising young cooperation by dwelling on the issue.

The question that remains is whether arbitrators are free to apply the CISG in cases where a choice of law is missing. The answer to this question hinges on whether arbitrators in international arbitration proceedings are bound by the rules of application contained in the CISG. These rules contain instructions regarding when the CISG is to be applied and their desired effect was to limit the applicability of the CISG in contrast to the ULF and ULIS, so as to enhance the acceptance of the CISG among potential Contracting State, making its application by courts in Contracting States dependent on a connection between the contract and Contracting States. International arbitration takes place outside of the strict confines of domestic legal systems; arbitrators have more freedom in regard to the application of law. It does not seem appropriate to bind arbitrators to the rules that resulted from a compromise between States. This thesis will show that arbitrators are not, in fact, bound by the rules, and are free to apply the CISG whenever it best serves the interests of the parties.

---

72 2015 ICC Dispute Resolution Bulletin, p. 15; 2016 ICC Dispute Resolution Bulletin, p. 17; 2017 ICC Dispute Resolution Bulletin, p. 20, 2018 ICC Dispute Resolution Bulletin, p. 14.

§ 2. Article 1(1) CISG – Rules of Application

The CISG determines its own applicability. The Convention contains provisions on the territorial, temporal and personal sphere of application of the uniform law. An important part of this is played by Article 1(1) of the CISG. After a brief overview over the provision (**A.**), its legal nature will be determined (**B.**). This will pave the way for the analysis of whether arbitrators are bound by them in the next chapter.

A. Overview over the Provision

Article 1(1) of the CISG states:

> *This Convention applies to contracts of sale of goods between parties whose places of business are in different States:*
> *(a) when the States are Contracting States; or*
> *(b) when the rules of private international law lead to the application of the law of a Contracting State.*

The connection with Contracting States can be based on one of of two alternatives, set forth in lit. a and lit. b. These requirements are not novel, as they had already been included in the ULF and ULIS as reservations.[73] Moving them out of the sphere of optional reservations for Contracting States and upgrading them to necessary requirements for the application of the Convention made the scope of the CISG much more measured than the scope of the ULF and ULIS had been. It also streamlined the applicability of the Convention, ensuring that at least in most Contracting States the applicability of the CISG is subject to the same requirements, instead of courts being confronted with a web of different prerequisites for every Contracting State.[74]

---

[73] See *supra*, p. 12.
[74] Schlechtriem/Schwenzer/*Schwenzer*/*Hachem*, ed. 4 2016, CISG Art. 1 paras. 1, 2.

§ 2. Article 1(1) CISG – Rules of Application

I. Connections with Contracting States

Article 1(1)(a) of the CISG declares the Convention applicable "to contracts of sale of goods between parties whose places of business are in different States **when the States are Contracting States**". This is called the *autonomous applicability* of the Convention[75], as it accesses the uniform law autonomously, or independently from the applicability of any one signatory State's sales law. The Convention is applicable because the dispute has a connection with two Contracting States. These two Contracting States, together with all other Contracting States, form a common legal system in the area of international sales that is detached from the particularities of their domestic legal systems.[76] The CISG is applicable as the *tronc commun* of two States that are closely connected to the dispute.

Article 1(1)(b) of the CISG stipulates that the Convention is applicable "to contracts of sale of goods between parties whose places of business are in different States **when the rules of private international law lead to the law of a Contracting State**". This is known as *indirect applicability* or the *Vorschaltlösung*.[77] It requires the application of the private international law of the court's forum. When this leads to the law of a Contracting State, then lit. b determines that the CISG is applicable.

As stated, the ULIS and ULF contained the possibility of making the applicability of the uniform laws subject to private international law in a reservation, thus limiting the universal applicability of the conventions. In the context of the CISG, applicability owing to private international law actually expands the scope of the Convention. Article 1(1)(b) enables the Convention's application even when the requirements of Article 1(1)(a) are not met because one or even both of the parties to the contract do not have their places of business in Contracting States. The indirect applicability of the Convention still met with resistance in the drafting process from States that wanted their own non-uniform sales law to apply when their legal system was selected by private international law. Thus, a new reservation was added in Article 95 of the CISG, according to which the State making the reservation ("Reservation State") "will not be bound by

---

75 Staudinger-BGB/*Magnus*, 2018, CISG Art. 1, para. 85.
76 Kröll/Mistelis/Perales Viscasillas/*Mistelis*, 2018, CISG Art. 7, para. 7.
77 See only Staudinger-BGB/*Magnus*, 2018, CISG Art. 1, para. 93. It will be shown that this is a misnomer, since the application of private international law does not take place before the application of Art. 1(1)(b) of the CISG, but rather within its application, see *infra*, pp. 42 et seqq.

subparagraph (1)(b) of article 1 of this Convention".[78] The effect of this reservation is a matter of debate, but it will be shown that determining the legal nature of the Article 1(1)(b) has an impact on this effect, as it does on several other contentious issues.[79]

II. Further Requirements of Applicability

Beyond the connection with a Contracting State, there are other requirements that have to be met in order for the Convention to be applicable: The first part of the sentence of Article 1(1) of the CISG calls for an international sale of goods, giving the Convention its name.

1. Internationality

The internationality of the sales contract is defined by the fact that the parties have their places of business in different States. "Place of business", for lack of a statutory definition, must be interpreted autonomously pursuant to Article 7(1) of the CISG. If a party uses a place openly to participate in trade and if this location displays a certain degree of duration, stability and independence, it is generally considered a place of business in the sense of Article 1 of the CISG by domestic courts.[80] If a party has several places of business or none, Article 10 of the CISG stipulates the selection of the place of business with the closest relationship with the transaction or, in the absence of a place of business, the party's habitual residence. The parties must have their places of business in different States at the time of the conclusion of the contract.[81] Conversely, if both parties have their places of business in the territory of the same State, performance of the contract abroad is not sufficient for the CISG to be applicable.[82]

---

[78] Such a reservation has been made by Armenia, China, Czechia, St Vincent and the Grenadines, Singapore, Slovakia and the United States, see link in fn. 33.
[79] This will be discussed on pp. 48 et seqq.
[80] Schlechtriem/Schwenzer/*Schwenzer/Hachem*, ed. 4 2016, CISG Art. 1 para. 23 with further references.
[81] Kröll/Mistelis/Perales Viscasillas/*Mistelis*, 2018, CISG Art. 1 para. 42; Staudinger-BGB/*Magnus*, 2018, CISG Art. 1 para. 80.
[82] Staudinger-BGB/*Magnus*, 2018, CISG Art. 1 para. 59; MüKo-HGB/*Mankowski*, ed. 4 2018, CISG Art. 1 para. 31.

§ 2. Article 1(1) CISG – Rules of Application

This approach to determining the internationality of a contract constitutes a simplification in contrast to the ULIS and ULF. The latter contained the same subjective criterion of the parties' seats of business being situated in the territory of different States, but additionally required that an objective criterion be met as well, such as that the offer and acceptance be effected in the territories of the different States.

2. Sale of Goods

The term "sale of goods" must be interpreted in accordance with the material provisions of the CISG. The general obligations resulting from such a contract of sale according to the CISG are set forth in Articles 30 and 53 of the CISG and include the delivery of goods, documents and transfer of property by the seller and the payment of the purchase price and taking the delivery on the side of the buyer.[83] Thus, contracts of sale in the sense of the CISG are "reciprocal contracts directed at the exchange of goods against the 'price'".[84]

The goods that are the object of sale lack a definition in the legal text. However, the rules of non-conformity (Articles 35 et seqq. of the CISG) are flexible enough to govern a variety of different types of goods, which suggests a broad understanding of the term, including goods which the drafter could not have foreseen.[85] While under the ULIS the goods still had to be movable (Articles 1(1), 6), entailing movability at the time of delivery,[86] the notion that non-corporeal goods such as software can also be considered goods in the sense of the CISG is becoming more popular.[87] The sale of rights, however, is not governed by the Convention.[88]

---

[83] Schlechtriem/Schwenzer/*Schwenzer/Hachem*, ed. 4 2016, CISG Art. 1 para. 6. The CISG expressly mentions several different types of sale contracts. In Article 31(1), 67, it makes reference to contracts involving the carriage of goods, in Article 35(2)(c) to sales by sample or model. According to Article 65, contracts in accordance with specifications made by the buyer are included just as instalment contracts are according to Article 73. Further types of contracts are generally thought to fall within the scope of the CISG as well, see ibid., Art. para. 7.
[84] Ibid., CISG Art. 1 para. 6.
[85] Ibid., CISG Art. 1 para. 16.
[86] *Schlechtriem/Schroeter*, Internationales UN-Kaufrecht, ed. 6 2016, p. 43.
[87] Schlechtriem/Schwenzer/*Schwenzer/Hachem*, ed. 4 2016, CISG Art. 1 para. 18.
[88] *Schlechtriem/Schroeter*, Internationales UN-Kaufrecht, ed. 6 2016, p. 43.

B. Legal Nature

Article 2 contains exceptions for contracts that are not governed by the Convention. Chief among these is the consumer contract as set forth in Article 2(a) of the CISG, the purpose of which is to ensure that domestic consumer protection laws are not overridden.[89] Other excluded sales are the sale by auction (lit. b), on execution or otherwise by authority of law (lit. c), of stocks, investment securities, negotiable instruments or money (lit. d), of ships, vessels, hovercraft or aircraft (lit. e) and of electricity (lit. f).

B. Legal Nature

What is the legal nature of Article 1(1) of the CISG? The provision determines the applicability of the CISG. Rules that determine the applicability of a body of law can either be conflict of laws rules, which determine the governing law amidst a number of potentially applicable legal systems, or they can be internal rules of distribution, which determine the governing law within a legal system that has already been determined to be applicable and are otherwise regular substantive rules. The rules of application in uniform law conventions inhabit a unique position, functioning as gatekeepers to a law resulting from an international agreement. They strike a balance between achieving maximum applicability of that international law and legitimizing its application by domestic courts in the stead of domestic law. In his seminal book on uniform laws, Kropholler demonstrated that rules of application of international uniform laws always have two separate functions: on the one hand, they separate the international situations from the domestic situations, since only the former are governed by the uniform law.[90] On the other hand, the rules of application set forth the application of the uniform sales law without the necessity of first applying autonomous or uniform rules of private international law. In this latter aspect, the rules of application are *lex specialis* to general conflict of laws rules.[91]

While rules of application in uniform laws generally cause confusion in regard to their legal nature and exact functioning, Article 1(1) of the CISG poses an especially vexing challenge. The provision is read as containing

---

89 Ibid., p. 44. Note, however, that the consumer contract is defined by the private use of the goods purchased.
90 *Kropholler*, Internationales Einheitsrecht, 1975, p. 190.
91 Ibid.

two separate rules. Article 1(1)(a), by way of the autonomous application of the CISG, leads to the direct applicability of the CISG, without any recourse to private international law. In the rare cases that the legal nature of the rule is discussed, it is described as a unilateral conflict rule[92] or, intriguingly, as a rule that is not technically a conflict rule but should be treated as such.[93] Article 1(1)(b), on the other hand, is overwhelmingly seen not as a conflict of laws rule, but as an internal substantive rule of the legal system of every Contracting State.[94] Because rules of private international law are expressly referenced, the rule is interpreted as merely exclaiming that once the law of a Contracting State has been determined to be applicable to the facts at hand, the CISG and not the Contracting State's domestic sales law should govern the facts. Thus, the conflict of laws aspect that Kropholler generally saw in rules of application of uniform laws is denied in regard to Article 1(1)(b) of the CISG.

It will be shown that Article 1(1) is actually one unilateral conflict of laws rule with two alternative connecting factors, which are set forth in lit. a and lit. b. To this end, the structure and function of conflict of laws rules, in particular of unilateral conflict of laws rules, will be demonstrated (**I.**). It will then be shown that both Article 1(1)(a) (**II.**) and Article 1(1)(b) (**III.**) are two variants of one unilateral conflict rule, i.e. Article 1(1) (**IV.**), which leads to the direct applicability of the CISG.

I. Structure and Function of Conflict of Laws Rules

1. Function

As the name suggests, a necessary prerequisite for the existence of a conflict of laws rule is that there is a conflict of different laws.[95] Laws can conflict in different ways, and different types of conflict rules resolve these conflicts: intertemporal conflict rules resolve conflicts between older and newer laws, interlocal conflict rules determine the applicability of various

---

92 *Lohmann*, Parteiautonomie und UN-Kaufrecht, 2005, p. 38.
93 *Janssen/Spilker*, RabelsZ 2013, 131, 142.
94 *Czerwenka*, Rechtsanwendungsprobleme, 1988, p. 162 ("Abgrenzungsnorm"); *Lohmann*, Parteiautonomie und UN-Kaufrecht, 2005, pp. 51 et seq; *Schlechtriem*, Internationales UN-Kaufrecht, ed. 4 2007, p. 12, para. 17.
95 "Es ist eine Binsenweisheit, dass für internationales Privatrecht nur Raum ist, wo Rechtsverschiedenheiten bestehen. Ohne Rechtskollisionen kein Kollisionsrecht." *Zweigert/Drobning*, RabelsZ 1965, 146, 147.

B. Legal Nature

conflicting territorial legal systems within a State, and interpersonal conflict rules clarify which rules only apply to specific groups of people within a State.[96] The fourth group of conflict rules are international conflict rules, and only these are meant when international private law is referenced.[97] They determine the applicable law among various potentially applicable laws of different national legal systems. This is necessary if a set of facts has connections to various legal systems, which therefore all potentially have a legitimate interest in regulating that set of facts. The appropriate law among these legal systems then has to be declared applicable.[98] As such, international conflict rules do not have a direct impact on the outcome of the case – they do not produce obligations or rights. Rather, they determine which legal system should have a say over whether rights or obligations arise out of a particular set of facts.

Not every rule that determines a law as applicable to certain situations is automatically an international conflict rule. Such rules must be distinguished from mere substantive rules whose applicability is limited in some way, be it territorially ("spatially conditioned internal rules"[99]), personally or factually. The purpose of such a rule is not to make a decision between two national legal systems, but rather to delimit the application of a part of a legal system. This can entail a restriction of its applicability to a certain territory of the State of which it is part of the legal system, such as a speed limit that only pertains to a specific stretch of road. It can, however, also restrict the application of a law that is part of a national legal system to certain types of situations or persons. For example, German inheritance law sets a deadline of six weeks for an heir to disclaim an inheritance. This deadline is extended to six months if the deceased had their last residence abroad.[100] Thus, the provision extending the deadline is only applicable to specific cases. It does not declare German law applicable to the situation, but instead relies on the prior applicability of German law and merely sets forth one special rule of German law for the outlined situations. Another much broader example is consumer law with all of its protective measures,

---

96 *Kegel/Schurig*, Internationales Privatrecht, ed. 9 2004, pp. 36-45.
97 The term international private law is often used to refer to laws governing a broader group of issues, including matters of court jurisdiction and enforcement of court decisions. Here, it will be used to refer only to such rules that determine the prevailing law in a conflict of different potentially applicable laws.
98 *Kegel/Schurig*, Internationales Privatrecht, ed. 9 2004, p. 56.
99 *Siehr*, FS Drobning, p. 448.
100 Sec. 1944(1) and (3) of the BGB.

applicable only to situations involving consumers.[101] The provision in consumer law determining that it is only applicable to these situations is not a rule of private international law, but an internal rule of distribution.[102]

In order to determine whether a rule can be categorized as either an international conflict rule or an internal rule of distribution, a test can be helpful. This test will be referred to as the Alternatives Test. According to the Alternatives Test, an analysis of the *alternative* to the application of the rule in question sheds light on its legal nature.[103] Put differently, the nature of the rule is revealed by considering what would happen if the rule were not applied. An internal rule of distribution selects a part of a legal system – specific rules that govern specific types of facts – *leges speciales*. The alternative to applying that rule is that the specific rules of that legal system are not applicable, but rather, the general rules – *leges generales*.[104] Thus, in the absence of the application of the internal rule, rules of the same national legal system are applicable. An international conflict rule, on the other hand, selects rules of a national legal system over rules of another national legal system. The alternative to applying the conflict rule is that another legal system is applicable.[105] Thus, if a rule determines application of a legal system that would otherwise not be applicable, that rule is an international conflict of laws rule.

2. Structure

Nowadays, conflict of laws rules are typically multilateral, meaning they can lead to the selection of a multitude of potential legal systems. A structure consisting of so-called operative facts and connecting factors determines the law most appropriate to govern a situation, and its outcome is

---

[101] An example for this is sec. 355 et seq. of the BGB, which grant a special right of withdrawal from consumer contracts to the consumers. These provisions thus only apply factually if the contract in question is a consumer contract, which requires that the parties qualify as trader and consumer, and personally if the person exercsising the right of withdrawal is a consumer.

[102] Private international can also contain rules dealing with the law applicable to consumer contracts in particular. However, such rules will refer to the legal system of a certain State, and within that domestic legal system international rules of distribution then identify which rules belong to consumer law.

[103] *Kegel/Schurig*, Internationales Privatrecht, ed. 9 2004, pp. 56 et seq.

[104] *Schurig*, Kollisionsnorm und Sachrecht, 1981, p. 58.

[105] Ibid., pp. 60 et seq.

B. Legal Nature

not pre-determined. Conflict of laws rules can also be unilateral, in which case they use the same elements to justify the selection of one particular law. As will be shown below, Article 1(1) of the CISG is a unilateral conflict of laws rule.[106] These can easily be confused with internal rules of distribution, seeing as both determine the circumstances under which a specific set of laws is applicable. However, as explained above, while internal rules determine the applicable law within a legal system, thus on a national level, unilateral conflict of laws rules determine one law's applicability over the law of another legal system, thus on an international level.

An international conflict rule gives the court instructions on how to determine the legal system that is best suited to govern a legal question because the legal system is closely connected with the dispute. This involves a process in which the legal question in need of an answer is distilled out, and then the legal system best suited to address the question is determined due to its connection with the facts. In private international law terminology, the tools for this process are termed operative facts (*Anknüpfungsgegenstand* or *catégories*) and connecting factors (*Anknüpfungspunkte/-momente* or *éléments de rattachement*).[107]

Operative facts stand for the sum of legal questions that require an answer[108] or, depending on the perspective, the category of rules being determined through the conflict rules.[109] The category of rules governing that situation – disassociated from any legal system – are described by the content that they regulate.[110] By way of illustration, Article 10 of the Introductory Act of the BGB stipulates: "The name of a person is governed by the law of the country of which the person is a national." In this case, the operative facts are "the name of a person". In order to determine whether the rules of a foreign legal system can be seen as falling within the scope of the operative facts set forth in a conflict of laws rule, e.g. whether a provision in Spanish law can be deemed a rule for regulating names,

---

106 See *infra*, pp. 64 et seq.
107 *Schurig*, Kollisionsnorm und Sachrecht, 1981, pp. 78 et seq., especially p. 87; *Kegel/Schurig*, Internationales Privatrecht, ed. 9 2004, p. 310 et seq; *Kropholler*, Internationales Privatrecht, ed. 6 2006, pp. 104 et seq; *Bar/Mankowski*, IPR I, ed. 2 2003, p. 553.
108 *Junker*, Internationales Privatrecht, ed. 2 2017, p. 75.
109 *Bar/Mankowski*, IPR I, ed. 2 2003, p. 554.
110 *Lipstein*, Principles of the Conflict of Laws, National and International, 1981, p. 93.

the court carries out a "qualification" or "categorization" (*Qualifikation*).[111] This can be difficult because operative facts often use general terms that are broader and more abstract than the legal terms found in domestic substantive law, or because the set of facts have no direct legal counterpart in the *lex fori*.[112]

The legal system best suited to govern the operative facts is determined through connecting factors. A connecting factor is an element – such as nationality, domicile, or the place in which an object is located[113] – that links the set of facts exclusively to one legal system, at least ideally.[114] Due to its connection with the set of facts, that legal system is regarded as best suited to govern them. In the case of Article 10 of the Introductory Act of the BGB, the connecting factor is the nationality of the person in question. Thus, once the court has concluded what category of rules it is looking for (by qualifying the facts), it has determined the operative facts. The conflict rule containing those operative facts tells the court what territorial reference point of the situation is the one that determines the applicable law, i.e. which connecting factor is decisive. The connecting factor includes information on which person in a situation involving several people, what point of time of a legal relationship and what factor in particular are decisive.[115] To take an example that is more closely related to the CISG, Article 4(1)(a) of the Rome I Regulation sets forth a conflict rule for sales contracts. It states:

> *A contract for the sale of goods shall be governed by the law of the country where the seller has his habitual residence.*

Here, the operative facts can be seen in "a contract for the sale of goods"; the connecting factor is the habitual residence of the seller.

In the following, Art. 1(1)(a) and (b) of the CISG will be examined to determine their legal nature.

---

111 *Junker*, Internationales Privatrecht, ed. 2 2017, p. 102.
112 Ibid., pp. 103-104. An example for this latter situation is the trust, which is a product of Anglo-American law but has no counterpart in civil law countries.
113 *Bar/Mankowski*, IPR I, ed. 2 2003, p. 553; *Lipstein*, Principles of the Conflict of Laws, National and International, 1981, p. 94.
114 *Bar/Mankowski*, IPR I, ed. 2 2003, p. 557.
115 *Junker*, Internationales Privatrecht, ed. 2 2017, p. 77.

II. Article 1(1)(a) of the CISG

Article 1(1)(a) of the CISG reads:

> *This Convention applies to contracts of sale of goods between parties whose places of business are in different States when the States are Contracting States.*

As will be shown, this article can be categorized as a conflict of laws rules because it has both the structure and function of such a rule.

1. Structure

As was just laid out, conflict rules contain both operative facts and connecting factors. Within Article 1(1)(a) of the CISG, the position of operative facts is taken by "contracts of sale of goods between parties whose places of business are in different States". The legal questions this provision seeks to pair with a specific governing law are any matters pertaining to an international sales contract as set forth in Article 1(1), first sentence. This includes both the formation of such contracts and the obligations and rights resulting from them – thus any and all questions arising in connection with such a contract.[116] The internationality of the contract is part of the operative facts. If the contract is not international in the sense of the Convention because the parties do not have their seats of business in different States, Article 1(1) of the CISG does not apply and the court will go directly to its forum's general private international law. In cases decided by courts in EU Member States, the sales contract would then be governed by Article 4(1)(a) of the Rome I Regulation.

The text of Article 1(1)(a) itself – "when the States are Contracting States" – plays the part of connecting factor. It connects a sales contract to the CISG when both parties have their places of business in Contracting States. Thus, the provision makes use of a typical connecting factor: the

---

116 In contrast, the rule of application in the ULF, which governed only the formation of international sales contracts used the operative facts "shall apply to the **formation** of contracts of sale of goods entered into by parties whose places of business are in the territories of different States" (Art. 1(1), first sentence of the ULF). Art 1(1) of the ULIS, which dealt with all other questions relating to such contracts, used the same operative facts as are now used in Art 1(1) of the CISG, i.e. "shall apply to contracts of sale of goods entered into by parties whose places of business are in the territories of different States".

place of business of a party. The place of business a party, much like the habitual residence of a person, is a popular connecting factor as it guarantees a close connection from a territorial perspective.

What is peculiar in regard to Article 1(1)(a) of the CISG is that it uses not one, but two connecting factors that have to be met cumulatively. Most conflict rules use one connecting factor, connecting the facts to one legal system, which is then applicable, such as the seat of business of one of the parties. When conflict rules contain several connecting factors, these typically apply alternatively or subsidiarily (*Anknüpfungsleiter*).[117] Very rarely does a conflict rule contain more than one connecting factor that lead to the same legal system and must apply cumulatively.[118] This is called a "cumulative connection" (*kumulative Anknüpfung*) and is supposed to raise the threshold for the applicability of the law.[119] An example of such a cumulative connection is Article 14(1) no. 1 of the Introductory Act to the BGB, which determines that if both spouses are nationals of the same State, the general effects of marriage are governed by that State's law. Another example is Article 311–15 of the French Code Civil, which determines that French law governs the *possession d'état* of a child when father, mother and child all have their domestic habitual residence in France.[120] These typical cases of a cumulative connection impact several different individuals. The requirement of the connecting factors of each person leading to the same legal system ensures equal treatment, at least regarding the applicable law.

As in these rules, Article 1(1)(a) of the CISG makes the application of the CISG dependent on two connecting factors in requiring that both

---

117 *Rauscher*, Internationales Privatrecht, ed. 4 2017, pp. 80 et seqq.
118 See Art. 14(1) of the Introductory Law to the Germany Civil Law Code, which sets forth a conflict rule for the general effects of marriage. This provision utilizes a combination of subsidiary connecting factors, which then also contain cumulative requirements, because the governing law should be of a legal system that both spouses have a connection with. The connecting factors here are primarily the common nationality of the spouses and, if they have different nationalities, secondarily the country in which both spouses have their habitual residence.
119 *Rauscher*, Internationales Privatrecht, ed. 4 2017, p. 86.
120 Cf. *Kropholler*, Internationales Privatrecht, ed. 6 2006, p. 139. Notice that Art. 311–15 of the Civil Code is a unilateral conflict of laws rule, as it only determines the applicability of French law and makes no determination regarding the applicable law for cases in which the connecting factors do not connect the case to France, i.e. all necessary family members do not have their residence in France.

parties' seats of business be situated in Contracting States of the CISG. However, in contrast to the examples given, the connecting factors will never point to the same national legal system, because the parties will not have their seats of business in the same State. In its first sentence, Article 1(1) requires that the parties have their seats of business in *different* States. Thus, the cumulative connecting factors in lit. a can only be met if the parties have their seats of business in different Contracting States. This is a result of the CISG's nature as a uniform law for international contracts. But it is a uniform law that all Contracting States share, and as such the connecting factors nevertheless point to the same law. While not selecting one common national legal system shared in some aspect by both parties, Article 1(1)(a) of the CISG does select one law and as such fulfills the same function as any domestic conflict of laws rule with cumulative connecting factors. Whereas in conventional conflict of laws rules, the domestic legal system pointed to by the connecting factor is considered the most appropriate to govern the case precisely because the facts are connected with it in more than one way, Article 1(1)(a) selects the CISG as the most appropriate law to govern international sales contracts because they have these two connections to States that have adopted the CISG.

2. Function

a) Conflict of Laws Analysis Not Superfluous

It has been argued that uniform substantive law conventions do not require a conflict of laws analysis to determine their applicability.[121] The rules of application in such conventions therefore would not constitute conflict rules, but rather substantive law provisions.[122] After all, where there is uniform law, there are no conflicts of laws. Where there are no conflicts of laws, no conflict rules are needed.[123] In fact, it was the express intention of the drafters of the ULIS and the ULF to substitute private international law rules, as Winship points out, quoting a report by UNIDROIT:

---

121 *Zweigert/Drobning*, RabelsZ 1965, 146, 161.
122 *Meyer-Sparenberg*, Kollisionsnormen, 1990, pp. 86 et seq.
123 See only *Winship*, Cornell Int'l L.J. 1988, 487, 501.

> *From the beginning of its work on sales, the Rome Institute acknowledged that it sought to substitute uniform rules for choice-of-law rules. The Report printed with the 1935 draft text states that: '[t]he Institute is of opinion [sic] that the utility of public international law rests largely on the fact that it furnishes within the sphere of its application a definite law which will eliminate the difficulties arising from the conflict of laws.'*[124]

The texts of the ULF and the ULIS even contained provisions excluding the application of private international law, stating: "Rules of private international law shall be excluded for the purposes of the application of the present Law, subject to any provision to the contrary in the said Law" (Article 2 of the ULIS, Article 1(9) of the ULF). If, then, uniform laws make private international law superfluous and no conflicts analysis is needed, the rules of application in substantive uniform law conventions cannot be conflict rules.

Article 1(1)(a) of the CISG seems to continue in this vein. It does not rely on general rules of private international law in order to determine the applicability of the Convention.[125] The CISG, unlike the ULF and the ULIS, does not contain a provision that expressly excludes private international law for the purposes of the application of the Convention. Lit. a – unlike lit. b – does not directly reference rules of private international law. Via Article 1(1)(a), the CISG has the power to position itself above any reference to private international law. It may therefore be used to further the argument that uniform laws and thus also he CISG do not require conflict of laws rules to determine their applicability.

However, unless there was a truly global uniform law, the notion that uniform law makes conflicts of law disappear is illusory.[126] Even the CISG – which has had an extraordinarily high rate of success when measured

---

124 *Nadelmann*, Yale L.J. 1964, 449, 457.
125 Schlechtriem/Schwenzer/Schroeter/*Ferrari*, ed. 7 2019, Art. 1 para. 63; Kröll/Mistelis/Perales Viscasillas/*Mistelis*, 2018, para. 47; MüKo-BGB/*Huber*, ed. 8 2019, Art. 1 para. 45. Originally, there was some confusion about whether this provision did not actually still necessitate a conflicts analysis. This would have entailed that, in order for the Convention to be applicable, private international law would determine the law of a Contracting State as applicable and, additionally, that both parties had their places of business in Contracting States. Either private international law would have to lead to the law of a State where one of the parties has their place of business, or it would have to lead to the law of a third country that is also a Contracting State. This approach would lead to the applicability of the Convention only under quite limited circumstances.
126 *Kropholler*, Internationales Einheitsrecht, 1975, p. 160.

by the number of signatories – is not ratified globally. Therefore, even if a body of uniform law is applicable, determining that this is the case involves ensuring that no laws of non-Contracting States or autonomous laws of Contracting States are applicable in its stead.[127] If the uniform law is declared applicable because it is the most appropriate law to govern the situation[128], this is a decision based on conflict of laws criteria.[129] The principle of substantive provisions overriding conflict of laws rules is unhelpful because it is the very applicability that is in question.[130] Provisions such as Article 2 of the ULF/ULIS can be interpreted as excluding all private international law not contained in the uniform law.[131] A conflict of laws analysis, however, is still necessary and the rules of application can serve as conflict of laws rules.

b) Alternatives Test

And a conflict of laws analysis is what Article 1(1)(a) of the CISG offers. Article 1(1) of the CISG solves a conflict of legal systems. The internationality element ensures that courts can only consider the application of the CISG when confronted with an international sales contract. In such a situation it is not immediately obvious which legal system is applicable. The court therefore has to make a choice between the legal systems of different States. At this point, Article 1(1) of the CISG comes into play, mandating the application of the Convention. It constitutes a rule that decides a conflict of laws, and it does so in favor of the Convention.

To demonstrate this, the Alternatives Test[132] can be applied: What would be the alternative to applying Article 1(1) of the CISG? Would it lead to a different rule of the same legal system, or to a different legal system? The former is true. For a court applying Article 1(1) of the CISG, the alternative would not be to apply the same rules of a legal system of which the CISG is part. Rather, the court would instead apply its general

---

127 "*Si l 'on veut faire du droit uniforme sans conflit de lois, on fait un peu comme ceux qui font de la physique sans mathématique,*" Battifol, Trav. Com. fr. d. i. p. 1964-1966, p. 101 et seq., cited by *Kropholler*, RabelsZ 1974, 372, 386. To this same end *Drobning*, FS Overbeck, p. 18.
128 *Winship*, Cornell Int'l L.J. 1988, 487, 499.
129 *v. Bar*, Typen des Einheitsrechts, p. 57.
130 Schlechtriem/Schwenzer/*Schwenzer/Hachem*, ed. 4 2016, Art. 1 para. 6.
131 *Meyer-Sparenberg*, Kollisionsnormen, 1990, p. 88.
132 See *supra*, p. 31.

§ 2. Article 1(1) CISG – Rules of Application

private international law, determining the applicability of the rules of a national legal system. If Article 1(1)(a) were an internal rule of distribution, the alternative to its application would be other rules of the same legal system, since it would merely designate the applicability of internal rules. This is said of lit. b, since its wording can be interpreted that way.[133] However, the Convention is not embedded in a national legal system. It is not exclusively part of any one of the Contracting States, but rather communal law of all Contracting States.[134] The alternative to Article 1(1) of the CISG determining the applicability of the Convention is a provision determining the applicability of the law of an individual national legal system.

While the alternative to Article 1(1)(a) of the CISG is the applicability of the domestic law of specific national legal system, the CISG itself is no such law. Private international law, however, designates the applicability of State law.[135] It decides conflicts of national legal systems in favor of one of those national legal systems. Such systems are characterized by originating from a national legislature of a State and applying in the territory of that State. However, this is not a relevant difference to the CISG. The CISG is part of the Contracting States' legal systems, regardless of the particular method by which the individual Contracting States incorporate the Convention into their legal systems. Article 1(1)(a) does not designate the CISG as applicable as part of one Contracting State's legal system, but rather as part of all Contracting States' legal systems. The Convention is State law, since in all Contracting States, the national legislatures have given the Convention the force of law. A rule that determines its applicability therefore determines the applicability of State law. The difference is that as a body of law, its territory is that of all Contracting States. Article 1(1)(a) determines the CISG to be applicable not as part of one Contracting State's legal system, but as the State law of the forum – which is a Contracting State – and also all other Contracting States.

The fact that the Convention not a legal system that exhaustively covers all potential legal questions does not change this assessment. First, conflict rules typically only select part of a national legal system, specifically the rules of that system that match the operative facts. For example,

---

133 This is discussed below, see pp. 4 et seq.
134 *Kropholler*, Internationales Einheitsrecht, 1975, p. 185; *Czerwenka*, Rechtsanwendungsprobleme, 1988, p. 30; *Drobning*, FS Overbeck, p. 17.
135 *Kegel/Schurig*, Internationales Privatrecht, ed. 9 2004, p. 4; *Kropholler*, Internationales Privatrecht, ed. 6 2006, p. 55.

B. Legal Nature

Article 4(1) of the Rome I Regulation only selects the rules governing sales contracts from the legal system of the State in which the seller has his habitual residence. It does not select any other of that legal system's rules. If matters unrelated to the contract have to be regulated, a new conflict analysis is necessary. Second, most modern systems of private international law allow parties to opt for a *dépeçage*, meaning they can choose different legal systems to govern different parts of their contracts, thereby only selecting a number of rules from each legal system as relevant. Thus, the fact that the CISG only governs sales contracts should not stand in the way of determining it as applicable through a conflict rule.

One might argue that even for the area of law that the CISG governs, i.e. sales contracts, the rules may be incomplete and some matters may remain unregulated. A national legal system, conversely, can offer solutions for how to fill potential gaps in its individual areas of law, such as its sales law. The CISG stands alone, without a domestic legal system surrounding it which might help fill its gaps. However, as shown above, it contains instructions on how to fill internal gaps, to be found in Article 7(1). External gaps can be filled with a new conflicts analysis. As such, it is self-sufficient. The lack of a legal system surrounding the CISG does not leave the courts applying it with any unanswered questions. The alleged incompleteness of the Convention cannot serve as an argument against its conflictual eligibility.[136]

III. Article 1(1)(b) of the CISG

The notion that the text of Article 1(1)(b) of the CISG could constitute a connecting factor is far more controversial than regarding Article 1(1)(a). Article 1(1)(b) stipulates:

> *This Convention applies to contracts of sale of goods between parties whose places of business are in different States [...] when the rules of private international law lead to the application of the law of a Contracting State.*

In contrast to Article 1(1)(a), it directly references private international law, making its application a necessary requirement for the application of the CISG. Only if private international law leads to the law of a Contracting State as applicable law is the CISG applicable. The structure and

---

136 Cf. *Roth*, FS Jayme, pp. 766 et seq., arguing in favor of parties being able to conflictually choose non-State bodies of law.

49

§ 2. Article 1(1) CISG – Rules of Application

wording of the Article 1(1)(b) are much more open for interpretation than is the case for Article 1(1)(a) of the CISG. It is regularly categorized as a mere internal rule of distribution.[137] However, the provision can and should be interpreted as a conflict of laws rule, as will be shown in an analysis of the systematic effects such an interpretation has within the CISG.

1. Ambiguous Wording

Most often, the provision is interpreted as an internal rule of distribution and as such as a substantive rule. It is read as stating that once the private international law of the forum has been applied and those conflict rules have led to the application of the law of a Contracting State, lit. b clarifies that the CISG is a part of that State's legal system and should be applied if the contract in question is an international contract of sales.[138] As such it would not itself constitute a rule of private international law. It would only become relevant once the applicable legal system has already been identified. Within that legal system, Article 1(1)(b) merely points to the applicable rules. As one scholar put it, while lit. a is a conflict rule, lit. b is just a "more elegant, if indirect, way of expressing the principle: 'The provisions of this Convention constitute the law of Contracting States applicable to contracts of sales of goods between parties whose places of business are in different states.'"[139]

However, it is entirely feasible that the rule does not send an "elegant, if indirect" message, but instead a quite straightforward one that is simply being misinterpreted, likely because of the rule's use of an admittedly unusual connecting factor. Lit. b is read in isolation instead of in the

---

137 *Czerwenka*, Rechtsanwendungsprobleme, 1988, p. 162 ("Abgrenzungsnorm"); *Lohmann*, Parteiautonomie und UN-Kaufrecht, 2005, pp. 51 et seq; *Schlechtriem*, Internationales UN-Kaufrecht, ed. 4 2007, p. 12, para. 17.

138 *Czerwenka*, Rechtsanwendungsprobleme, 1988, p. 162; Staudinger-BGB/*Magnus*, 2018, CISG Art. 1 para. 95 (lit. b as clarification regarding which of the two sales laws is applicable within a Contracting State's legal system); *Lohmann*, Parteiautonomie und UN-Kaufrecht, 2005, pp. 52; *Schlechtriem*, Internationales UN-Kaufrecht, ed. 4 2007, p. 12 para. 17; Schlechtriem/Schwenzer/*Schwenzer/Hachem*, ed. 4 2016, CISG Art. 1 para. 35 ("within the domestic law of a CISG Contracting State, Article 1(1)(b) thus has the function of alllocating sales issues to the CISG"); MüKo-HGB/*Mankowski*, ed. 4 2018, CISG Art. 1 para. 48 ; *Neumayer*, RIW 1994, 99, p. 101 (referring to lit. b as "interne Verteilungsnorm" – an internal rule of distribution).

139 *Petrochilos*, Rev. hell. 1999, 191, 195.

context of the rest of Article 1(1), which starts with the words: "This Convention applies", to which lit. b adds "when the rules of private international law lead to the application of the law of a Contracting State."[140] Article 1(1) sets forth one consequence: the applicability of the CISG. The requirements for this consequence are contained in lit. a and lit. b, of which one has to be met. The wording does not suggest a distinction in the legal effect based on which alternative requirement is met. The consequence of both is the same, i.e. the applicability of the CISG.

Read correctly, lit. b is connecting the facts at hand with the Convention as applicable law, just like lit. a.[141] The requirement set forth in lit. b is that "the rules of private international law lead to the application of the law of a Contracting State".[142] This is certainly not a classic connecting factor, as these latch on to one tangible aspect of a set of facts, such as a nationality, a habitual residence, or – like lit. a – a place of business, any of which directly link the facts to one State. The requirement set forth in lit. b, i.e. the conflict of laws analysis, does connect the facts to a law – to be specific, to the Convention. The connecting factor is that the outcome of a conflict of laws analysis selects the law of a Contracting State. If this is the case, the facts are closely enough connected to the Convention to justify its applicability.

The court applying lit. b will apply its forum's private international law and in particular the conflict rule applicable to sales contracts and use it and its connecting factor to determine which State's law would govern the case according to it. If that State is a Contracting State, then the CISG is applicable, not as a part of exclusively that State's legal system, but rather as part of the forum's and all other Contracting States' law. For example, if the forum is in an EU Member State and there is no choice of law by the parties[143] the relevant conflict rule would be Article 4(1)(a) of the Rome I Regulation, which contains the connecting factor "habitual residence of the seller". If the habitual residence of the seller is located in a Contracting State, the requirement set forth in the connecting factor of lit. b is met and the facts have a close connection with the Convention, which is therefore applicable. The legal system of the Contracting State is

---

140 *Schlechtriem/Schroeter*, Internationales UN-Kaufrecht, ed. 6 2016, p. 22.
141 Ibid., p. 22 paras. 38, 39; *Schroeter*, FS Kritzer, p. 447.
142 *Schlechtriem/Schroeter*, Internationales UN-Kaufrecht, ed. 6 2016, p. 22 para. 38.
143 The effect of a choice of law of a party on the applicability of the CISG will be discussed below, pp. 53 et seq.

only relevant in that its theoretical applicability serves as a justification to apply the Convention. It is not actually applicable.

Taken literally and interpreted correctly, Article 1(1) of the CISG thus contains one conflict rule with two alternatively ("or") applicable connecting factors.[144]

2. Systematic Interpretation

This result is supported by a systematic interpretation of the provision. Article 1(1)(b) of the CISG is a complex rule that is entangled with several different issue within the CISG. These issues are, first, whether applying "the rules of private international law" includes giving effect to a *renvoi*, second, the effect of a reservation under Article 95 of the CISG, third, what law is applicable to an agreement to opt out of the CISG, and finally, whether the Convention is applied as domestic or foreign law. All of these issues are directly influenced by the legal nature of Article 1(1)(b). Curiously, while the rule is commonly believed to be an internal rule of distribution, the preferred solutions for these issues are much better explained by recognizing the provision as a rule of private international law.

a) *Renvois* Within "the Rules of Private International Law"

The application of rules of private international law is a requirement for the application of the CISG via Article 1(1)(b) of the CISG. The nature of the rule has an effect on how exactly private international law is applied, for example in regard to giving effect to a *renvoi*. As explained above, many see the rule as an internal rule of distribution. These same scholars also believe that the provision should be read to exclude a potential *renvoi* set by the legal system of the Contracting State, following the lead of the Secretariat Commentary.[145] That means that when the private international

---

144 The relationship of lit. a and lit. b will be discussed below, pp. 63 et seq.
145 Honsell/*Siehr*, ed. 2 2009, Art. 1 para. 17; *Lohmann*, Parteiautonomie und UN-Kaufrecht, 2005, pp. 58-60; MüKo-HGB/*Mankowski*, ed. 4 2018, CISG Art. 1 para. 52; Schlechtriem/Schwenzer/Schroeter/*Ferrari*, ed. 7 2019, CISG Art. 1 para. 74; Staudinger-BGB/*Magnus*, 2018, CISG Art. 1 para. 106; *Vékás*, IPrax 1987, 342, 344.

law of the court's forum selects the legal system of a Contracting State, then Article 1(1)(b) would ensure that the CISG is applicable regardless of whether the reference to the legal system included conflict rules of the Contracting State or not.

The private international law of each State includes decisions on what legal system to apply to what legal questions, and whether this reference to a foreign legal system includes a reference to its private international law. Arguing that lit. b as an internal rule of distribution can influence the extent of the reference in the private international law of another State would entail that a strictly internal rule of distribution of one State's substantive law could have an effect on how the private international law of another State is interpreted. The justification for such an endowment of an internal rule with the powers of a conflict of laws rule is that it ensures that the CISG is applied, which has a bias in favor of its own enforcement.[146] However, while the goal is desirable, a mere internal substantive rule could never have an effect on how private international law, especially that of a different State, is applied. Private international law is blind regarding the law that it is referring to, otherwise it would not be neutral. Thus, by the time substantive rules are taken into account, the analysis of private international law has to have been completed; substantive rules cannot influence the analysis retroactively.

The way a rule can have such an effect, however, is if it itself is a conflict rule. The wording of Article 1(1)(b) requires that "the rules of private international law lead to the law of a Contracting State." This wording leaves the specifics unclear: does "the rules of private international law" mean only the forum's private international law, or does it include other conflict rules that might be referred to within a general reference (*Gesamtverweis*)? Put differently, should "the law of a Contracting State" be understood as the legal system – including its private international law – or only as the substantive law of the Contracting State? The wording of the provision does not exclude the possibility that the conflict rules make a general reference to another State's legal system and thus lead the application of foreign rules of private international law, as well.[147] Theoretically, a court could follow any number of references to foreign legal systems until finally a direct reference is made to the substantive law of a Contracting State.

---

146 MüKo-HGB/*Mankowski*, ed. 4 2018, CISG Art. 1 para. 52.
147 *Neumayer*, RIW 1994, 99, 101 (although regarding lit. b as an internal rule of distribution).

While this outcome could technically be justified with the broad wording of the provision, a complex chase through different legal systems does not serve the purpose of Article 1(1)(b). The requirement that the rules of private international law lead to the law of a Contracting State serves as a connecting factor between the dispute and the CISG, ensuring that courts in Contracting States only apply the CISG when there is a connection between the dispute and a Contracting State. Any kind of reference to the law of a Contracting State, not just a reference to its substantive law, establishes a close connection to the Contracting State and thus the CISG. The technicalities of what kind of reference it is and whether the Contracting State's private international law would refer to a different State's law should not have an impact on this outcome. The CISG is not being applied as part of the State's substantive law anyway, so that the type of reference itself is irrelevant. Instead, it is being applied directly, and the reference by the rules of private international law merely serves as a threshold to ensure that the court does not impose the Convention on disputes with no connection to the CISG. Article 1(1)(b) of the CISG can therefore be interpreted broadly.

While the effect of Article 1(1)(b) as a conflict rule is up to interpretation, it is possible and preferable to interpret it to mean that any reference to the law of a Contracting State by the forum's private international law satisfies its requirements. However, this is only possible because it does, in fact, constitute a conflict of laws rule, while reading the same effects into a mere substantive rule would mean violating basic rules of private international law. Thus, the desired outcome of having a *renvoi* be ignored within the application of Article 1(1)(b) of the CISG can easily be achieved by recognizing that it is a conflict of laws rule, and functions as such.

b) Effect of Article 95 Reservation

Article 1(1)(b) is also connected to Article 95 of the CISG, which reads:

> *Any State may declare [...] that it will not be bound by subparagraph (1)(b) of article 1 of this Convention.*

The effect of such a reservation is unclear. Unity can be found regarding the notion that courts in Reservation States should not apply Article 1(1)(b) of the CISG when determining the law applicable to a dispute, even when its own private international law directs it to the law of a Non-Reser-

B. Legal Nature

vation State.[148] After all, the Reservation States have clearly stated that they do not want to be bound by the provision. In the reverse situation, however, when a court of a Non-Reservation State applies its private international law and is led to the law of a Reservation State, there are varying opinions on whether the reservation should have an effect in such a situation. Should the courts in the Non-Reservation State be obliged to respect the reservation made by another State?

The reciprocity of the Convention is referenced in arguments regarding the reservation. Given that the Convention is based on reciprocity, the courts applying the CISG have to apply it the same way that the courts would in the State whose law is applicable.[149] If the applicable law is that of a Reservation State and the courts located there cannot apply Article 1(1)(b), then foreign courts applying the Reservation State's law should follow suit and apply the Reservation State's autonomous, non-uniform law. Others argue the opposite, stating that the main objective of the Convention is to be applied as often as possible in order to have the most beneficial impact on international trade, regardless of how the State's courts would apply its own law in the same situation.[150] While States are welcome to make reservations from the Convention and thus direct its application though their own courts, the courts of Non-Reservation States should apply the Convention in its complete form. Only thus could the fullest possible effect of a uniform law convention be guaranteed.

However, a clear determination of the legal nature of Article 1(1)(b) gives guidance on this issue without relying on notions of reciprocity, which can apparently be manipulated to serve conflicting arguments. The legal nature of the rule determines which courts have to apply it as part of which State's legal system. If Article 1(1)(b) were an internal rule of distribution and therefore a substantive rule, it would be part of the legal

---

148 Staudinger-BGB/*Magnus*, 2018, CISG Art. 1 para. 108; Internationales Vertragsrecht/*Saenger*, ed. 3 2018, CISG Art. 1 para. 19; Schlechtriem/Schwenzer/*Schwenzer/Hachem*, ed. 4 2016, CISG Art. 1 para. 37; *Piltz*, Internationales Kaufrecht, ed. 2 2008, para. 2-104; *Siehr*, RabelsZ 1988, 587, 610; *Lohmann*, Parteiautonomie und UN-Kaufrecht, 2005, p. 60. *Mankowski* contradicts himself at this point, first stating that a court in a Reservation State can only apply the CISG via Article 1(1)(a) of the CISG, but that it also has to apply the CISG if its private international law leads to the application of the law of a Non-Reservation State, see MüKo-HGB/*Mankowski*, ed. 4 2018, CISG Art. 1 paras. 54 and 56.
149 Bianca/Bonell/*Evans*, 1987, Art. 95 para. 3.4; *Karollus*, UN-Kaufrecht, 1991, pp. 31, 34; *Vékás*, IPrax 1987, 342, 345 et seq; *Pünder*, RIW 1990, 869, 871 et seq.
150 Honsell/*Siehr*, ed. 2 2009; *Czerwenka*, Rechtsanwendungsprobleme, 1988, p. 159; *Siehr*, RabelsZ 1988, 587, 604.

system that is being applied: The court would be applying it as a provision of the legal system, foreign or not, that its rules of private international law have directed it to apply. If, however, the provision is a conflict rule, it is part of the private international law of the court that is deciding the dispute, part of the *lex fori*. The court applies it as one of its own conflict rules. As a conflict rule, Article 1(1)(b) determines the CISG as the applicable law. Depending on the exact categorization, a reservation under Article 95 affects the application of the CISG in different ways. Do the States want to exclude the binding effect of a conflict rule, or the binding effect of an internal rule of distribution?

If the rule were seen as an internal rule of distribution, States making a reservation would essentially be saying that they want foreign and domestic courts applying their law to always apply their non-uniform sales law. Once a court determines the Reservation State's legal system as applicable, there is no Article 1(1)(b) that could direct that court to apply the CISG.[151] The German legislature ostensibly took this position in its law accompanying the ratification of the CISG[152], Article 2 of which states:

> *If the rules of private international law lead to the application of the law of a State that has made a reservation pursuant to Article 95 of the CISG, then Article 1(1)(b) of the CISG does not apply.*[153]

This is also the interpretation some States had in mind that were lobbying for the inclusion of a reservation from Article 95: both the German Democratic Republic (GDR) and the Czechoslovak Socialist Republic (CSSR) wanted their domestic sales law to apply to international sales instead of the CISG whenever their legal system was to govern a dispute.[154] As an internal rule of distribution, the purpose of Article 1(1)(b) would be to achieve the opposite. Therefore, the effect of that provision had to be eliminated for cases in which their legal systems would be found applicable.

---

151 Honsell/*Siehr*, ed. 2 2009, Art. 1 para. 16.
152 Gesetz zu dem Übereinkommen der Vereinten Nationen vom 11. April 1980 über Verträge über den internationalen Warenkauf sowie zur Änderung des Gesetzes zu dem Übereinkommen vom 19. Mai 1956 über den Beförderungsvertrag im internationalen Straßengüterverkehr (CMR), BGBl. II p. 586.
153 "Führen die Regeln des internationalen Privatrechts zur Anwendung des Rechts eines Staates, der eine Erklärung nach Artikel 95 des Übereinkommens von 1980 abgegeben hat, so bleibt Artikel 1 Abs. 1 Buchstabe b des Übereinkommens außer Betracht."
154 Bianca/Bonell/*Evans*, 1987, CISG Art. 95 para. 2.3; Staudinger-BGB/*Magnus*, 2018, CISG Art. 95 para. 3.

A reservation pursuant to Article 95, according to which States are not bound by the internal rule Article 1(1)(b), would have the desired effect. For example, if a court in France – a Non-Reservation State – were to apply the law of the United States – a Reservation State – to an international sales contract, then the French court would have to apply the autonomous sales law of the United States. However, it would also mean that courts in Reservation States, when their forum's private international law leads to the law of a Non-Reservation State, would have to apply Article 1(1)(b), e.g. a US court would have to apply the CISG if its private international law led to French law. After all, France wants the CISG to apply to international sales contracts instead of its autonomous sales law; otherwise it would have made a reservation.

This consequence is incompatible with the prevailing view that courts in Reservation States should never apply Article 1(1)(b), even though it is held by the same people that believe Article 1(1)(b) to be an internal rule of distribution. If one believes that it is an internal rule, should a reservation not only have an effect when the internal rules of a Reservation State are applied? Why should a reservation by the United States affect whether autonomous French sales law or the CISG is applied? Thus, if the categorization of Article 1(1)(b) as an internal rule were accepted in all its consequences, then a reservation pursuant to Article 95 would mean that courts in Reservation States would still have to apply the provision as a part of foreign Non-Contracting States' legal systems.

The only way to reach the conclusion that courts in Reservation States do not have to apply Article 1(1)(b) is if it is seen as a conflict rule, as part of the private international law of each Contracting State. Then, if a State makes such a reservation and thereby declares that it does not want to be bound by it, it is casting the rule from its own private international law. In applying its private international law, the State's courts should be prohibited from taking Article 1(1)(b) into account when determining the law governing a dispute. The only way such courts could find the CISG to be applicable is via Article 1(1)(a), i.e. when both parties have their seats of business in Contracting States. Courts in the United States, for example, can only ever apply the CISG to cases in which both parties have their seats of business in Contracting States. If this is not the case, then the State's general private international law will determine the applicable non-uniform law. French courts, on the other hand, can apply the CISG if French private international law leads to the application of US law, because Article 1(1)(b) as a French conflict of laws rule says they can.

Accordingly, the effects of a reservation under Article 95 vary depending on how one determines the legal nature of Article 1(1)(b), and are preferable when Article 1(1)(b) is recognized as a conflict rule. It is the only interpretation that can carry the one aspect everybody seems to agree on: that courts in Reservation States should not have to apply the CISG pursuant to Article 1(1)(b). Such courts cannot be bound by the provision when determining the applicable law by applying their private international law. Courts in Non-Reservation States, on the other hand, are free to apply it as one of their forum's conflict rules. If their rules of private international law, applied as a requirement of Article 1(1)(b) of the CISG, then lead to the law of a Reservation State, the CISG is applicable. It is irrelevant to the court of a Non-Reservation State whether the Reservation State considers itself bound by the conflict rule or not, since the former is not generally applying the latter's conflict rules. The reservation is only relevant to a court if made by the forum of the court. Thus, clarity on the legal nature of Article 1(1)(b) untangles the debate surrounding the impact of Article 95 Reservations.

c) Law Applicable to Opt-Out

Finally, it is not clear what law is applicable to an agreement by the parties to opt out of the CISG. Again, the legal nature of Article 1(1) of the CISG influences this debate. In order to demonstrate this, it is helpful to first set out what effect a choice of law by the parties has within the parameters of the CISG.

aa) Choice of Law

The CISG offers an opt-out mechanism. This means that the CISG is generally applicable if the requirements in its rules of application are met and that parties can then opt out of the application of the Convention if they wish. This follows from Article 6 of the CISG, which stipulates that

> [t]he parties may exclude the application of this Convention or [...] derogate from or vary the effect of any of its provisions.

In practice, this has the following consequences: If both parties have their seats of business in different Contracting States, the CISG is generally applicable pursuant to Article 1(1)(a) of the CISG. The parties can subsequently avoid the application of the CISG only if they explicitly exclude its application. Even if the parties do not both have their places of business in Contracting States, the CISG is applicable if the rules of private international law lead to the law of a Contracting State pursuant to Article 1(1)(b) of the CISG. Private international law typically places high priority on party autonomy and will thus give effect to a choice of law by the parties.[155] If the parties choose the law of a Contracting State, this satisfies the requirements of Article 1(1)(b), as the rules of private international law then technically lead the law of a Contracting State, by virtue of the valid choice of law. Under these circumstances, it is still possible for the parties to opt out of application of the CISG pursuant to Article 6 of the CISG. They can either state that they do not want the CISG to apply or they can specifically select the domestic sales of the Contracting State to be applicable, which is interpreted as an opt-out.

According to statistics published by the ICC, the CISG was chosen directly by the parties in 13 contracts subject to arbitration proceedings under the ICC in 2014 and 2015.[156] Even such a direct choice of the CISG, as straightforward as it would first appear, does not automatically guarantee application of the Convention.[157] Instead, the court in a Contracting State must first look at Articles 1(1)(a) and (b) to establish the application of the CISG. If the requirements of lit. a are met, the CISG is applicable purely because both parties have their seats of business in Contracting States. If this is not the case, the court will take Article 1(1)(b) into account. Here, the direct choice of the CISG can be considered, but only within the limits of the court's rules of private international law.[158] Since the requirement is that these rules find the law of a Contracting State to be applicable, the

---

155 See only Art. 3(1), first sentence of the Rome I Regulation: "A contract shall be governed by the law chosen by the parties."
156 2015 ICC Dispute Resolution Bulletin, p. 15; 2016 ICC Dispute Resolution Bulletin, p. 17.
157 The direct choice of the CISG is sometimes incorrectly named as a third path to the application of the CISG next to Art. 1(1)(a) and (b), see e.g. *Mistelis*, CISG and Arbitration, p. 379.
158 Whether the choice of the CISG can lead directly to the applicability of the Convention, or whether such a choice first has to be interpreted as the choice of a legal system of a Contracting State and then specifically the CISG depends on the rules of private international law. The possibility of a direct choice of the law of a treaty, beyond its scope, is seen as beneficial by some scholars, and it was discussed, but ultimately rejected, during the drafting of the Rome I Regulation, see *supra*, p. 16.

choice of the CISG can be interpreted as the law of a Contracting State and the Convention as part of it.[159]

Under Article 1(1)(b) of the CISG, the effect of a choice of law by the parties is twofold: in a first step the general choice of the law of a Contracting State by the parties leads to application of the CISG, but it can in a second step also constitute an opt-out of the Convention. The validity of the choice of law is determined by the court's forum private international law since the requirement is that those rules of private international law lead to a Contracting State's laws. The choice of the parties has to select "the law of a Contracting State". Any reference to an area of law within that legal system that can be interpreted as an explicit or implicit deselection of the CISG is to be treated separately as an agreement to opt out of the CISG, a matter of Article 6 of the CISG.[160]

In order to opt out of the CISG, it is not necessary for the parties to choose a domestic law to be applicable instead of the CISG – a mere choice against the CISG suffices. The parties may want the autonomous, non-uniform sales law of a Contracting State to govern their dispute. However, unless there are clear indications of such intent, the choice of a Contracting State's law must be interpreted to include the CISG.[161] The CISG must be considered part of the legal system of the Contracting States and as a body of law for international contracts of sale it is superior to domestic sales laws. In order to enhance its effectiveness, an opt-out cannot be given too low a threshold. Even choices in favor of "German commercial law" or "German substantive sales law" still include the CISG, since it is German law in the sense that it is part of the German legal system.[162] An express

---

159 This process may seem like an artificial and ultimately superfluous step to finally establish the direct applicability of the CISG, which was the initial goal of the parties anyway, but it is the natural result of the CISG's deference to rules of private international law of the Contracting States, ensuring that these are not entirely overridden. If those rules did not enable a party choice of law at all, then a choice of the CISG would simply have to be ignored. If the rules do give effect to a choice, the extent of party autonomy in this regard matters. In the end, a direct choice of the Convention will lead to its direct applicability via Article 1(1)(b) of the CISG.
160 Schlechtriem/Schwenzer/Schroeter/*Schroeter*, 2019, Intro Artt 14-24 CISG paras. 14b and 14c.
161 BGH NJW 1999, 1259; Staudinger-BGB/*Magnus*, 2018, Art. 1 para. 104; Kröll/Mistelis/Perales Viscasillas/*Mistelis*, 2018, CISG Art. 6 para. 12; MüKo-HGB/*Mankowski*, ed. 4 2018, CISG Art. 6 para. 7.
162 MüKo-HGB/*Mankowski*, ed. 4 2018, CISG Art. 6 para. 7.

exclusion or similar can be expected from the parties.¹⁶³ As long as this is not the case, the choice of a Contracting State's law includes the CISG and leads to its applicability according to Article 1(1)(b) of the CISG.

bb) Applicable Law

The question of what law should govern an agreement by the parties to opt out of the CISG can now be addressed. There are different approaches. On the one hand, it is suggested that the law governing such an agreement should be the law that the parties choose in lieu of the CISG ("bootstrap theory").¹⁶⁴ In the absence of a positive choice by the parties, the law objectively applicable according to the rules of private international law should apply to the agreement. On the other hand, most argue that the CISG itself should apply to the agreement, specifically Articles 14 to 24, which govern contract formation.¹⁶⁵ This debate is relevant because opt-out clauses are often contained in general terms and conditions, which are designed to stand up to scrutiny under domestic laws, but not necessarily under the CISG.

A categorization of the legal nature of Article 1(1) of the CISG, however, gives a clear and satisfying answer to the question of the applicable law. Because Article 1(1) of the CISG is a conflict of laws rule, the Convention is directly applicable when the requirements of either Article 1(1)(a) or (b) of the CISG are met. This direct applicability of the Convention is established before the parties can opt out of it pursuant to Article 6 of the CISG. Such an agreement deselecting the Convention necessarily takes place within the scope of the CISG. Only after its applicability to the contract has been determined does the agreement to opt out of it even become relevant.

---

163 What law is applicable to such an opt-out is a matter of debate. Since this question is relevant for both when the Convention is applicable pursuant to lit. a and pursuant to lit. b, and since it is a consequence of the qualification of both of these provisions as conflict rules, it will be discussed below, see pp. 58 et seqq.
164 Honsell/*Siehr*, ed. 2 2009, Art. 6 para. 4.
165 MüKo-HGB/*Mankowski*, ed. 4 2018, CISG Art. 6 para. 9; *Lohmann*, Parteiautonomie und UN-Kaufrecht, 2005, pp. 242 et seq; Staudinger-BGB/*Magnus*, 2018, CISG Art. 6 para. 10; Schlechtriem/*Schroeter*, Internationales UN-Kaufrecht, ed. 6 2016, p. 27; Internationales Vertragsrecht/*Saenger*, ed. 3 2018, CISG Art. 6 para. 2..

§ 2. Article 1(1) CISG – Rules of Application

As a result, the bootstrap theory is ill-suited to determine the law applicable to an opt-out agreement regarding the CISG. By way of an example, the bootstrap-theory is employed in the Rome I Regulation, according to which choice of law by the parties are governed "by the law which would govern it under this Regulation if [choice of law] were valid".[166] Thus, the choice of law has to satisfy the requirements of the law chosen by the parties. Only if the choice is not valid (or in case there is no choice of law at all) is the applicable law determined according to objective criteria. Because of this mechanism, it is entirely reasonable that the party choice is measured by the law chosen by the parties. No other law is applicable to that choice at this point – there is a legal vacuum in this regard – since the objectively applicable law is only determined in the absence of a valid choice. Thus, no other law can legitimately invalidate the choice of law.

This mechanism is the opposite of what takes place when the CISG is applicable according to Article 1(1). Because Article 1(1) is a conflict of laws rule, the procedure is reversed: The applicability of the CISG is determined first, either by virtue of Article 1(1)(a), or due to subjective or objective criteria in private international law pursuant to Article 1(1)(b). An agreement to opt out of the CISG is only taken into account once the applicability of the CISG has been established. The purpose of this mechanism is to enhance the applicability of the Convention. Only when the parties specifically do not want the CISG to apply should that choice be examined according to Article 6. Article 6 is the extension of the party autonomy granted by the CISG and enhances the possibilities of what the parties can choose on a conflict of laws level. Given this sequence, it is natural that an agreement to opt out of the CISG, and no other law, should satisfy the requirements regarding the formation of contracts set forth in the CISG. The bootstrap theory, which offers a party autonomy-friendly solution for situation which suffers from a legal vacuum, is not appropriate for an opt-out of the CISG, which takes place in the opposite of a legal vacuum.

The purpose of the Convention's mechanism of applicability, i.e. to maximize the cases governed by the Convention, justifies the fact that the

---

166 Art. 3(5) of the Rome I Regulation: "The existence and validity of the consent of the parties as to the choice of the applicable law shall be determined in accordance with the provisions of Articles 10, 11 and 13." Art. 10(1) of the Rome I Regulation: "The existence and validity of a contract, or any term of a contract, shall be determined by the law which would govern it under this Regulation if the contract or term were valid."

parties should only be able to opt out of the mechanism if it satisfies the CISG standard for the formation of agreements. Applying the CISG has the added benefit that it ensures that all opt-out agreements are held to the same uniform standard, which enhances legal certainty. If the parties have indeed opted out validly, their choice of another law instead of the CISG is then measured by the standard set by the private international law of the forum, which may well call for an approach following the bootstrap theory.[167]

A baffling consequence of categorizing Article 1(1)(b) of the CISG as a mere internal rule of distribution would be that the law according to which the validity of an opt-out of the CISG would have to be assessed would differ depending on whether the CISG is applicable pursuant either to lit. a or to lit. b. In the case of Article 1(1)(a) of the CISG – a conflict rule – the opt-out would have to be judged by the standard set by the CISG, as just explained. If, in contrast, the CISG is applicable according to Article 1(1)(b) as an internal rule, the opt-out would need to be measured by the same standards of the choice of law in general. The choice of law in favor of a Contracting State's legal system is measured by the standards set forth by the private international law of the forum, and the choice of that State's non-uniform, domestic sales law – an opt-out of the CISG – would need to be measured by those standards as well because it also takes place on a conflict of laws level. Only once that conflict of laws analysis is complete could Article 1(1)(b) as a substantive law rule take effect, and it would then set forth the applicability of the CISG only if the parties have not already preemptively opted out of it. Thus, the opt-out would need to be measured by the same standards as the choice of law by the parties.

It makes little sense to judge the validity of an opt-out by the parties by different standards depending on which of Article 1(1)(a) or (b) of the CISG leads to the applicability of the Convention. Recognizing that those two provisions are merely parts of one single conflict of laws rule and that the application of either has the same effect – the direct applicability of the CISG – enables us to measure an agreement to opt out of that applicability by the same standards, i.e. the standards set forth by the CISG. In effect, all clauses, whether negotiated or standard, that aim to deselect the Convention must satisfy the requirements of the Convention.

---

167 *Hachem*, Applicability of the CISG - Articles 1 and 6; Bianca/Bonell/*Bianca*, 1987, CISG Art. 6 para. 2.3; Schlechtriem/Schwenzer/Schroeter/*Ferrari*, ed. 7 2019, CISG Art. 6 para. 15; Staudinger-BGB/*Magnus*, 2018, CISG Art. 6 para. 60; MüKo-HGB/*Mankowski*, ed. 4 2018, CISG Art. 6 para. 5.

§ 2. Article 1(1) CISG – Rules of Application

This is justified by the goal of maximizing the applicability of the CISG that all Contracting States have agreed to by signing the Convention. If this means that standard clauses that would be valid under their domestic law are not valid under the CISG or vice versa, this must be tolerated in the interest of the proliferation of the Convention and of legal certainty.

d) CISG Applicable as Domestic Law

The final argument in favor of interpreting Article 1(1)(b) of the CISG as a conflict of laws rule instead of an internal rule of distribution is that this enables all courts in Contracting States to always apply the CISG as domestic law. Article 1(1)(a) of the CISG unquestionably always leads to the applicability of the Convention as domestic law: The rules of the Convention are applied as part of the forum's legal system and as such, they are domestic law for the court, not foreign law. This ties into the notion that the territory of the CISG is the territory of all Contracting States and that as a uniform body of law, it is domestic law for the courts in all Contracting States.[168]

If Article 1(1)(b) of the CISG was seen as a mere internal rule of distribution, the CISG would need to be treated as foreign law, even if applied by a Contracting State. After all, the court would be applying a foreign legal system, and the CISG as part of that foreign legal system. Given that the exact same law is part of the applying court's legal system, this is a pointless distinction. Accordingly, even authors that see lit. b as an internal rule of distribution argue that the CISG must be applied as domestic law, even though it is technically being applied as part of a foreign legal system.[169]

Treating lit. b as a conflict rule resolves this dissonance and ensures that uniform application of the uniform law matches the legal nature of its rules of application. In this case, it also leads to the applicability of the Convention as law of the forum, i.e. as domestic law. Even though application of private international law rules takes place, this does not lead to application of the CISG as part of the law of a different Contracting State, and as such, technically, as foreign law. Rather, this selection process

---

[168] See *supra*, fn. 134.
[169] Staudinger-BGB/*Magnus*, 2018, CISG Art. 1 para. 84; Schlechtriem/Schwenzer/Schroeter/*Ferrari*, ed. 7 2019, CISG Art. 1 para. 76; *Maultzsch*, FS Schwenzer, 1218; *Pünder*, RIW 1990, 869, 873; *Vékás*, IPrax 1987, 342.

is merely the precursor for direct application of the CISG, which the court of the Contracting State applies as its own law. As a result, the Convention is applied directly and not as the foreign law of one Contracting State, but rather as the law of the forum under both lit. a and lit. b. Consequently, the Convention constitutes domestic law for courts in every Contracting State, as is preferable since the courts in all Contracting States are at least theoretically familiar with the Convention.

This distinction is especially relevant in jurisdictions in which a distinction is made between foreign and domestic law, such as Germany.[170] Firstly, the relevance lies in whether foreign law is treated as a matter of law or of fact. In some jurisdictions, foreign law is considered a matter of law, which means that the court is charged with applying it. To this end, the court can request the input of an expert. The parties may also offer their views on the matter, but these are not binding on the court, as opposed to statements made regarding questions of fact. In Germany and the Netherlands, this flows from the principle *iura novit curia*, which translates to "the court knows the law"; in other jurisdictions such as Belgium, Italy, France and Portugal, this is explicitly codified.[171] However, in common law jurisdictions, foreign law is actually treated as a matter of fact. In this case, it is the parties' job to prove the content of foreign law and the court is only in charge of applying and interpreting it.[172] This can make a big difference for the outcome of the case, because the court is bound by undisputed claims regarding the content of the law, which could potentially be quite different from the actual content. There is no reason that a court in a Contracting State should have to apply the CISG as foreign law and submit to the presentations of the parties regarding the Convention's content. Any court in a Contracting State should be able to treat the CISG as domestic law, as it is no more foreign to it than its domestic sales law.

Another level at which the difference between foreign and domestic law becomes critical in some jurisdictions is in its application by higher courts.[173] In Germany and several other jurisdictions, the application of foreign law in lower instances cannot be fully reviewed by higher courts

---

170 *Lohmann*, Parteiautonomie und UN-Kaufrecht, 2005, p. 50; *Czerwenka*, Rechtsanwendungsprobleme, 1988, pp. 162 et seq.
171 *Trautmann*, Ermittlung ausländischen Rechts, p. 446.
172 Ibid.
173 *Geimer*, Internationales Zivilprozessrecht, ed. 8 2020, para. 2610 et seq.

§ 2. Article 1(1) CISG – Rules of Application

(*irreversibles Recht*).[174] Instead, the higher courts are bound by the findings of the lower courts, while they would be free to apply and interpret domestic law as they saw fit. As is the case with treating the CISG as fact and not as law, binding higher courts in Contracting States to the finding of lower courts disregards the fact that these courts should be as familiar with the CISG as with their domestic sales law. Even if they are not, perhaps because they deal with a greater number of national rather than international sales contracts, the CISG and related commentary is available in many languages and asserting its content as well as its correct application and interpretation does not present the same hurdles as does foreign domestic law.

Of course, it is possible that the private international law of a Non-Contracting State could make a general reference to the entire legal system of a Contracting State, including its private international law. Only in the rare case[175] where a Non-Contracting State's court would come to apply the CISG – because the private international law of a Contracting State led to the application of the CISG via Article 1(1)(a) or (b) of the CISG – would the CISG ever be applied as foreign law. In such cases, treating the CISG like law of a foreign State is sensible. Because the forum did not become a signatory to the Convention, the CISG is not part of the forum's legal system. It is as foreign as the domestic sales law of any other country. Interpreting lit. b as a conflict rule thus justifies the desirable application of the Convention as domestic law for Contracting States and foreign law for Non-Contracting States.

3. Conclusion

An interpretation of the wording and systematic effects of Article 1(1)(b) of the CISG show that it is a conflict of laws rule. Just like Article 1(1)(a), it effects the direct application of the CISG, as State law of the forum and all other Contracting States.

---

174 For Germany, see sec. 545 of the Civil Code of Procedure.
175 References in private internationa law are rarely general references. In the EU for example Article 20 of the Rome I Regulation excludes private international law from its references, making any reference to the law of another State a reference to that State's substantive law. A reference to the law of a Contracting State would not include the rule of application of the CISG. Thus, EU Member States that are Non-Contracting States of the CISG (such as the UK until it leaves the EU) could never be tasked to apply the CISG.

IV. Consequences for Article 1(1) of the CISG as a Whole

1. Structure

Following the analysis regarding Article 1(1)(a) and (b), Article 1(1) of the CISG is not a conglomeration of rules of different legal natures. Instead, it is a unilateral conflict of laws rule with alternative connecting factors.

a) Alternative Connecting Factors

Both Article 1(1)(a) and 1(1)(b) of the CISG constitute conflict of laws rules. In fact, they both constitute part of the same conflict of laws rule: Article 1(1) of the CISG. This has an influence on their relationship to one another. Typically, Article 1(1)(a) is believed to be applicable primarily, and only if its requirements are not met, Article 1(1)(b) is to be applied.[176] It is not entirely clear what the reason for this preferential treatment of the so-called autonomous application of the CISG is, but one reason could be that lit. a and lit. b are generally believed to have different legal natures. Lit. a would naturally have to be applicable first, since it is seen as a conflict of laws rules. Lit. b as a presumed internal rule could only be applicable if general private international law leads to the application of the law of a Contracting State, which would only be consulted if the requirements of lit. a are not met. The primacy of lit. a is a product of the presumed legal nature of both rules.

Given that lit. a and lit. b are not distinct rules, but both merely connecting factors of one single conflict of laws rule, their relationship is not dictated by such a difference. It would still be possible that one of the connecting factors is primarily applicable; this is a method used in other conflict of laws rules.[177] However, the wording of Article 1(1) of the

---

[176] MüKo-HGB/*Mankowski*, ed. 4 2018, CISG Art. 1 para. 47; Kröll/Mistelis/Perales Viscasillas/*Mistelis*, 2018, CISG Art. 1 para. 4.
[177] Art. 14(1) of the Introductory Act of the EGBG, for example, reads:
"The general effects of the marriage are governed by
1. the law of the country of shared nationality of the spouses or last shared nationality during the marriage if one of them is still the national of that country, otherwise
2. the law of the country in which both spouses have their habitual residence or lastly had it during the marriage, if one of them still has his or her habitual residence there, otherwise

CISG – which uses a simple "or" between lit. a and lit. b – suggests that the provisions are alternatively applicable, with no one clause primarily applicable. If the requirements of one clause are not met, the requirements of the other still could be. Practically, however, it would not make a difference if one of the clauses was primarily applicable. It would still lead to the applicability of the CISG according to either lit. a or lit. b. One could merely complain if a court were to apply the CISG according to lit. b even if the requirements of lit. a were met and lit. b would therefore not have been applicable. However, since the results are the same, it is unlikely that this would have any negative consequences.

b) Unilaterality

Doubts have been raised regarding the private international law character of Article 1(1) of the CISG due to the fact that it does not rely on the same mechanism as most conflict rules: it does not enable the addressee to find the applicable law among a variety of different legal systems. Janssen/Spilker believe that

> [i]n order to be considered as a rule of international private law, a legal provision must **offer solutions to a conflict of laws in the abstract** (i.e. by determining the applicable law in the light of several options).[178] [emphasis added]

Article 1(1) of the CISG does not give neutral instructions that could lead to any law, as long as the connecting factor connects the facts at hand to that law. Instead, it stipulates its own applicability when certain connecting factors are present. The presumption is that, accordingly, it is the law most appropriate for governing the contract. It does not give instructions as to which law should be applicable if the requirements are not met, i.e. if the connection of the facts to the CISG is not close enough. Instead, it then cedes the search for the applicable law to general private international law, instead of for example stating that the non-unified sales law of the State of the seller's place of business should be applicable in its stead. As such, the critics explain, Article 1(1)(a) and (b) are specific and not abstract: they merely determine the scope of application of the

---

   3. the law of the country with which the spouses are jointly most closely connected."

178 *Siehr*, RabelsZ 1988, 587.

Convention and are therefore "technically speaking [...] not a rule of private international law"[179].

While it is true that Article 1(1) is a specific rule, this does not disqualify the provision as a private international law rule. It merely renders it a unilateral conflict rule instead of a multilateral conflict rule. Unilateral conflict of laws rules differ from the standard multilateral conflict rules in one important way: Instead of specifying that the law of any State to which the connecting factor leads is applicable, they always determine the applicability of one specific law. While multilateral conflict rules determine which of several possible laws are applicable, unilateral rules specify when the particular legal system of which they form part is applicable.[180] As Dicey, Morris & Collins put it:

> *A statute containing a particular or unilateral conflict rule answers the question, When does a system of law of which the state forms part apply? A statute containing a general or multilateral conflict rule answers the more general question, What law applies?*[181]

Such unilateral conflict of laws rules contain the same elements as multilateral conflict rules. Just like multilateral rules, unilateral rules set forth operative facts defining the situations for which they seek to determine the applicable law. The difference lies in the connecting factor. Instead of using an open connecting factor, which can lead to any law that is connected to the case via the connecting factor, its sets forth a connecting factor that has to be connected to the State in question in order for that State's law, and no other law, to be applicable.

While the Introductory Act of the BGB originally comprised mainly unilateral conflict of laws rules,[182] such rules have become very rare, as they do not mesh with the modern understanding that all legal systems are equal and capable of governing any situation justly. One example of German private international law still using a unilateral conflict of laws rule is Article 17a of the Introductory Act of the BGB, which sets forth:

---

179   Ibid.
180   *Kegel/Schurig*, Internationales Privatrecht, ed. 9 2004, pp. 301 et seq; *Kropholler*, Internationales Privatrecht, ed. 6 2006, pp. 106 et seq.
181   Dicey, Morris and Collins on The Conflict of laws, ed. 15 (2012), p. 21.
182   See only *Kropholler*, Internationales Privatrecht, ed. 6 2006, pp. 106 et seq.

> *Prohibitions regarding trespass, approaching and contact pertaining to a marital home located in Germany are governed by German substantive law.*[183]

The prohibitions regarding trespassing, approaching and contact pertaining to the marital home constitute the operative facts. The connecting factor is the location of the home and household goods *in Germany*.[184] This is not a reference to the law of the State in which they are located regardless of which State that may be. It is a reference exclusively to German law, solely for the case that the marital home and household goods are located in Germany.

As is the case with multilateral conflict of laws rules, the connecting factor in unilateral conflict rules serves to connect the facts to the most appropriate law. However, which law is the most appropriate has already been established. In the example of Article 17a of the Introductory Act of the BGB, the drafter considered German law the most appropriate and a unilateral reference to it justifiable because time is typically of the essence in the situations it governs, e.g. conflicts regarding the right to use the marital home and bans on entry or contact. The determination of a foreign law can be cumbersome, and a lengthy process may well expose a spouse to danger if bans on entry or contact are being sought.[185] Furthermore, the foreign law finally determined to be applicable may not even contain rules for these matters.[186] German law has therefore been predetermined as appropriate in these cases, and its application only a matter of whether the – relatively narrow – requirements of the provision are met.

Article 1(1) of the CISG is such a unilateral conflict rule. It has only one goal: to determine the applicability of the CISG to an international contract of sales. The connecting factors in litt. a and b set forth requirements that connect the sales contract to Contracting States. If the requirements are met, the connection between the contract and the CISG is strong enough to warrant its application. The unilateral reference to the CISG is justified because it is the law best suited to govern international sales

---

183 "Die Nutzungsbefugnis für die im Inland belegene Ehewohnung und die im Inland befindlichen Haushaltsgegenstände sowie damit zusammenhängende Betretungs-, Näherungs- und Kontaktverbote unterliegen den deutschen Sachvorschriften."
184 Staudinger-BGB/*Mankowski*, 2010, EGBGB Art. 17a para. 5.
185 Ibid., EGBGB Art. 17a para. 2.
186 Ibid.

contracts, given that it is a neutral law of international origin with rules specifically tailored for the needs of cross-border transactions.[187]

2. Effect

It was already shown in the individual analyses of Article 1(1)(a) and (b) that the effect of each is the direct application of the CISG. In both cases, the provision functions as a conflict of laws rule, determining the application of a law, not as *lex specialis* within one legal system, but instead of the domestic sales laws of any particular legal system. As such, the provision has the effect that conflict rules have following the Alternatives Test. Article 1(1) of the CISG is binding on courts in Contracting States under international public law, and not on courts in Non-Contracting States. Courts in Contracting States must apply the Convention as part of their own State's private international law, just like any other conflict of laws rules, whether these stem from international treaties or not. Among a Contracting State's private international law, Article 1(1) of the CISG is *lex specialis* and only if its requirements are not met are the other rules of private international law applied. Courts in Non-Contracting States, on the other hand, are not bound by either Article 1(1)(a) or Article 1(1)(b).[188] Their forum States have not ratified the Convention and as such they have no duty under international law to enforce it. If their private international law refers directly to the law of a Contracting State, the CISG does not become applicable to the contract.[189] Instead, the non-uniform sales law of the Contracting State governs the transaction.

---

187 See *supra*, pp. 20 et seqq.
188 This is also the view of the majority authors arguing that Article 1(1)(b) is an internal rule of distribution, see Schlechtriem/Schwenzer/*Schwenzer*/*Hachem*, ed. 4 2016, CISG Art. 1 para. 31; Staudinger-BGB/*Magnus*, 2018, CISG Art. 1 para. 95; Internationales Vertragsrecht/*Saenger*, ed. 3 2018, CISG Art. 1 para. 16; *Pünder*, RIW 1990, 869, 870; *Siehr*, RabelsZ 1988, 587, 610. *Neumayer* accepts the consequences of categorizing lit. b as an internal rule of distribution and believes that Non-Contracting States should also be bound by it, see *Neumayer*, RIW 1994, 99, 101.
189 This is where the authors just named disagree. Since Art. 1(1)(b) of the CISG is part of the foreign legal system, it has to be applied as part of that law by Non-Contracting States.

§ 2. Article 1(1) CISG – Rules of Application

C. Conclusion

Article 1(1) of the CISG is a conflict of laws rule, both in structure and in function. It functions as a unilateral conflict rule, stipulating only the application of the CISG. If the requirements are not met, a new conflicts of law analysis must be conducted. Regarding its structure, Article 1(1) comprises operative facts – "contracts of sale of goods between parties whose places of business are in different States" – and two alternatively applicable connecting factors, contained in lit. a and lit. b. In lit. a, the connecting factor is that both parties have their seats of business in Contracting States. Lit. b, on the other hand, makes the application of the CISG reliant on the selection of a Contracting State's legal system through the rule of the forum's private international law. The result of the conflict of laws analysis serves as a connecting factor. This is supported by a systematic analysis, because the categorization as a conflict of laws rule leads to preferable outcomes in a set of contentious issues: when lit. b is seen as a conflict of laws rule, this gives a legally sound explanation for the popular notions that a *renvoi* does not have to be given effect when applying rules of private international law within Article 1(1)(b) of the CISG, that a reservation under Article 95 of the CISG only binds courts in Reservation States and does not affect the application of the CISG by courts in Non-Reservation States, that the CISG is applicable to agreements to opt out of the CISG, and that courts in Contracting States must always apply the CISG as domestic law.

In view of the fact that Contracting States are bound by the rules of application in the CISG, this leaves us with the following question: Are international arbitral tribunals bound by the conflict of laws rule Article 1(1)(a) and (b) of the CISG as well? The answer hinges on several different aspects, which will be discussed in the next chapter.

§ 3. Binding Effect of Article 1(1) in International Commercial Arbitration

Are arbitrators bound by Article 1(1) of the CISG? Must they apply the Convention when the requirements of this provision are met? Conversely, are they free to apply it when the requirements are not met? As established in the foregoing chapter, Article 1(1) of the CISG is a conflict rule, a rule of private international law. As a consequence, international arbitrators are bound by it if they are bound by private international law in general. Whether this is the case, however, is the subject of a debate that has been raging for many decades. Most States around the world have both traditional private international law, which Article 1(1) of the CISG is part of, and arbitration-specific conflict of laws rules. It is unclear whether international arbitrators are bound by both, either or none of these types of rules.

In the following, the question will be approached from the perspective of the jurisdiction of States: Are States competent to regulate what law governs the merits in international arbitration proceedings by setting forth conflict of laws rules for private international commercial law? If so, which State in particular is competent? This concerns the States' jurisdiction to prescribe, or legislative jurisdiction, i.e. their "competence under international law to regulate the conduct of natural and juridical persons".[190] International arbitrators can be bound by States' laws only if the States making those rules have the jurisdiction to do so. This vantage point – the competence of States – is crucial because creating rules of private international law is an inherent function of any State's sovereignty. However, the concept of international arbitration is older than the modern concept of sovereign States[191]: It came into existence not because sovereign States allowed it to but because parties decided that they needed it as a mechanism to resolve disputes. The emergence of a world order in which the

---

190 *Crawford*, Brownlie's Principles of Public International Law, 2012, p. 456.
191 While the sovereignty of nations as we understand it today was first recognized in theory by *Bodin* in the late 15th century and in practice towards the end of the 17th century (see *Besson*, 'Sovereignty' in *The Max Planck Encyclopedia of Public International Law*, vol. IX paras. 15 et seqq.), arbitration already existed in Greek and Roman times.

§ 3. Binding Effect of Article 1(1) in International Commercial Arbitration

sovereignty of individual States is seen the root of all power demands that international arbitration find its place in this system while maintaining its functionality. It will be demonstrated that arbitrators are not bound by the general rules of private international law, including Article 1(1) of the CISG. Instead, arbitrators are merely bound by arbitration-specific conflict rules contained in arbitration laws, which are generally vague and broad.

First, the legal framework at work in international commercial arbitration will be laid out (**A.**). By way of an introduction, the web of laws and rules potentially applicable in international arbitration proceedings will be outlined, to show when exactly rules of private international law such as Article 1(1) of the CISG become relevant. Then, the debate surrounding the localization of international commercial arbitration will be introduced. As regards the question of whether arbitration proceedings are subject to any one State's authority, this is significant for the discussion at hand and the arguments brought forward in the debate will be dissected at different points throughout this chapter.

Next, a closer look will be taken at the notion of prescriptive jurisdiction, and under what circumstances a State might have jurisdiction to prescribe conflict rules in international arbitration (**B.**). It will be shown that the location of an arbitral seat in the territory of a particular State does not grant that State an inherent right to prescribe conflict rules applicable in the proceedings, neither due to tribunals being quasi-courts, nor due to a genuine link to the arbitral procedure. Instead, a customary rule of international law has emerged according to which States can include a broadly worded conflict of laws rule in their arbitration laws, applicable when a seat of arbitration is located in their territory.

Next, the desire to apply the Rome I Regulation in international arbitration will be addressed separately, due to its prominence and perceived benefits for arbitration. An analysis of the Regulation will show that neither did its drafters intend for such application, nor is it well-suited to govern disputes in international arbitration proceedings (**C.**).

After that, it will be demonstrated that the legal freedom of arbitrators is accompanied by a practical freedom (**D.**). As a consequence of the broadly worded arbitration-specific conflict rules, arbitrators have developed their own methods for determining the applicable substantive law, which will be introduced last.[192] The application of conflict rules is not subject to

---

192 See pp. 158 et seqq.

court review, which severely limits the effect of any conflict rules could have even if States had jurisdiction to bind arbitrators with them.[193]

Finally, the consequence of this freedom will be analyzed regarding the CISG in one aspect in particular: its application as non-State law (**E.**).

A. Legal Framework of Arbitration Proceedings

I. Overview over Potentially Applicable Laws and Rules

The international nature of international commercial arbitration places arbitration proceedings amid a number of international and national laws that might competently govern them. Parties agreeing to subject any future disputes to international commercial arbitration will for the most part not be aware of the tangle of laws that they are entering into, nor will they have to, because the force of laws will not be felt until a court is asked to review the process. What is relevant to the parties first and foremost is the scope of their arbitration agreement. Typically, they will agree on where the arbitration proceedings will take place, i.e. the place or seat of arbitration, and they may select the rules of an arbitration institution. Finally, they may agree on a law to govern the merits of their dispute. All of these aspects will typically be chosen with the aim of utmost neutrality and practicality. The appeal of international arbitration is that neither party is forced to submit to court proceedings in the home State of the other party and that the parties can decide on how the proceedings take place.

1. Institutional Rules

Arbitration institutions are private institutions that offer services regarding the administration and supervision of arbitration procedures. There are many around the world, the most well-known and influential being the International Chamber of Commerce's (ICC) arbitral institution called International Court of Arbitration.[194] Other important institutions are the London Court of International Arbitration (LCIA), the International

---

193 See pp. 163 et seqq.
194 See https://iccwbo.org/dispute-resolution-services/ (last accessed 28 October 2018).

§ 3. Binding Effect of Article 1(1) in International Commercial Arbitration

Center of Dispute Resolution (ICDR) of the American Arbitration Association (AAA), the Singapore International Arbitration Center (SIAC), the Deutsche Institution für Schiedsgerichtsbarkeit (DIS) and the Hong Kong International Arbitration Center (HKIAC).

The most relevant function of arbitration institutions is that they provide a set of rules organizing the arbitration process. These rules contain provisions similar to domestic arbitration statutes, but they are often more detailed and only contain provisions directly affecting the arbitration procedure, such as regarding the selection of the arbitrators or the taking of evidence. Since these rules are not anchored in legislation, they are not binding, but if adopted by the parties, institutional arbitration rules are incorporated into the contract and become part of the agreement. Arbitrators are familiar with the rules of the leading arbitration institutions, and the rules of the different institutions often share similarities.

If no arbitrational institution is chosen, the process is referred to as *ad hoc* arbitration.[195] The parties' individual agreements then constitute the entirety of the arbitration agreement. The parties may incorporate the UNCITRAL Arbitration Rules into their contract by reference. These rules are similar to the aforementioned institutional rules but are not tied to any specific institution. There are, however, some commentaries on their text, which gives arbitrators a measure of security in applying and interpreting the rules.

2. The Arbitral Seat and the *Lex Loci Arbitri*

The parties typically also select a seat of arbitration. In the absence of such a choice, some institutional rules provide for a selection by another entity, such as the arbitration institution itself[196] or by the arbitration tribunal[197]. The seat is where the arbitration proceedings nominally take place, although this is not a requirement according to most institutional rules and domestic arbitration statutes.[198] The ICDR has filtered out a number of factors that have proven relevant for the choice of the location of the arbitral seat, including where parties, attorneys, documents and witnesses are located, where records, sites and materials that might need to

---

195 *Blackaby et al.*, International Commercial Arbitration, ed. 6 2015, pp. 15 et seq.
196 See Art. 18(1) of the ICC Arbitration Rules, Art. 16 of the LCIA Rules.
197 1978 and 2010 UNCITRAL Arbitration Rules.
198 The function of the arbitral seat be discussed *infra*, pp. 111 et seqq.

A. Legal Framework of Arbitration Proceedings

be inspected can be found, where the contract was to be or was performed, and where previous court actions have taken place.[199] Ideally, the seat of arbitration should be easily accessible to all parties but also neutral, thus lacking a connection to the dispute or either one the parties involved.

The choice of arbitral seat has several implications.[200] First of all, the award will be considered to be have the nationality of the State in which the seat is located.[201] The only meaningful relevance of this determination is for whether an award is "foreign" in the sense of the New York Convention on the Recognition and Enforcement of *Foreign* Arbitral Awards[202], which will be discussed next.[203] Outside of this context, claiming that an international award has a nationality of any kind is misleading. Simply because an arbitration award results from proceedings taking place in the territory of a particular State does not make the award a product of that State's legal system.

A far more relevant implication of the location of the arbitral seat is the applicability of domestic arbitration statutes. In as many as 118 jurisdictions in 85 States worldwide[204], the national arbitration statute is modeled after the UNCITRAL Model Law. The result is a certain degree of uniformity among the national arbitration laws, although the Model Law is not binding and States are free to deviate from it in any way they see fit. The Model Law suggests – and most, if not all domestic arbitration statutes modeled on it adopt this stance – that the arbitration statute is applicable when the seat of arbitration is located in the territory of the State. The choice of an arbitral seat is then automatically also a choice of the State's domestic arbitration statute, called *lex loci arbitri*. This is especially relevant for this thesis because most arbitration statutes contain

---

199 ICDR, Locale Determinations in International Cases 1, available at www.adr.org.
200 For an in-depth discussion, see *Born*, International Commercial Arbitration, ed. 2 2014, chapter 14, pp. 2051 et seqq.
201 Ibid., p. 1541.
202 Available at http://www.newyorkconvention.org/.
203 See *infra*, pp. 77 et seq.
204 See https://uncitral.un.org/en/texts/arbitration/modellaw/commercial_arbitration/status. Arbitration statutes are not necessarily implemented on a federal level. For example, in Canada, the provinces and territories are in charge of making rules of arbitration, as are the states and territories in Australia. In these cases, there are several jurisdiction in one State that have an arbitration statute modeled on the UNCITRAL Model Law, which is why the number of States is lower than the number of jurisdictions.

a provision regarding the law applicable to the merits of the dispute, i.e. an arbitration-specific conflict rule.

The choice of arbitral seat and with it, the seat's *lex loci arbitri* result in the jurisdiction of the local courts for certain auxiliary measures, though only if requested by the arbitration tribunal.[205] The most important function of the courts at the seat of arbitration is that they can set aside the award if so requested. This does not effectively eradicate the award on an international level – it still very much exists in the eyes of foreign courts.[206] The fact that an award has been set aside can, however, serve as a ground for the refusal of a foreign court to recognize or enforce the award in its forum State.

This shows that the seat of arbitration has certain relevance, as it serves as an anchor for the international proceedings in a national legal system, at least to a certain extent. This has led to the assertion that the seat is comparable to the forum of a court, representing more than a merely supportive hosting function. How the relationship between the arbitral seat and the arbitration proceedings is viewed has implications for the role of the State that serves as a seat of arbitration under public international law: does the fact that the seat of an arbitration procedure is located in the territory of a particular State equip that State with jurisdiction to legislate on the arbitration proceedings? Does this jurisdiction extend to making rules of private international law applicable in those proceedings? It will be shown below that the answer to both questions is yes, due to a customary rule of international law.[207]

3. Recognition and Enforcement of Arbitration Awards

One aspect that is beyond the influence of the parties' arbitration agreement is the enforcement of the arbitration award abroad. This process is governed by the New York Convention on the Recognition and Enforce-

---

205 See Artt. 5, 17 J, 27, 34, 35 UNCITRAL Model Law.
206 Art. V(1)(e) of the New York Conventions stipulates that the annulment of the award at the seat of arbitration is merely a facultative ground for refusing the recognition and enforcement of an arbitration award, and one that has to be brought forward by the parties and cannot be raised *sua sponte* by the courts. For more on the New York Convetion see *infra*, pp. 115 et seq., 151 et seqq.et seqq.
207 See *infra*, pp. 177 et seqq.

A. Legal Framework of Arbitration Proceedings

ment of Foreign Arbitral Awards of 1958[208] ("New York Convention"), one of the most successful treaties in existence signed by 168 signatory States.[209] It sets forth a set of ground rules regarding international arbitration agreements and awards, stipulating that arbitration agreements are to be respected by courts of signatory States and that courts should refer parties that are subject to such an agreement to arbitration. It further declares that arbitration awards should be recognized as binding and enforced, and then gives an exhaustive list of grounds on which the losing party can resist the recognition and enforcement of a foreign award in any signatory State.[210] While the Convention governs neither the process nor the merits of arbitral proceedings, its influence stems from its enormous practical relevance.

II. The Localization Debate

International commercial arbitration by definition has points of contact to a number of different States. Unlike court proceedings or even domestic arbitration proceedings, for the regulation of which one single State is always competent, it is unclear which State has authority over which international arbitration proceedings. This issue is at the core of the localization debate. The "localization" of international arbitration proceedings in a specific State would give that State the competence to regulate the proceedings, including setting forth rules of private international law directed at the arbitrators. The theories regarding the localization of international arbitration inhabit a spectrum. The existing theories can roughly be divided into approaches that attempt to localize international arbitration in a particular State, and approaches that delocalize it.

---

208 See fn. 202.
209 https://uncitral.un.org/en/texts/arbitration/conventions/foreign_arbitral_awards/status2.
210 These grounds are mirrored in the UNCITRAL Model Law both for the annulment and the enforcement of awards, streamlining the bases on which both active and passive recourse can be taken against an unfavorable award.

§ 3. Binding Effect of Article 1(1) in International Commercial Arbitration

1. Localization

The purest version of localization of international arbitration is the seat theory.[211] Supporters of the seat theory agree that the arbitral process is governed by one *lex arbitri*, "a unique law which globally governs an arbitration and by the standards of which the validity of the arbitral proceedings and the ensuing award are evaluated"[212]. The law that is deemed to be applicable is the law of the seat of arbitration, although the reasons for this differ.

Firstly, one approach is to localize the arbitral process at the seat for territorial reasons.[213] As will be discussed below[214], States have legislative jurisdiction over activity taking place in their territory. In international arbitration, this results in recognizing any State's right to make laws regulating arbitral proceedings that take place in its territory. As Mann put it:

> *Is not every activity occurring on the territory of a State necessarily subject to its jurisdiction? Is it not for such State to say whether and in what manner arbitrators are assimilated to judges and, like them, subject to the law? Various States may give various answers to the question, but that each of them has the right to, and does, answer it according to its own discretion cannot be doubted.*[215]

The seat or place of arbitration is typically selected by the parties in the arbitration agreement, or it can be determined by the arbitral institution or the arbitral tribunal, and it is the place where the arbitral process physically takes place, at least nominally. In the view of the territorialists, this constitutes a territorial connection of the arbitral process to the seat of arbitration. Following this logic, any State has the jurisdiction to make laws applicable to arbitral proceedings that have their seat in its territory. This is the approach followed by many national arbitration statutes that have implemented the UNICTRAL Model Law, which declares the provisions of the Model Law applicable "only if the place of arbitration is in the territory of this State"[216]. National arbitration laws thereby "unilateral[ly define] their international scope of application, and within such

---

211 *Petrochilos*, Procedural Law, 2004, pp. 22 et seqq.
212 Ibid., p. 20; *Paulsson*, LSE Law, Society and Economy Working Papers 2010, 1, 4, 5.
213 *Petrochilos*, Procedural Law, 2004, pp. 22-26.
214 See *infra*, pp. 85 et seqq.
215 *Mann*, Lex Facit Arbitrum, p. 246.
216 Article 1(2) of the UNCITRAL Model Law.

A. Legal Framework of Arbitration Proceedings

scope only exceptionally will they allow the application of another law [...]".[217] This has been described as "the 'closed geometry' of arbitration statutes".[218]

Another approach leads to the same result, but its starting point is a different one: party choice. In 1957, the *Institut de Droit International* adopted a resolution on "Arbitration in Private International Law".[219] It stated that the parties' choice of a place of arbitration included a tacit choice of the arbitration law of the place, as well. The resolution was based on a report by Professor Sauser-Hall from 1952.[220] He followed a hybrid theory, which, while acknowledging that arbitration has a contractual element, focused on the idea that arbitration agreements function as choices of forum, ousting national courts.[221]

Aside from the seat theories, which detect the seat of arbitration and extrapolate the procedural law from there, there are some far less popular methods that have a more legal approach. One method determines the *lex arbitri* by applying the procedural law that the parties choose.[222] Respecting such a choice is based on the general acceptance of party autonomy as a fundamental element of private international law. A different method applies the *lex arbitri* of the State whose national courts would have jurisdiction over the issue if it were not for an arbitration agreement.[223]

2. Delocalization

The other side of the debate argues in favor of a notion of international arbitration that is not anchored in just one legal system, but rather is delocalized to varying degrees. An extreme approach to delocalizing arbitration is the "transnational" approach, which "accepts that international arbitration transcends national legal orders and that it constitutes a transnational

---

217 *Petrochilos*, Procedural Law, 2004, p. 9 para. 1.24.
218 Ibid., p. 9, fn. 24.
219 Resolution on Arbitration in Private International Law, (1957) 47ii Ann IDI 491, available at http://www.idi-iil.org/app/uploads/2017/06/1957_amst_03_en.pdf.
220 *Petrochilos*, Procedural Law, 2004, pp. 26, 27.
221 Ibid., p. 27.
222 Ibid., p. 30; *Rubino-Sammartano*, J. Int'l Arb. 1988, 85, p. 87. This was the approach of the German Code of Civil Procedure before it was amended in 2008.
223 *Petrochilos*, Procedural Law, 2004, p. 34.

§ 3. Binding Effect of Article 1(1) in International Commercial Arbitration

system of justice sometimes labeled as the 'arbitral legal order'"[224], and which is a concept that originated among the French scholars Goldman, Fouchard and Lalive.[225] The transnational approach was based on the fact that the international arbitration community had long since started to develop its own rules, and the belief that these are valid without having to rely on domestic legal systems. This had produced a unique legal system, comparable to the system of public international law, that does not fit neatly in the thinking of traditional national legal systems.[226]

The transnational approach is justified using the arbitrator's duty to issue an enforceable award. An arbitrator seeking to issue an enforceable award must take all national legal systems into account where such enforcement proceedings could potentially take place, which could turn out to be several systems. The arbitrator would be forced to model the award to be compatible with as many potential enforcement States' legal systems as possible, letting the least favorable norm prevail, *in defavorem arbitrandum*.[227] Proponents of the transnational approach argue that instead of relying on national laws, the arbitrator should ensure that the award is compliant with international standards, common to a wide variety of legal orders.[228] These international standards are essentially what transnationalists consider to constitute the international arbitral legal order.

The second, less drastic approach to delocalization is called the pluralist or multilocal approach and emphasizes the fact that while the opinion of the courts of the arbitral forum can potentially be disregarded for the reasons outlined above, the decisions by the courts in the State of enforcement have direct consequences. The enforcement courts ultimately decide whether the winning party can access the unsuccessful party's assets. In contrast, if the annulment court's decision can be disregarded, that decision is of academic interest at best outside of its forum but will not necessarily have any real-life impact.

This view, notably held by Jan Paulsson,[229] thus wants to move away from a strict model intent on anchoring international arbitral proceedings

---

224 *Gaillard*, Transcending National Legal Orders for International Arbitration, p. 372.
225 *Goldman*, RdC 1963-I, 347, 347 et seqq; *Fouchard*, L'arbitrage commercial international, 1965, pp. 103-104; *Lalive*, RdC 1967-I, 569, 649.
226 *Gaillard*, Legal Theory of International Arbitration, 2010, pp. 35 et seqq.
227 Ibid., p. 35.
228 These standards do not have be shared by all legal systems, see ibid., pp. 48 et seq.
229 *Paulsson*, Int'l & Comp.L.Q. 1981, 358.

in any one place, as this is not consistent with the reality of parties subject to arbitration, but also shies away from placing international arbitration on an entirely transnational legal platform, divorced from all national legal systems. Paulsson states that

> [i]f theoreticians are reduced to insisting that protection which has proved effective in practice is aberrant because it has its source outside the conceptual system they have elaborated, perhaps the time is ripe to expand the notion of the legal framework of transnational arbitration.[230]

The final product is a system in which an international arbitral award is regarded as "floating" until the point in time which its recognition or enforcement is sought (which may never happen). The arbitral process is legitimized only in the recognition or enforcement of an award, when it meets the enforcing State's criteria.[231] Because of this *a posteriori* legitimization, "the seat of the arbitration is of no ultimate importance"[232]. It is not entirely disregarded, but considered to be just one relevant legal order among others.[233] The arbitral award simply does not need to rely on being legitimized by the *lex loci arbitri*, because, in practice, it can survive without it. This approach has also been titled the "Westphalian" approach due to the equal reverence it gives each State and its legal system, with no hierarchical regard to the State of the seat of arbitration.[234]

3. Discussion

The multilocal or Westphalian approach is preferable among these theories. It prevails over the transnational approach on the one hand because while the proponents of the transnational approach hold a vision of international arbitration that is desirable in its independence of national legal system, its simply is not a reality (yet). The idea of a transnational arbitral legal order does not hold water. It was thoroughly inspected and ultimately convincingly rejected by Schultz[235]. His criticism hinges on the fact that the purpose of a legal order is to enable the addressees to model

---

230 Ibid., p. 363.
231 *Gaillard*, Transcending National Legal Orders for International Arbitration, p. 371.
232 Ibid.
233 *Gaillard*, Legal Theory of International Arbitration, 2010, p. 25.
234 Ibid.
235 *Schultz*, J.I.D.S. 2011, 59.

§ 3. Binding Effect of Article 1(1) in International Commercial Arbitration

their behavior after it, in a way that they can anticipate repercussions when they do not.[236] Given that the arbitral legal order consists mainly of arbitral awards, predictability would only exist if the awards had precedential power, were sufficiently well reasoned and fairly widely published.[237] A real appeals procedure would enhance the semblance of arbitration having its own legal order.[238]

However, the lack of such a transnational arbitral legal system may be less of a problem than the proponents make it out be. In their main criticism of the multilocal approach, they overestimate the lengths to which arbitrators will generally go to make an enforceable award:

> *Arbitrators do not examine the validity of the arbitration clause, or of their appointment, under the laws of every country that might conceivably be approached as an enforcement forum. Nor do they have a duty to do so. Indeed, that task would be impossible, unless they could read the parties' minds, predict future tracing of assets, and find a crystal ball to reveal where the res judicata embodied in an award might variously be brought to bear by any number of affected parties.*[239]

Rather, it seems more likely that an arbitral tribunal will attempt to craft an award valid in the few States where enforcement will most likely be sought, instead of all potential enforcement States. The lack of an arbitral forum with binding guidelines on the arbitral process will not lead a pragmatic arbitral tribunal to be gagged by the sheer volume of legal systems against which the award might eventually be tested. Thus, a transnational arbitral legal order is not needed to relieve the arbitrator of excessive obligations.

On the other hand, the localization theories fail to make a compelling case as to why the State of the arbitral seat or any other State should have ultimate authority over international arbitration proceedings. The choice of procedural law by the parties is no useful basis because parties rarely actually choose a procedural law of a State. Localizing an arbitration procedure in the State that would otherwise have adjudicative jurisdiction is not helpful because more than one State will have adjudicative jurisdiction over disputes resulting from international transactions as are subject to international commercial arbitration proceedings. The other arguments in

---

236 Ibid., pp. 84, 85.
237 Ibid., pp. 77-80.
238 Ibid., p. 83.
239 *Paulsson*, The Idea of Arbitration, p. 40.

favor of localization will be addressed later, through the lens of what a State's competence to set forth conflict of laws rules for international arbitration could be based on: the territorial approach within the seat theory sees territoriality as a basis of jurisdiction, the second version of the seat theory bases legislative jurisdiction on party choice. It will be shown that neither aspect can inherently serve as a basis for jurisdiction to regulate arbitration proceedings and thus for localizing the arbitration proceedings at the seat of arbitration.

B. Competence to Make Conflict Rules Applicable in International Commercial Arbitration

Which State has the competence to make rules of private international law that have to be applied by international commercial arbitration tribunals?

States are sovereign, meaning that they have supreme authority within their territory.[240] One aspect of this authority is that they have jurisdiction – that they can decide how they want to act in a legislative, judicial and executive manner.[241] This includes the competence of States to make rules on how and according to what substantive law civil law disputes are decided in their territory.[242] This ability to make laws is referred to as legislative jurisdiction. Given that conflict of laws rules are also laws, the State needs legislative jurisdiction to set forth such rules. What basis legislative jurisdiction can have will be shown first (**I.**).

The legislative jurisdiction of a State to make rules of private international law is an essential complement to any State's court system and partakes in the exclusive jurisdiction that each State enjoys regarding the settlement of disputes in its territory. From this follows that States would be competent to set forth conflict of laws rules for international arbitration tribunals if these could be considered organs of a particular State's, which they cannot (**II.**).

However, States might still be competent to set forth conflict of laws rules for international commercial arbitration based on their legislative jurisdiction, either by way of a genuine link to the arbitration proceedings they want to regulate, such as the location of the arbitral seat in their terri-

---

240 *Besson*, 'Sovereignty' in *The Max Planck Encyclopedia of Public International Law*, vol. IX p. 367 para. 1, p. 374 para. 56.
241 *Oxman*, 'Jurisdiction of States' in ibid.vol. VI p. 547 para. 1.
242 *Geimer*, Internationales Zivilprozessrecht, ed. 7 2015, pp. 196 et seq.

§ 3. Binding Effect of Article 1(1) in International Commercial Arbitration

tory, or due to a rule of customary international law. While the arbitral seat is arguably too weak a link to establish legislative jurisdiction (**III.**), there is clear evidence of a customary law basis for such a competence to set forth arbitration-specific conflict of law rules (**IV.**).

I. Legislative Jurisdiction

1. The Lotus Decision

The basis and limitations of State jurisdiction were laid out by the PCIJ in the *Lotus* decision of 1929.[243] The case dealt with a collision between the French mail steamer *Lotus* and the Turkish collier *Boz-Kourt* on the high seas in 1926. The *Boz-Kourt* sank and eight Turkish nationals died. The French steamer, after doing its best to rescue the remaining shipwrecked, put into port in Constantinople. Turkey instituted criminal proceedings against the officer of the watch aboard the *Lotus*, as well as against the captain of the Turkish steamship, and sentenced both to a term of imprisonment. The French Government contended that Turkey had acted contrary to the principles of international law by doing so, and the governments of both countries agreed to bring the question to the PCIJ.

The PCIJ framed the question as to whether States needed some title to jurisdiction recognized by international law in order to have jurisdiction or whether jurisdiction existed as long as it did not come into conflict with a principle of international law. The case was thus whittled down to the inquiry at its core of whether international law is fundamentally permissive or prohibitive. The court decided by a one-vote margin that "[r]estrictions upon the independence of States cannot [...] be presumed" because international law is based on the free will of independent States. Following this view, States are allowed to exercise jurisdiction as they see fit unless there is a prohibitive rule to the contrary. In his dissent, Judge Loder described the majority position as "based on the contention that under international law everything which is not prohibited is permitted. In other words [...] every door is open unless it is closed by treaty or by established custom."[244]

---

243 Lotus, 1927 P.C.I.J. (ser. A) No. 10, p. 4; available at https://www.icj-cij.org/files/permanent-court-of-international-justice/serie_A/A_10/30_Lotus_Arret.pdf (last accessed on 7 February 2018).
244 Lotus decision (fn. 243), p. 34.

2. Genuine Link

This extremely broad approach to jurisdiction was heavily criticized following the decision. Many critics contended that the opposite must be true: States are prohibited from exercising jurisdiction unless there is a permissive rule to the contrary.[245] It is unclear whether the majority opinion in *Lotus* even meant to make such a sweeping statement regarding absolute freedom of action as a general principle.[246] In practice, a consensus has emerged that does require permissive principles in order for a State to claim jurisdiction. This notion of permissive principles is, however, interpreted quite broadly, in effect giving the States broad jurisdiction. States have jurisdiction, specifically legislative jurisdiction, when a genuine link exists between the State and the situation.[247] In order to claim such a genuine link, States have to be able to "advance a legitimate interest based on personal or territorial connections of the matter to be regulated."[248] Due to a lack of treaties regulating the permissive principles in detail, the proper scope of a State's law has to be ascertained at any given time by way of an analysis of current customary law.[249] Accepted permissive principles include the principles of territoriality, personality, protective and universality, which may thus all serve as bases of legislative jurisdiction.

The territoriality principle states that States have jurisdiction regarding events taking place completely or partially in their territory and regarding the status of things located in their territory.[250] It is a direct consequence of the Westphalian underpinnings of the law of jurisdiction and is the most important basis for legislative jurisdiction, and the only basis of enforcement jurisdiction.[251] While it is sufficient that part of an action takes place in the territory of a State, a contentious issue is whether an action taken abroad merely having an effect in another State gives that State legislative jurisdiction based on the territoriality principle (the so-called effects doctrine).[252] This is relevant in competition law, where States claim

---

245 *Ryngaert*, Jurisdiction, 2008, p. 21.
246 See *Handeyside*, Mich. J. Int. Law 2007, 71, pp. 76 et seq.
247 *Herdegen*, Völkerrecht, ed. 17 2018, p. 182; Cf. *Mann*, RdC 1984-III, 9, p. 29 ("sufficiently close legal connection").
248 *Ryngaert*, Jurisdiction, 2008, p. 22.
249 Ibid., p. 28.
250 *Mills*, Confluence, 2009, pp. 234, 235; *Herdegen*, Völkerrecht, ed. 17 2018, p. 183.
251 *Mills*, Confluence, 2009, p. 235.
252 *Geimer*, Internationales Zivilprozessrecht, ed. 7 2015, p. 199 para. 375.

jurisdiction over agreements made abroad that have a negative effect on competition in their territory.[253]

The personality principle is not nearly as relevant as a basis for prescriptive jurisdiction. There is the *active* personality principle on the one hand, due to which States have jurisdiction over the rights, obligations and status of its nationals. This includes issues such as taxation, social security and voting entitlements, or in international law regarding diplomatic protection.[254] The *passive* personality principle, on the other hand, gives jurisdiction when the protection of persons from foreign nationals under the law of their home State is concerned. As such, it constitutes a basis for jurisdiction over crimes committed abroad against nationals. This is particularly relevant for acts of terrorism or organized crime, regardless of where they take place, as long as they target nationals of the State claiming jurisdiction.

The protective principle serves as a basis of jurisdiction for laws ensuring the safety or protection of important public matters, even if the harmful actions are taking place abroad.[255] For example, espionage abroad can be sanctioned under this principle. The universality principle ensures that any State in the world has the legislative jurisdiction to make laws protecting matters that the entire State community has an interest in. Classic examples for the universality principle that give any State jurisdiction are cases of genocide, slave trade, war crimes, aircraft hijackings and specific terrorist acts.[256] These principles are not likely to serve as a basis of legislative jurisdiction in civil matters.

In international commercial transactions, it is typical that genuine links can be established to several different States, conferring legislative jurisdiction to a number of States:

> Concurrent jurisdiction is indeed the inevitable result of the classical public international law approaches: especially in the economic field the effects of certain practices may fan out globally nowadays, thereby possibly providing connections that are sufficient for more than one State to exercise their jurisdiction.[257]

---

253 Ibid., para. 376, referencing Art. 101 TFEU in the context of EU competition law.
254 *Mills*, Confluence, 2009, p. 247.
255 *Herdegen*, Völkerrecht, ed. 17 2018, p. 187.
256 See the Restament (Third) of the Foreign Relations Law of the United States, § 404.
257 *Ryngaert*, Jurisdiction, 2008, p. 20.

In such a case, there is a conflict of rightfully applicable laws that must be decided using the rules of private international law.

3. Treaty or Customary Law

A State that can show no genuine link to the dispute that it wants to regulate may still base its right to do so on a treaty or on customary law. Both are sources of public international law, which are reflected in Article 38 of the Statute of the International Court of Justice.[258] Although the provision, which is from 1920, has been criticized for being out of date, it is flexible enough to work in practice. It refers to three sources of public international law: (1) international conventions, whether general or particular, establishing rules expressly recognized by the contesting states, (2) international custom, as evidence of a general practice accepted as law, and (3) the general principles of law recognized by civilized nations. It does not establish any particular hierarchy among these sources. Instead, the hierarchy of different sources must be determined on a case by case basis, using the international law principles of interpretation, such as *lex specialis derogat legi generali* and *lex posterior derogat legi priori*.

A convention or treaty is "an international agreement concluded between States in written form and governed by international law, whether embodied in a single instrument or in two or more related instruments and whatever its particular designation", according to Article 2(1) of the Vienna Convention on the Law of Treaties[259]. International organizations can also be party to treaties.[260] The subject of treaties can be an obligation to act or refrain from acting a certain way, but can also be matters of status, such as the authority over territories. "Law-making" treaties create legal obligations that cannot not be met through one-time observance, but rather constitute general norms that govern the conduct of the parties.[261] One extremely successful example that has been discussed and will be expanded upon below is the New York Convention.[262] Like any agreement, treaties are based on consent and as such only bind the States that agree to

---

258 See https://www.icj-cij.org/en/statute.
259 https://treaties.un.org/doc/publication/unts/volume%201155/volume-1155-i-18232-english.pdf.
260 *Herdegen*, Völkerrecht, ed. 17 2018, p. 121.
261 *Crawford*, Brownlie's Principles of Public International Law, 2012, p. 31.
262 See fn. 202.

it when they become party to it. However, if they codify a general practice they can assist in the creation of customary law, a second important source of public international law.

Customary law is defined in the text of Article 38 of the ICJ Statute as "general practice accepted as law". It stems from the notion that conduct can create legitimate expectations in others, which in turn begets legal obligations.[263] It is generally accepted that two elements are necessary to constitute customary law: State practice combined with corresponding *opinio iuris*.[264] The element of State practice usually manifests as actions or omissions by States and can be of domestic or international nature.[265] For a practice by States to become relevant in the context of customary law, it has to be consistent, at least to a certain extent.[266] If this is the case, a specific duration is not required. It is not necessary for all States to actively participate in the formation of a norm in order for it to become customary law; if the issue is one that only particularly affects a number of States, the actions of these States will be decisive.[267] Otherwise, the practice has to be uniform, meaning that the vast majority of States has to participate in it. The *opinio iuris* is the psychological element, meaning that the States believe that certain conduct is required under international law. The International Court will often simply infer an *opinio iuris* from a certain practice, but has also been rigorous in finding it in some important cases, such as the Lotus case.[268] Customary law has a universal effect, in principle binding all States. If a State does not want to be bound by customary law it has to be a persistent objector. While treaties bind only signatory States, they can provide evidence of customary rules, even if they are only bilateral.[269]

Finally, "general principles recognized by civilized nations" fill the gaps where neither treaties nor customary law contain a solution. The reference to civilized nations indicates not a regression to a Eurocentric point of view, but rather that an overall assessment is required of all those legal systems that have developed a certain standard that reflects the fundamen-

---

263 *Thirlway*, Sources of International Law, p. 124.
264 See only *Wolfrum*, 'Sources of International Law' in *The Max Planck Encyclopedia of Public International Law*, vol. IX p. 304 para. 25.
265 Ibid., para. 26.
266 *Crawford*, Brownlie's Principles of Public International Law, 2012, p. 24.
267 *Ryngaert*, Jurisdiction, 2008, pp. 37, 38.
268 See *supra*, p. 109 and fn. 333.
269 *Crawford*, Brownlie's Principles of Public International Law, 2012, p. 31.

tal values of the modern State community.[270] The term general principles has been defined as "sweeping and rather loose standards of conduct that can be deduced from the various rules by extracting and generalizing some of their most significant common points."[271] Most general principles are established by comparison of the bigger private law systems. Some important examples are the principle of good faith[272], which includes the prohibition of *venire contra factum proprium*. Examples of procedural nature are the principle of *res iudicata*[273] and the right to be heard before a court.[274] While general principles are a source of public international law that should not be underestimated, they cannot serve as a basis of legislative jurisdiction and as such, will not be analyzed in the following.

II. Arbitral Tribunals as "Quasi-Courts" of a State

As stated above, it is inherent to a State's sovereignty that it has the power to organize its judicial system through both procedural and private international law. In terms of legislative jurisdiction, the ability to make such laws is a fundamental fact of public international law. There can be no doubt that if international arbitrators were organs of any State – such as the State where the arbitral seat is located or the arbitral institution has its headquarters – they would have to apply the laws of a State, including the private international law. No one seriously argues that they are such organs – this claim could far too easily be disproven: their existence is not based on an inaugural law and they are not subject to constitutional or other supervision. However, the argument could be made that because international arbitration has become such an important tool of dispute resolution and displaces court proceedings in so many instances, it is

---

270 *Herdegen*, Völkerrecht, ed. 17 2018, p. 161.
271 *Cassese*, International Law, 2001, p. 151.
272 ICJ, Case concerning the Land and Maritime Boundary between Cameroon and Nigeria, Preliminary Objections, ICJ Reports 198, p. 275.
273 ICJ, Question of the Delimitation of the Continental Shelf between Nicaragua and Colombia beyond 200 Nautical Miles from the Nicaraguan Coast [Nicaragua v. Colombia], Preliminary Objections, paras. 55 et seq.
274 *Gößling*, Europäisches Kollisionsrecht, 2019, p. 6; *Herdegen*, Völkerrecht, ed. 17 2018, p. 162.

§ 3. Binding Effect of Article 1(1) in International Commercial Arbitration

comparable in many ways to court proceedings.[275] In order to ensure that citizens participating in international arbitration proceedings actually receive justice and conversely cannot shield their dispute from the oversight of States with an appreciable interest in it, arbitration tribunals should be treated like courts – specifically, like courts of the seat of arbitration. One important step would be to bind them to the private international law of that State. This would ensure that they determine the applicable law in a predictable manner and give effect to public policy and overriding mandatory rules as set forth in the rules of private international law.

Whether arbitral tribunals must be considered "quasi-courts" is the issue at the core of the debate regarding the nature of international commercial arbitration.[276] Is it judicial in nature, and thus just a different outlet for sovereign power usually exercised through national court proceedings, or is it a purely contractual construct, reliant entirely on party consent?

1. Theories Regarding the Nature of Arbitration

Arbitrators in international proceedings have a different relationship with States than do national courts. Traditional voices contend that arbitrators, even international arbitrators, are embedded in a national legal system just like national courts are, typically the legal system at the seat of arbitration.[277] The consequence of this is that the *lex fori* rule can be neatly applied to international arbitrators as well, seeing as they owe the same deference as national courts to the national legal system of which they form a part.

In its most pure form this is the content of the judicial theory of arbitration.[278] According to it, arbitral tribunals merely borrow from the national courts' power to administer justice. The State has a monopoly over the administration of justice; only the State can exercise judicial

---

275 Regarding the "institutionalization" of international arbitration, see *Voit*, JZ 1997, 120, as the basis for the amendment of the German arbitration statute in 1998.
276 For an overview see *Born*, International Commercial Arbitration, ed. 2 2014, § 1.05, pp. 213 et seq.
277 *Mann*, Lex Facit Arbitrum, pp. 245 et seq.
278 See generally *Kröll et al.*, Comparative International Commercial Arbitration, 2003, pp. 71 et seqq.

power.²⁷⁹ When an arbitral tribunal administers justice, it is exercising sovereign power.²⁸⁰ This cannot be authorized through a party agreement, but instead only by the State whose powers the arbitrators are exercising, by delegating these powers to the tribunal. This notion that arbitrators dispense justice in the fashion of national courts is reinforced with the fact that arbitral awards have procedural effects similar to those of court decisions.²⁸¹ They bind the parties, have the force of *res iudicata* and can be subject to enforcement. They can also be nullified through legal remedies. The existence of legal remedies is testament to the fact that the award is integrated into the national legal system.

The opposite of the judicial theory is the contractual theory.²⁸² It contends that the arbitral tribunal does not derive its power from any one State's legal system and its courts, but from the arbitration agreement alone. The arbitral award has been considered to share in the contractual nature of the arbitration agreement.²⁸³ One way to make sense of this is to view the arbitrators as representatives of the parties, making an agreement on behalf of the parties.²⁸⁴

In between these two extremes resides the so-called hybrid theory.²⁸⁵ It states that arbitration has both contractual and judicial elements and cannot be categorized as purely one or the other. While the contractual basis of arbitration is stressed, it is also acknowledged that arbitrators exercise a public – or judicial – role.²⁸⁶

2. Discussion

While arbitrators do adopt judicial functions, they differ in meaningful ways from national courts in several key aspects, namely the source of

---

279 *Samuel*, Jurisdictional Problems, 1989, p. 55; *Solomon*, Verbindlichkeit von Schiedssprüchen, 2007, p. 296.
280 *Sandrock*, FS Stoll, p. 688; *Habscheid*, JZ 1998, 445, 446.
281 *Solomon*, Verbindlichkeit von Schiedssprüchen, 2007, p. 295; *Bajons*, FS Kralik, p. 10.
282 *Born*, International Commercial Arbitration, ed. 2 2014, p. 214; *Solomon*, Verbindlichkeit von Schiedssprüchen, 2007, pp. 290 et seqq.
283 *Solomon*, Verbindlichkeit von Schiedssprüchen, 2007, p. 290; *Kröll et al.*, Comparative International Commercial Arbitration, 2003, pp. 73, 74 para. 5-17.
284 *Solomon*, Verbindlichkeit von Schiedssprüchen, 2007, p. 290.
285 *Born*, International Commercial Arbitration, ed. 2 2014, p. 214; *Kröll et al.*, Comparative International Commercial Arbitration, 2003, pp. 79 et seqq.
286 *Born*, International Commercial Arbitration, ed. 2 2014, p. 214.

§ 3. Binding Effect of Article 1(1) in International Commercial Arbitration

their adjudicative power, their relationship to the law, and the result of their adjudicative process. The hybrid theory is the most accurate in its categorization of international arbitration.

a) Source of Power

While courts derive their power from the legal system of their forum, the source of arbitrators' power is the party agreement.

Courts derive their power to adjudicate from their forum State. The laws of the legislature organize life within the territory of the State; courts enforce those laws. The State has a monopoly on the use of force, and as a necessary prerequisite also a monopoly on administering justice.[287] If citizens have a claim pursuant to the laws of the State, they must go to the courts to have the claim recognized and potentially enforced; they are not allowed to use force against their fellow citizens in pursuit of their claim.[288] The party against whom the claim is made has no choice but to take part in the court proceedings or suffer the consequences. In exchange for this subjugation, both parties are constitutionally guaranteed a fair process. This ensures peaceful, non-violent coexistence by channeling the resolution of disputes to neutral judges. Courts are therefore a vital part of a law-based State.

When parties submit their dispute to arbitration, they are deciding to circumvent the national court system to a large extent. To make such a decision, they need party autonomy. It seems plausible that parties should only be able to bar a legal system from exercising its adjudicatory jurisdiction in any matter if that system grants them the necessary party autonomy to do so. If the parties decide not to rely on one States' court system, only that State can decide to what extent the parties are allowed to resolve their dispute privately. Once arbitrators are allowed to displace courts to a certain extent, those arbitrators are seemingly being granted the power to adjudicate the matter by that legal system, enabling them to exercise sovereign power.[289] As F.A. Mann put it:

> No one has ever or anywhere been able to point to any provision or legal principle which would permit individuals to act outside the confines of a

---

287 See only *Randelzhofer*, HBdSR, pp. 706 et seq.
288 Sachs/*Sachs*, ed. 8 2018, Art. 20 para. 162.
289 *Schlosser*, Schiedsgerichtsbarkeit, ed. 2 1989, para. 46.

system of municipal law; even the idea of the autonomy of the parties exists only by virtue of a given system of municipal law and in different systems may have different characteristics and effects. Similarly, every arbitration is necessarily subject to the law of a given State.[290]

While this argument is plausible in purely domestic cases in which only one legal system's courts are competent, its flaws become evident as soon as international elements open up potential jurisdictions of other States' courts. In international cases, more than one legal system is affected, and the parties are ousting the courts of each affected legal system by choosing to go to international arbitration. The parties are not derogating from court proceedings of one legal system, but of every legal system that has adjudicative jurisdiction.

Does every affected legal system have to grant the parties the right to arbitrate? The answer to this question lies within the nature of party autonomy. Party autonomy (*Parteiautonomie*) is understood as the right of parties to choose the law applicable to their legal relationship. Going beyond merely substantive *private* autonomy (*Privatautonomie*), which enables parties to deviate from non-mandatory rules in the applicable law through agreement, *party* autonomy on a conflict of laws level enables parties to choose an entire legal system over another, including its mandatory rules.[291] The applicable private international law rules decide to what extent parties are permitted to make such a choice of law. However, the parties can select accommodating conflict of laws rules by choosing to go to court in a country with liberal private international law.[292]

This right to choose the applicable law is thus not created by any one legal system, but merely tolerated by each legal system to a differing extent. It exists regardless of whether a legal system stipulates that it should. If all jurisdictions potentially competent to adjudicate an international case decided to limit party autonomy, then it would not be given effect – not because it did not exist in the first place, but because it was not granted an outlet. As such, it is a pre-State right. Its basis can be found in the

---

290 *Mann*, Lex Facit Arbitrum, p. 245.
291 *Mäsch*, Rechtswahlfreiheit und Verbraucherschutz, 1993, pp. 77 et seq.
292 This explains why parties typically do not have the freedom to choose a foreign law in a purely domestic case. Since they cannot choose a different jurisdiction in which to go to court, the case will invariably be measured by the standards of their domestic international private law. This law can effectively limit the parties right to choose a foreign legal system to govern their contract.

freedom that every individual has[293], as is expressed in the existence of human rights.[294] These, too, exist despite potentially not being recognized by individual States. While they lack impact if positive laws that attach exercisable rights to them do not exist, that does not attenuate the existence of human rights. Admittedly, the existence of a freedom that cannot be exercised because of the constrictions imposed by a State is of little use to its holder. This aspect certainly gives credence to the notion that in the end, it is the forum that decides whether or not it wants to grant a particular freedom – be it human rights or party autonomy.[295] However, in the realm of international transactions the power of each State is limited by the mere fact that, to a certain extent at least, the parties have the ability to choose which State's constrictions they are willing to submit to – a mechanism known as forum shopping, which is not nearly as negatively connoted as it once was.

The parties' right to resolve their dispute privately is an element of the same freedom. Both the right to choose the applicable law and the right to choose not to go to court are versions of party autonomy. However, it is immediately clear that the choice of arbitration has farther reaching consequences. Parties are opting for an entirely different form of dispute resolution, enjoying its advantages and accepting its disadvantages. They are exchanging highly regulated and constitutionally safeguarded proceedings for privacy, flexibility and the expert knowledge of arbitrators – and

---

293 As Jayme put it: "L'autonomie de la volonté des parties pour choisir la loi applicable à un contrat international fait partie des libertés plus vastes de l'individu, qui comprennent aussi le droit 'au développement' de ses capacités économiques en vue d'atteindre le mieux-être matériel." *Jayme*, Annuaire de l'Institut de Droit International, 64-I, p. 65.

294 *Basedow*, RabelsZ 2011, 32, 38 et seq. and in particular 50, 51. *Leible* sees the justification for the ability of States to grant party autonomy in the importance of the human will and the respect that is owed individual decisions. Finally, he calls it an "Ausfluss eines überpositiven Autonomie- und Freiheitsgedankens", see *Leible*, FS Jayme, pp. 487, 488.

295 *Renner*, Zwingendes transnationales Recht, 2010, pp. 47, 48, pointing out that parties can only opt out of the applicability of an entire legal system if the domestic conflict of laws allow for this; *Leible*, FS Jayme, p. 487, referring to Neuhaus' "archimedischer Punkt", meaning that the extent freedom of the parties relies on private international law, and not on the will of the parties itself.

B. Competence to Make Conflict Rules Applicable

possibly a speedier process and lower costs.[296] The resulting award is binding on them, unless it contains certain narrowly reviewable flaws.[297]

In the same manner that the parties' right to choose the applicable law meets its first test when a court is seized and applies its forum's private international law[298], their right to choose arbitration is evaluated when a court is seized and applies its forum's arbitration law, be it in order to give effect to an arbitration clause or because it is asked to set aside or enforce an award. The right to arbitrate is not created by that court's *lex fori*, it is only recognized or potentially limited by it.[299] Thus, the right for parties to arbitrate instead of going to court is not granted by one legal system. Rather, it flows from party autonomy, which is a manifestation of individual freedom that exists *a priori*. Therefore, arbitral tribunals do not derive their power from any one legal system, but solely from the parties' agreement to subject their dispute to arbitration.

Thus, arbitrators are not exercising any State's sovereign power when resolving that dispute. This has implications in two directions: international arbitrators have greater freedom than courts do in how they approach their mandate, and they are far more limited in their power to execute it, because they cannot use force like courts can.

---

296 These aspects are classically hailed as the advantages of international arbitration, see *Blackaby et al.*, International Commercial Arbitration, ed. 6 2015, pp. 27 et seq. However, the length and cost of an international arbitration process can be quite similar to that of national court proceedings in complex cases. Still, the rising popularity of international arbitration is a sign that its other characteristics are attractive in and of themselves to justify opting out of national court proceedings.
297 See *infra*, pp. 163 et seqq.
298 *Basedow*, RabelsZ 2011, 32, 39.
299 In Germany, the law used to state that only matters on which parties could come to a settlement before court could be subject to arbitration, see MüKo-ZPO/*Münch*, ed. 5 2017, § 1031, para. 5. The fact that arbitrability is no longer limited in such a way is seen as an argument in favor of the notion that arbitrators are increasingly fulfilling purely judicial functions, which are not subject to party autonomy. This argument is flawed. In reality, the legal system in Germany simply limits party autonomy to a different extent in international arbitration than it does in domestic court proceedings. It does not mean that arbitrators were exercising functions that they could not be endowed with solely by party autonomy, and that this were proof of them exercising State power.

b) Application of Law

Arbitral tribunals fulfill a function similar to courts: They resolve disputes in a binding fashion through the application of law. However, the fact that arbitral tribunals do not exercise sovereign power in doing so grants them some freedoms that courts, which are constitutionally limited, do not have. The arbitral tribunals' *modus operandi* has a different relationship to the law. Courts, on the one hand, do more than simply apply national law – they have the responsibility of maintaining it. Arbitrators, on the other hand, do not necessarily resolve disputes by applying national or any other law, and even when they do apply national law, they do not have the same responsibility for the law that courts do.

aa) No Maintenance of the Law

Courts are organs of a State and play an important constitutional role. They apply the laws that the legislature has made, and simultaneously examine those laws for constitutionality. While the legislature, composed of representatives of the body politic, codifies the will of the (majority of the) people[300], the judicature is tasked with applying the result to facts. In doing so – in taking a general and abstract rule and finding its concrete application in a case – the courts are essentially continuing the process of making law.[301] This goes beyond the role of a judge as the *bouche de la loi*[302], merely a mouthpiece, automatically transferring law to fact, because to a certain degree of the court exercises discretion.[303] Beyond applying the law, courts are tasked with ensuring that the rules they apply are constitutional, acting as a check on the legislature.[304] Once courts detect a potential unconstitutionality they are obligated to ask a constitutional court to decide on the constitutionality of the law. In Germany, national courts confronted with a flawed law are obligated to present it to the

---

300 *Reinhardt*, Konsistente Jurisdiktion, 1997, 314.
301 *Starck*, Gesetzesbegriff, 1970, p. 268; for civil law counties beyond Germany, see *Iturralde*, Precedent as subject of interpretation, p. 105; for Switzerland see *Hotz*, Richterrecht zwischen methodischer Bindung und Beliebigkeit?, 2008, pp. 114 et seq.
302 *Starck*, Gesetzesbegriff, 1970, p. 147; *Voßkuhle*, Rechtsschutz gegen den Richter, 1993, p. 93.
303 v. Mangoldt/Klein/Starck/*Sommermann*, ed. 7 2018, GG Art. 20 para. 286.
304 Ibid., GG Art. 20 paras. 210 et seq.

B. Competence to Make Conflict Rules Applicable

constitutional court, the *Bundesverfassungsgericht* (BVerfG). This obligation arises from Article 20(3) of the German Constitution, the *Grundgesetz*, which stipulates that courts are bound by (constitutional) laws and it is regulated in Article 100 of the Grundgesetz.[305] Through this mechanism, courts contribute to the maintenance of the legal system by not only applying laws, but ensuring that the laws are constitutional and that the leeway that the laws allow is used in a constitutional manner in any given case. This makes them guardians of the law and, more importantly, of the constitution.

Arbitrators are not charged with maintaining a legal system this way. Even if they were to exercise sovereign power, they are not equipped to ensure the constitutionality of the laws they are applying. If, in the process of applying a national law, the suspicion arises that the law is unconstitutional or if the arbitrators are unsure of how to interpret it in a manner consistent with constitutional or EU law, they are essentially powerless. In Germany, courts in the sense of Article 100 of the Grundgesetz are defined "objectively independent panels, tasked by a formally valid law with the role of a court and designated as courts"[306]. Because arbitral tribunals are not tasked by law with the role of a court, they are not considered to meet these requirements,[307] despite the fact that a broad interpretation of the word is used to ensure access to justice.[308] This obstacle could be overcome if tribunals were able to request assistance from a national court, which could make the application to the BVerfG for them. However, a court can only make such an application when the law is decisive in a case that the court itself is deciding on[309], and this requirement is not met when the case is being adjudicated by an arbitral tribunal and the court is only lending assistance. Arbitrators are effectively barred from having the BVerfG check the law for constitutionality and are forced to apply the law regardless of their doubts.

The only way to prevent potentially unconstitutional law from having an effect in the particular case is if its application would result in an award that violated international public policy. The award could then be set aside pursuant to section 1059(2) no. 2(b) of the German Code of

---

305 Ibid., GG Art. 20 para. 272.
306 Decision of the BVerfG of 17 January 1957, BVerfGE 6, 55, 63.
307 Detterbeck in Sachs/*Sachs*, ed. 8 2018, GG Art. 100, para 4; *Benda et al.*, Verfassungsprozessrecht, 2012, p. 316 para. 767.
308 v. Mangoldt/Klein/Starck/*R.-Sieckmann*, ed. 7 2018, GG Art. 100, fn. 69.
309 Detterbeck in Sachs/*Sachs*, ed. 8 2018, GG Art. 100, para 14.

Civil Procedure. It is questionable whether national courts asked to set the award aside would be able to apply to the BVerfG at such a late stage, since they are not allowed to make a *révision au fond*, a full review of the case. They are restricted to assessing whether the effects of the award violate public policy.[310] Even if they were able to set an award aside because of the unconstitutionality of the substantive law applied, this does not mean that the award could not be recognized and enforced abroad.[311]

When courts in EU Member States have doubts regarding the interpretation of EU law, they may – or in the case of courts of last instance, they must – request a preliminary ruling by the European Court of Justice ("ECJ") on the matter pursuant to Article 267 of the Treaty on the Functioning of the European Union (TFEU)[312],[313] According to the provision, "any court and tribunal of a Member State" can raise a question for a preliminary ruling. The ECJ does not consider arbitral tribunals to be tribunals in the sense of this provision and to be equipped to guarantee the correct interpretation of EU law. In the *Nordsee* case, an arbitral tribunal requested a preliminary judgment from the ECJ and asked whether the arbitration panel itself constituted a "court or tribunal" in the sense of Article 267 of the TFEU, which would be a prerequisite for even submitting such a request. While the ECJ admitted that "there are certain similarities"[314] between national courts and international arbitral tribunals, it found that the similarities were not enough to elevate arbitration panels to "courts or tribunals" of Member States in the sense of Article 267 of the TFEU. It justified this with the fact that the arbitration was not

---

310 See *infra*, pp. 163 et seq.
311 Art. V(2)(b) of the New York Convention (fn. 202) stipulates that the annulment of the award at the seat of arbitration is merely a facultative ground for the enforcement court to refuse to recognize and enforce the award.
312 Consolidated versions of the Treaty on European Union and the Treaty on the Functioning of the European Union 2012/C 326/01, https://eur-lex.europa.eu/legal-content/EN/TXT/?uri=celex%3A12012E%2FTXT.
313 Preliminary rulings enable the ECJ to decide on the interpretation of the EU Treaties, as well as the validity and interpretation of acts of the institutions, bodies, offices or agencies of the Union. Such rulings may be requested any court or tribunal in any Member State if it considers a question in this regard to be necessary to enable it to give judgment. If the court or tribunal is of last instance, in that there is no judicial remedy against its decision under national law, then the court or tribunal must bring the question to the ECJ (see Article 267 (2) and (3) of the TFEU). See *Horspool et al.*, European Union Law, ed. 10 2008, 5.30.
314 ECJ, judgement of 23 March 1982, case C-102/83, ECLI:EU:C:1982:107 – Nordsee, para 10.

B. Competence to Make Conflict Rules Applicable

mandatory and with the low level of involvement of the local authorities in the arbitral process.[315] The ECJ stated that any national courts asked to set aside or enforce the award could make the reference for a preliminary judgment.[316] This entails leaving the review of the interpretation of EU law to the post-award stage.[317]

This inability of arbitral tribunals to reflect upon the laws that they are applying, both on a domestic and a European level, and to ask high courts for help when in doubt shows that they play a fundamentally different role for the legal system whose laws they are applying. They have no power to initiate a process to remove "bad" laws or to ensure that they are applying EU law correctly.[318]

bb) Application of Non-State Law or No Law

Not only do arbitral tribunals have no tools to maintain the law of a specific legal system, they do not necessarily have to apply State law at all, unlike national courts.[319] It is a defining feature of international arbitration that tribunals can decide cases by applying non-State law, or even no law at all, as *amiables compositeurs*.[320] This is rooted in the history of

---

315 *Nordsee* (see fn. 313), paras 11 and 12. It had extended the right make such references for preliminary rulings to arbitral tribunals operating on a statutory basis in the decision of the ECJ of 30 June 1966, case C-61/65, ECLI:EU:C:1966:39 – Vaassen v Beambtenfonds Mijnbedrijf. The *Scheidsgerecht van het Beambtenfonds voor het Mijnbedrijf Heerlen*, which is the arbitration court of the miners' pension fund in the Netherlands, was seen as a court or tribunal in the sense of the provision because it "was foreseen by and organised according to the law as the mandatory dispute settlements mechanism: it had to apply the law in the same way as ordinary courts, and its member were appointed by the minister responsible for mining", see *Kröll et al.*, Comparative International Commercial Arbitration, 2003, p. 447 para. 19-5.
316 *Nordsee* (see fn. 313), para 14.
317 *Kröll et al.*, Comparative International Commercial Arbitration, 2003, p. 479 para. 19-10.
318 Among others, Gößling calls for a dynamic interpretation of the word "court" under European law that should include international commercial arbitration tribunals, *Gößling*, Europäisches Kollisionsrecht, 2019, pp. 87-95.
319 It is not unthinkable that national courts can apply non-State law. Including such an option in the Rome I Regulation was discussed, but the idea was rejected, see *Mankowski*, Interessenpolitik und europäisches Kollisionsrecht, 2011, 27 et seq. and *supra*, p. 20.
320 See chapter § 4, in particular pp. 183 et seq.

§ 3. Binding Effect of Article 1(1) in International Commercial Arbitration

international arbitration and has been cemented globally in arbitration statutes, institutional rules and treaties.

Parties may, in exercising their party autonomy, agree to have arbitrators decide on the basis of non-State law or as *amiables compositeurs*. In the absence of such a choice the decision made by the arbitrators must be based on national law. Most national arbitration statutes, international treaties and institutional rules follow this pattern. However, there are exceptions. The arbitration law of Ecuador states that arbitrators should by default make a decision *en equidad*, an equitable decision, and only apply a law if the parties expressly tell them to do so in their agreement.[321] Until quite recently, Bolivia and Peru had similar provisions in their laws, speaking of *"equidad"*, *"conciencia"* (conscience) and *"conocimiento y leal saber y entender"* (knowledge and legal learning and understanding") as the default basis for tribunals' decisions.[322] The civil code of procedure of Argentina required that arbitrators should decide as *"amigables componedores"* unless directed otherwise,[323] and only changed its law in 2018.[324] The latter countries' laws have been changed to prefer a decision according to law in order to assimilate to the global standard. However, the fact that the States originally opted for *ex aequo et bono* decisions to be the default in their arbitration statutes is testament to the importance of this mode of decision-making in international arbitration.

---

321 Ecuador, Ley de Arbitraje y Mediación (Law No. 000. RO/145 of 4 September 1997), Art. 3: "Las partes indicarán si los árbitros deben decidir en equidad o en derecho, a falta de convenio, el fallo será en equidad."
322 Peru, Ley de Arbitraje General 1006, Art. 3: "Salvo que las partes hayan pactado expresamente que el arbitraje será de derecho, el arbitraje se entenderá de conciencia." (http://www.sice.oas.org/DISPUTE/COMARB/Peru/lgenarb1.as p); Bolivia, Ley N°1779 1997, Art. 54: "Salvo pacto en contrario, el Tribunal Arbitral decidirá según la equidad y conforme a sus conocimientos y leal saber y entender." (https://www.lexivox.org/norms/BO-L-1770.html).
323 "Podrán someterse a la decisión de arbitradores o amigables componedores, las cuestiones que pueden ser objeto del juicio de árbitros. Si nada se hubiese estipulado en el compromiso acerca de si el arbitraje ha de ser de derecho o de amigables componedores, o si se hubiese autorizado a los árbitros a decidir la controversia según equidad, se entenderá que es de amigables componedores." Art. 766 (2) of the Codigo Procesal Civil y Comercial de la Nación of 1981 (http://servicios.infoleg.gob.ar/infolegInternet/anexos/15000-19999/16547/texact.htm).
324 Art. 81 of the International Arbitration Act of Argentina, Ley 27449 of 2018 now reads: "El tribunal arbitral decidirá ex aequo et bono o como amigable componedor sólo si las partes lo han autorizado expresamente a hacerlo así."

Even if arbitrators are asked to decide based on law, this does not necessarily mean State law. Arbitrators can be free to apply the infamous *lex mercatoria*, the UNIDROIT Principles and PECL or general principles of law. This can arguably also entail the application of international treaties, such as the CISG, independent from any national legal system.[325] Just like decisions *ex aequo et bono*, this freedom is often made dependent on an agreement by the parties; with no such agreement arbitrators must apply State law.[326] Criticism of this is at times fierce, and the proponents of binding arbitrators to private international law like national courts argue that it leads to legal uncertainty.[327] This relationship to law is, however, a cornerstone of international commercial arbitration.

This sets arbitral tribunals apart from national courts, which are barred from producing decisions based on the judges' conscience[328] or, as of now, from applying non-State law. They are bound by the law of the country of their forum. In cases with an international element, they must apply their forum's conflict of laws rules, which in turn regularly do not permit simply reaching an equitable solution or applying non-State law, but rather lead to domestic or a foreign State's laws and regulations.[329] The differences between the relationship arbitrators have with law and the relationship national courts have with law are considerable. They are born out of the constitutional role that courts play and show that arbitrators are not comparable to courts in that aspect, despite their similar functions regarding dispute resolution in general.

c) The Arbitral Award

Ultimately, the arbitral process culminates in an arbitral award. Due to an agreement by the parties to this end, such an arbitral award resolves a dispute and is binding on the parties. Ending disputes in a binding man-

---

325 *Magnus/Mankowski*, Joint Response to the Green Paper, 2002, p. 16. See also *infra*, pp. 173 et seq.
326 E.g. Art. 28(3) of the UNCITRAL Model Law, which uses the term "law" instead of "rules of law" in regard to the arbitrators' choice of law, or § 1051(2) of the German Code of Civil Procedure, which speaks explicitly of *"Recht des Staates"*.
327 MüKo-BGB/*Martiny*, ed. 7 2018, Art. 3 Rom I-VO para. 36; *Bar/Mankowski*, IPR I, ed. 2 2003, pp. 79 et seq.
328 *Spickhoff*, RabelsZ 1992, 116, 133.
329 Internationales Vertragsrecht/*Ferrari*, ed. 3 2018, Art. 3 Rom I-VO para. 20.

§ 3. Binding Effect of Article 1(1) in International Commercial Arbitration

ner may appear to be function unique to courts, as they have a monopoly on administering justice, which would mean that if arbitral tribunals are able to do the same, they must qualify as courts as well.[330] However, there are again important differences that set arbitral awards apart from court decisions.

The monopoly that the State has on administering justice has a consequence that arbitration could never achieve: only the State has the power to adjudicate without the consent of both parties. While parties have the right to choose a court within the parameters set forth by each legal system, any party can still be sued without such a choice of court agreement before courts that are competent pursuant to objective criteria of their forum's procedural law. Arbitral tribunals cannot adjudicate an issue if the parties have not agreed beforehand that they should have the power to do so. They have such power not because of sovereignty, but because of the party agreement. In making an arbitral award, the tribunal does not require sovereign power, since it is not able to enforce its decision the way courts can enforce theirs. A tribunal can look at the facts of a dispute and find a solution, whether based on law or not. The parties have agreed beforehand that this decision will be binding on them. That is the extent of it. This constitutes a voluntary type of jurisdiction that does not touch upon the States' monopoly on adjudicating with sovereign power.[331] The tribunal's decision is binding because the parties agree that it should be, not because it is the result of an exercise of sovereign power.

The contractual theory picks up on this aspect and contends that the arbitral award – the result of an agreement between parties – is itself no more than a contract, made on behalf of the parties by arbitrators as their legal representatives. However, arbitrators are not asked to reach a contractual agreement on behalf of the parties, but rather to resolve a dispute between the parties. The award has effects that go beyond a mere agreement; it has undeniably judicial elements because parties cannot void it like an ordinary agreement. Recognition of this fact by legal systems around the world has led to the New York Convention, which ensures that the award has the effect desired by the parties, namely its enforceability.[332]

---

330 *Yüksel*, J. Priv. Int. 2011, 149, 164-166.
331 *Solomon*, Verbindlichkeit von Schiedssprüchen, 2007, p. 325; *von Hoffmann*, Internationale Handelsschiedsgerichtsbarkeit, 1970, p. 37; *Schlosser*, Schiedsgerichtsbarkeit, ed. 2 1989, Rn. 458; *Schwab/Walter*, Schiedsgerichtsbarkeit, 2005, chapter 18 para 1, chapter 30 para 1.
332 Kronke/Naciemiento/Otto/*Kronke*, 2010, Introduction, p. 8

B. Competence to Make Conflict Rules Applicable

However, the fact that arbitration awards still need national courts to establish the enforceability of awards sets it apart from court decisions.

International arbitral awards can be likened to court decisions as regards the effect that court decisions have abroad, in that court decisions have a rational element but lack an imperative element.[333] The terms rational element and imperative element were coined by Batiffol in regard to laws.[334] Laws have a rational element, which is based on the fact that they are at their core decisions balancing competing interests and aimed at finding a universally correct abstract and general rule. The imperative element describes the effect that the law has: In the territory of the lawmakers who passed this law, it is an expression of *l'ordre du pouvoir* and as such has an imperative element.[335] This means that the law must be followed. Outside of this legislature's territory, the law lacks this imperative element, but retains the rational element, since it is still in essence a rational decision with a *vocation universelle*.[336] This logic can be extended to national court decisions, because they contain the same claim to validity as the laws they are interpreting.[337] They also have an inherently imperative nature only in the forum of the court and in order to be imperative abroad must first be recognized by foreign courts.[338] Finally, arbitral awards contain only a rational element, but not an imperative element. They constitute fair and balanced decisions concerning the facts at hand, but their awards lack an imperative element in any legal system, including at the seat of arbitration.[339] Even at the seat of arbitration, the awards have as much force as a foreign court decision or a foreign law. In order to gain an imperative element, a legal system must recognize an award through its court system as a decision that does not violate its basic notions of fairness and lend it its coercive powers to enforce it.

---

333 *Solomon*, Verbindlichkeit von Schiedssprüchen, 2007, p. 321.
334 *Batiffol*, Aspects, 1956, pp. 110-119; *Kegel/Schurig*, Internationales Privatrecht, ed. 9 2004, p. 193.
335 *Batiffol*, Aspects, 1956, pp. 110-119.
336 Ibid.
337 *Solomon*, Verbindlichkeit von Schiedssprüchen, 2007, pp. 325, 326.
338 An exception to this rule is that decisions made by courts of EU Member States generally no longer have to recognized by courts in other EU Member States in order to be enforced there due to the Regulation (EU) No 1215/2012, also known as the Brussels Ia Regulation (https://eur-lex.europa.eu/eli/reg/2012/1215/2015-02-26). For more on this, see *infra*, pp. 193 et seq.
339 Ibid., p. 327.

This is what sets arbitral awards apart from national court decisions. Every arbitral award needs to be recognized before it can be enforced. As long as it is not recognized by a national legal system, it remains a toothless form of dispute resolution and a party's refusal to comply with it has no consequences. If and when a State decides to grant the powers of a court decision to arbitral awards – through a national court on the basis of a law – this equalizes the effects of the award and a court decision, but not also the legal basis for these effects.[340]

While this makes the award less powerful than a domestic court decision, it makes it more powerful than a contract. If the arbitration award were a mere contract, as suggested by some authors[341], one party could not simply go to a court and demand that the contract be enforced. Instead, this party would need to sue the contractual partner, which would lead to a court decision that could then be enforced. The fact that the enforcement of the award can be directly requested from a domestic court reveals the fact that it has an effect extending beyond that of a mere contract, lending credence to the hybrid theory.

3. Conclusion

International arbitration is neither entirely contractual in nature nor entirely judicial. The hybrid theory therefore best describes the legal nature of international arbitration. However, for the discussion at hand regarding the jurisdiction of States to bind international arbitrators to their laws – including private international law – it is vital to note that arbitrators do not resemble national courts in that they organically belong to any legal system. They do not receive their power from a State whose sovereignty they exercise, but from the parties. If parties had not previously consented to arbitration, they could not be subjected to an arbitral process. Because arbitration tribunals differ from domestic courts in key aspects, they are not inherently subject to their sovereignty and it is not appropriate to treat them like State organs. Thus, while States have the right to decide how and according to what law civil law disputes are to be decided in their territory, this does not automatically extend to a right to dictate what substantive law is applicable in private dispute resolution, through rules such as Article 1(1) of the CISG.

---

340 Ibid., p. 330.
341 See fn. 282.

III. Seat of Arbitration as Genuine Link

Since international arbitral tribunals cannot be seen as part any one State's judicial system, the basis for any State's legislative jurisdiction to make conflict rules applicable in international commercial arbitration must be found elsewhere. The seat of arbitration itself could qualify as the genuine link necessary for establishing legislative jurisdiction over the matter of applicable substantive law. Contracts that contain international arbitration agreements typically have connections to a number of different States: the contractual partners will be nationals of and have their seats of business in different States and the contractual obligations will be performed in different States. Any of these connections can potentially serve as a genuine link, leading to concurrent legislative jurisdictions of several States. Of all potentially competent States, the State in which the seat of arbitration is located is the one that is believed to have authority over the arbitration proceedings, also to determine which substantive law is applicable. While it is feasible that this State is also connected to the dispute in additional aspects, for example that the contract was performed in its territory, this is often not the case. Instead, the seat of arbitration is typicallyselected for its neutrality, which results precisely from its lack of a connection to the parties and their contract. In order to determine if the location of the seat establishes a genuine link between the State and the arbitration process, the possibility of an alternative connection with the State in which it is located will be disregarded and it will be assumed that the location of the seat is the only connection. The seat alone must constitute a genuine link to the process.

1. Territoriality

The seat or place of arbitration is nominally the location in which the arbitration proceedings physically take place. States have legislative jurisdiction over actions taking place in their territory, as this gives them a territorial link to the actions, which is generally accepted as a genuine link as required for legislative competence. This argument is brought forward by the proponents of the territorial version of the seat theory, who believe that the location of the arbitral seat in a particular State gives that State the right to legislate on the arbitration proceedings.[342] The notion that

---

342 See *supra*, pp. 78 et seq.

§ 3. Binding Effect of Article 1(1) in International Commercial Arbitration

parties and arbitrators meet in the territory of a State in order to resolve their dispute, presenting their arguments, introducing evidence and finally handing down an award, does seem to give the State some interest in ensuring that the process is not deeply inadequate and that the parties do not face some grave injustice because they chose to meet in that State. However, the necessarily territorial aspect of the arbitral seat has effectively been abolished, robbing the territorial seat theory of its justification.

While the seat of arbitration was originally conceived as the meeting point for all participants in an international commercial arbitration procedure, it now constitutes an increasingly tenuous connection with the arbitration process. The arbitral seat has evolved from being the location where activity related to the arbitration procedure physically takes place into a mere legal concept: it is now the "legal or judicial home or place of the arbitration"[343]. Arbitration statutes and institutional rules commonly contain provisions stating that activity pertaining to the proceedings does not actually have to take place at the location of the arbitral seat.[344] For example, the ICC Arbitration Rules contain the following provision in Article 18: "The arbitral tribunal may, after consultation with the parties, conduct hearings and meetings at any location it considers appropriate, unless otherwise agreed by the parties." The UNCITRAL Model Law, on which many domestic arbitration statutes are based, states that the arbitration tribunal may meet anywhere it considers appropriate "for consultation among its members, for hearing witnesses, experts or the parties, or for inspection of goods, other property or documents."[345] This is convenient, because the seat of arbitration is regularly chosen by the parties during the drafting of their agreement and thus long before the proceedings even became necessary. The consequence is that the seat of the arbitration does not necessarily equate to the geographic location of the hearings or meetings in the arbitration.[346]

This has consequences for the quality of the seat of arbitration as a genuine link. If it is no longer the place where all or even any of the physical activity in an arbitration process takes place, then the territorial

---

343 *Born*, International Commercial Arbitration, ed. 2 2014, p. 1536.
344 E.g. § 34(2)(a) of the English Arbitration Act, 1996, Article 18(2) of the UNCITRAL Arbitration Rules, Article 18(2) of the 2012 ICC Arbitration Rules, Article 13(2) of the ICDR Arbitration Rules.
345 Art. 20(2) of the UNCITRAL Model Law.
346 *Born*, International Commercial Arbitration, ed. 2 2014, p. 2051.

link to the State in which the seat lies is weak or even nonexistent.[347] The territorial connection becomes a legal fiction, which is not enough to establish a genuine link of *territoriality* under public international law. A territorial connection with the arbitration proceedings only exists in cases in which the arbitration proceedings actually take place in the State of the arbitral seat. This is becoming increasingly unlikely in the age of modern technology, in which there are numerous digital options for making physical meetings superfluous. Many activities that would ordinarily have been done in person can be and have been replaced by group chats and video and telephone conferences, in particular since the COVID-19 pandemic forced the world to become more open to these options. In such cases, each participant is at their laptop or desktop computer or on their cellphone, yet physically located in different places, in different countries and continents. Arbitration proceedings being conducted entirely digitally may seem far off to some. However, the experience of months-long State-imposed travel bans and social distancing during the pandemic in 2020 and 2021 has shown that under certain circumstances, arbitrators may simply not have a choice if they want the case to move forward.

Once the actual physical activities no longer take place in the territory of the State, basing legislative jurisdiction on the territorial aspect as a genuine link becomes impossible.

2. Party Choice

Even if the seat does not convey a territorial link to the State in which it is located, the fact that it was chosen by the parties may well still serve as enough of a connection to grant the State certain rights regarding the arbitration proceedings. The *Institute de Droit International*, representing the seat theorists in the localization debate, made the application of the *lex loci arbitri*, including any arbitration-specific conflict of laws rule, contingent on the choice of the seat. This was stipulated in Article 1 of its resolution "Arbitration in Private International Law":

> Parties shall be free in the arbitral agreement [...] to exercise their free choice and to indicate the place where the arbitral tribunal must sit; this choice

---

[347] *Petrochilos*, Procedural Law, 2004, pp. 23, 24 paras. 2.12, 2.13; *Rubino-Sammartano*, International Arbitration, ed. 3 2014, p. 103.

> *shall imply that they intend to submit the private arbitration to the law of the seat of the country arbitration [...]. [sic]*[348]

The choice of the seat by the parties was thus interpreted as a choice of the *lex loci arbitri*, in effect giving the State legislative jurisdiction regarding any matter covered by the *lex arbitri*.

The notion that solely a choice by parties to resolve their dispute in a particular State can constitute a relevant connection with that State is not alien. In some States, parties are able to select the State as a forum for future litigation even if there is no connection between the State and the dispute.[349] The choice of forum effects jurisdiction of that State. Once adjudicative jurisdiction has been established, the application of the procedural and private international law of the chosen forum is an automatic consequence. In several ways, a choice of an arbitral seat seems comparable to a choice of forum. First, in many States the arbitration statute declares itself applicable when the seat of arbitration is located in the territory of the State. A consequence of the choice of the seat is thus the applicability of the procedural law and arbitration-specific conflict rule of the arbitral seat, much like the application of the forum's procedural and private international law results from a choice of forum. Second, arbitration statutes typically contain rules stipulating the jurisdiction of the domestic courts over matters regarding the arbitral procedure and the resulting award. Thus, the choice of a seat of arbitration triggers the jurisdiction of the State's courts in a fashion similar to a choice of forum.

Despite these similarities, the effect of a choice of forum is not the comparable to a choice of an arbitral seat in the context of establishing a connection with the State. The fact that a State's arbitration statute containing conflict rules addressed to the arbitration tribunal declares itself applicable does not automatically mean that that State has legislative jurisdiction in these matters. To the contrary, whether such jurisdiction exists is the subject of this analysis. What sets a choice of an arbitral seat apart from a choice of forum is the content of the choice: By selecting a domestic court for their litigation, parties are willfully subjecting their dispute to the authority of the State that is the forum of that court. The parties are aware that they are submitting to a dispute resolution mecha-

---

348 The resolution can be found under http://www.idi-iil.org/app/uploads/2017/06/1957_amst_03_en.pdf.
349 This is the case for EU Member States due to the Rome I Regulation, as long as the dispute is not exclusively connected with one single State, see e.g. Beck-OK BGB/*Spickhoff*, ed. 48 2018, Rom I-VO Art. 3 para. 35.

B. Competence to Make Conflict Rules Applicable

nism that is entirely instituted, run and controlled by the forum. When parties opt for international arbitration, they are specifically choosing a dispute resolution mechanism that is neutral in that it is divorced from any particular State. The location of the seat of the arbitration proceedings is a practical aspect that is in no way a submission of the dispute to the supreme authority of that State.

Furthermore, the choice of the seat is not necessarily made by the parties. A choice of forum requires just that: a choice by the parties in favor of a particular forum. Without such a choice, there is no way a State without any connection with the dispute could assert adjudicative competence over a case.[350] The seat, however, is not necessarily chosen by the parties.[351] Different institutional rules and arbitration statutes have different mechanisms for how to deal with the absence of a choice by the parties. There are four different ways in which the choice can fall to an entity other than the party.[352] First, the seat can be chosen by the tribunal, once it has been assembled. This approach is stipulated by the UNCITRAL Arbitration Rules.[353] Because it is also suggested by the UNCITRAL Model Law[354], this approach has been adopted in a number of domestic arbitration statutes. Second, the administrator of an arbitral institution can choose the seat, as is stipulated by the ICC Arbitration Rules[355], calling for a decision by the "Court", and the Arbitration Rules of the Stockholm Chamber of Commerce[356], referring the decision to the "Board". Third, the decision can be made in a provisional manner by the administrator, subject to final determination by the tribunal, as stipulated in the Arbitration Rules

---

350 *Geimer*, Internationales Zivilprozessrecht, ed. 7 2015, para. 377a.
351 *Hayward*, Conflict of Laws and Arbitral Discretion, 2017, p. 78 para. 2.67.
352 For a detailed analysis, see *Sabater*, J. Int'l Arb. 2010, 443; *Born*, International Commercial Arbitration, ed. 2 2014, § 14.07, pp. 2093 et seq.
353 Article 18(1) of the UNCITRAL Arbitration Rules: "If the parties have not previously agreed on the place of arbitration, the place of arbitration shall be determined by the arbitral tribunal having regard to the circumstances of the case. The award shall be deemed to have been made at the place of arbitration."
354 Art. 20(1) of the UNCITRAL Model Law: "The parties are free to agree on the place of arbitration. Failing such agreement, the place of arbitration shall be determined by the arbitral tribunal having regard to the circumstances of the case, including the convenience of the parties."
355 Art. 18(1) of the ICC Rules: "The place of the arbitration shall be fixed by the Court, unless agreed upon by the parties."
356 Art. 20(1) of the SCC Arbitration Rules: "Unless agreed upon by the parties, the Board shall decide the seat of arbitration."

§ 3. Binding Effect of Article 1(1) in International Commercial Arbitration

of the International Centre of Dispute Resolution[357] and in the Rules of Procedure of the Inter-American Commercial Arbitration Commission[358]. Fourth and finally, the rules may specify a place of arbitration directly, to be determined finally by the tribunal. This is the approach used in the Arbitration Rules of the London Court of International Arbitration, under which London is the default place of arbitration.[359] In any of these cases, the decision is not made by the parties. In such cases, there simply is no choice of an arbitral seat by the parties which could confer a connection to the State in which the seat is located.

The fact that specifying the seat of arbitration can even be delegated demonstrates that it is merely a technicality, albeit of potentially great practical significance. By itself, the fact that the choice of the seat of arbitration is often delegated to the tribunal shows the crucial difference between the choice of seat and the choice of forum. The choice of forum effects the jurisdiction of a court, which then decides on the case. The arbitration agreement effects the jurisdiction of the arbitral tribunal, which can then choose the seat, i.e. where the process should legally be anchored. This difference is also reflected in the fact that the choice of a forum by parties can effect the jurisdiction of a court that would not otherwise have jurisdiction. If there is no choice of forum, the parties may only go to court in a jurisdiction with a pre-determined connection with the dispute. The choice of a seat, on the other hand, can simply be delegated to somebody else and could fall on a State without any connection with the dispute, regardless of whether the parties make the choice themselves or not. In fact, a neutral place of arbitration is often preferred, as has been discussed before.

---

357 Art. 17(1) of the ICDR Arbitration Rules: "If the parties do not agree on the place of arbitration by a date established by the Administrator, the Administrator may initially determine the place of arbitration, subject to the power of the arbitral tribunal to determine finally the place of arbitration within 45 days after its constitution."

358 Art. 13(1) of the IACAC Rules of Procedure: "If the parties have not reached an agreement regarding the place of arbitration, the place of arbitration may initially be determined by the IACAC, subject to the power of the tribunal to determine finally the place of arbitration within sixty (60) days following the appointment of the last arbitrator."

359 Art. 16.2 of the LCIA Arbitration Rules: "In default of any such agreement, the seat of the arbitration shall be London (England), unless and until the Arbitral Tribunal orders, in view of the circumstances and after having given the parties a reasonable opportunity to make written comments to the Arbitral Tribunal, that another arbitral seat is more appropriate."

B. Competence to Make Conflict Rules Applicable

These differences show that the choice of a seat cannot establish a connection with the State in which the seat is located in the same way that a choice of forum can establish a link to the forum State.

3. Conclusion

The seat of arbitration is steadily losing its force as a territorial link to the State in which it is located, and it is not reliably the product of a choice by the parties, so that party choice is also not a consistent genuine link.

IV. Customary Law Basis for Arbitration-Specific Conflict Rule

It was just demonstrated that the seat of arbitration is primarily a legal concept and is losing its ability to serve as a territorial link between the dispute and the State in which the seat is located. However, the relevance of the location of the seat cannot be denied. As discussed above[360], the application of most arbitration statutes is contingent on the seat being – at least formally – located in the territory of the forum. In terms of private international law, the location of the arbitral seat serves as a connecting factor in the unilateral conflict rule contained in each arbitration statute.

This connection is the product of customary international law. As demontrated, in order for a usage to become customary law, there has to be State practice and an *opinio iuris*, i.e. a substantial number of States has to act a certain way, due to a notion that they are legally obliged to do so. In the case at hand, we are looking for general practice of States making conflict of laws rules applicable to arbitration and doing so precisely because they believe that they have jurisdiction in the matter.

1. State Practice

In the area of domestic statutes for international arbitration, it is not difficult to identify State practice, especially owing to the UNCITRAL Model Law.[361] As the name already shows, this is a model law, crafted by

---

360 See *supra*, pp. 74 et seq.
361 See *supra*, fn. 204.

the United Nations Commission on International Trade, UNCITRAL[362], that has been declared the "single most important legislative instrument in the field of international commercial arbitration".[363] Its creation was initiated to supplement the New York Convention with a protocol regarding party-adopted arbitration rules. In its final form, however, it constitutes a set of rules that can be adopted by States as their arbitration statute, or at least serve as an inspiration in the law-making process. The Model Law was drafted to overcome some common defects that persisted in domestic arbitration statutes, ranging from restrictions on parties regarding the submission of future disputes to international arbitration to limiting the competence of arbitrators to determine their own competence or to conduct the proceedings as deemed appropriate.[364] Legislation based on the Model Law has been adopted in 85 States, in a total of 118 jurisdictions.[365] Consequently, in all these jurisdictions, the statutes pertaining to international commercial arbitration proceedings will be quite similar, if not identical. Given the large number of States that have adopted the Model Law and the fact that the arbitration statutes in other States often contain similar provisions as well, there is ample opportunity for common State practice to emerge in this area of law.

Regarding the scope of application of arbitration statutes, the Model Law suggests the following clause in Article 1(2):

> *The provisions of this Law [...] apply only if the place of arbitration is in the territory of this State.*

The States adopting the Model Law or, similarly, arbitration statutes that declare themselves applicable when the seat of arbitration is in their territory, in turn demonstrate State practice that determines that the State in which the seat of arbitration is located is competent to regulate the procedure of arbitration proceedings and any additional issues covered by the Model Law. Crucially, the Model Law also contains the following provision, Article 28(2):

> *Failing any designation by the parties, the arbitral tribunal shall apply the law determined by the conflict of laws rules which it considers applicable.*

---

362 See fn. 28.
363 *Born*, International Commercial Arbitration, ed. 2 2014, p. 133.
364 *Hußlein-Stich*, Das UNCITRAL-Modellgesetz, 1990, p. 3; *Friedrich*, UNCITRAL-Modellgesetz, 2006, pp. 41, 42.
365 See fn. 204.

B. Competence to Make Conflict Rules Applicable

This itself constitutes a conflict of laws rule, set forth by the State in which the seat of arbitration is located.

Article 28 of the Model Law is not always implemented verbatim. There are several different methods employed in the drafting of conflict rules contained in arbitration statutes globally. The arbitration statutes of Australia[366], Chile[367], Hong Kong[368], Iran[369], Ireland[370], Nigeria[371], Russia[372], Serbia[373], Singapore[374], Slovakia[375], South Africa[376], Sri Lanka[377], Thailand[378] and the United Kingdom[379], among others, stipulate that the arbitral tribunal should find the applicable substantive law by applying the conflict of laws rules that it considers applicable or appropriate. This is popular phrasing because it is suggested by Article 28(2) of the UNCITRAL Model Law. A different approach, which is followed in the arbitration statutes of States such as Argentina[380], Austria[381], Cana-

---

366 Art. 28(3) of the Commercial Arbitration Act of the Australian Capital Territory of 2018, of the Commercial Arbitration Act of New South Wales of 2010, of the Commercial Arbitration Act of the Northern Territory of 2018, of the Commercial Arbitration Act of Queensland of 2013, of the Commercial Arbitration Act of Queensland of 2011, of the Commercial Arbitration Act of Tasmania of 2011, of the Commercial Arbitration Act of Victoria of 2011 and of the Commercial Arbitration Act of Western Australia of 2012.
367 Art. 28(2) of the International Arbitration Act, Ley 19971 of 2004 for England, Wales and Northern Ireland, Art. 7 of the Scottish Arbitration Act of 2010 in connection with Art. 47(1)(b) of the Scottish Arbitration Rules; Art. 23(1) of the Bermuda International Conciliation and Arbitration Act of 1993 in connection with Art. 28(2) of the UNCITRAL Model Law, Art. 62 of the Arbitration Act of the Virgin British Islands of 2013.
368 Sec. 64 of the Ordinance L.N. 38 of 2011.
369 Art. 27(2) of the Iranian Law for International and Commercial Arbitration of 1997.
370 Art. 6 of the Arbitration Act of Ireland of 2010, which implements the UNCITRAL Model Law.
371 Art. 47(3) of the Arbitration and Conciliation Act of Nigeria of 2004.
372 Art. 28(2) of the Law of the Russian Federation on International Commercial Arbitration, N 5338–1.
373 Art. 50(3) of the Arbitration Act, No. 46/2006.
374 Sec. 3(1) of the International Arbitration Act.
375 Sec. 30(1) of the Act No. 244/2002 on Arbitration, as amended in 2016.
376 Art. 6 of the International Arbitration Bill of South Africa of 2017, which gives the UNCITRAL Model Law the force of law.
377 Art. 24(2) of the Arbitration Act of Sri Lanka, No. 11 of 1995.
378 Sec. 34 of the Arbitration Act of Thailand, B.E. 2545 of 2002.
379 Sec. 46(3) of the Arbitration Act of 1996.
380 Art. 80 of the International Arbitration Act of Argentina, Ley 27449 of 2018.
381 Sec. 604 of the Austrian Code of Civil Procedure.

da[382], Colombia[383], France[384], Greece[385], India[386], Lithuania[387], Mexico[388], Spain[389] and Vietnam[390], stipulates that the tribunal should apply the law that it considers appropriate. Yet a different method is used in the arbitration statutes of China[391], Egypt[392], Germany[393], Japan[394], Korea[395], Portugal[396], Switzerland[397] and the United Arab Emirates[398], which specify that the tribunal should apply the law that it considers most closely connected with the dispute.

Virtually all arbitration statutes based on the Model Law contain a conflict of laws rule provided by the seat of arbitration. Following the criteria laid out above[399], this meets the requirements of a State practice in the context of customary law.

2. Opinio Iuris

State practice must be supported by *opinio iuris*, i.e. by the notion that the States are obliged to act the way they do, in order to establish customary law. Thus, it is necessary to find evidence that the arbitration statutes contain conflict of laws rules because the States believe that they have the right to legislate this aspect of international arbitration proceedings. Otherwise, the identical rule in arbitration statutes can only be categorized as usage. *Opinio iuris* is not always easy to identify, but it can be found

---

382   E.g. Sec. 32(1) of the Arbitration Act of Ontario of 1991.
383   Art. 101 of the Colombian Arbitration Act, Ley 1563 of 2012.
384   Art. 1511 of the French Code of Civil Procedure.
385   Art. 28(2) of Law 2735/1999.
386   Sec. 28(1)(b)(iii) of the Arbitration and Conciliation Act of India of 1996.
387   Article 39 of the Lithuanian Law on Commercial Arbitration, No I-1274 of 1996.
388   Art. 1445 of the Mexican Commerce Code.
389   Art. 34(2) of the Arbitration Act of Spain, Ley 60/2003 of 2003.
390   Art. 14.2 of the Vietnamese Law on Commercial Arbitration, No. 54-2010-QH12 of 2010.
391   Art. 126 of the Chinese Contract Law of 1999.
392   Art. 39 of the Egyptian Arbitration Act No. 27 of 1994.
393   Sec. 1051(2) of the German Code of Civil Procedure.
394   Art. 36(2) of the Japanese Arbitration Law, no. 138 of 2003.
395   Art. 29(2) of the Korean Arbitration Act, as amended by Act No.6083 in 1999.
396   Art. 52(2) of the Voluntary Arbitration Act of Portugal of 2011.
397   Art. 381(2) of the Swiss Code of Civil Procedure.
398   Art. 38(1) of the UAE Arbitration Law, Law No. (6) of 2018.
399   See *supra*, pp. 89 et seq.

in agreements or statements by State organs.[400] Two promising sources of *opinio iuris* in the matter of legislative jurisdiction regarding international commercial arbitration are the New York Convention and the *travaux préparatoires* to the Model Law

a) New York Convention

The New York Convention is one of the most successful treaties in existence: a formidable 168 State are party to it.[401] The New York Convention makes mention of the law applicable in arbitration proceedings in two different provisions: Article V(1)(a) and (d). Both of these specify grounds on which an award can be refused recognition and enforcement if so requested by the party against whom it is invoked. According to Article V(1)(a), such a ground can be based on the invalidity of the arbitration agreement. The standard for the arbitration agreement is the law chosen by the parties ("under the law to which the parties have subjected it"), or otherwise the law of the seat of arbitration ("under the law of the country in which the award was made")[402]. Article V(1)(d) stipulates that the award can be refused recognition and enforcement if the composition of the arbitration tribunal or the arbitral procedure violated the agreement of the parties, "or, failing such agreement, was not in accordance with the law of the country where the arbitration took place," i.e. the seat of arbitration.

These two provisions reflect an understanding on who has the legislative jurisdiction in these matters. In effect, the competence to make rules regulating arbitration agreements and arbitration procedures, the latter of which are subsidiary to any party agreement, rests with the State where the seat of arbitration is located. By agreeing on the applicability of the law of

---

400 *Wolfrum*, 'Sources of International Law' in *The Max Planck Encyclopedia of Public International Law*, vol. IX p. 304 para. 26.
401 See fn. 209.
402 The "country in which the award was made" does not necessarily align with the seat of arbitration. Notably, Art. V(1)(d) explicitly uses the term "country where the arbitration took place", thus differentiating between these two places. Depending on how the phrase in lit. a is interpreted, it could refer to the process of decision making, or the act of signing the decision by each of the arbitrators. Any of these steps could take place in a different location and none of them have to take place at the agreed upon or assigned seat of arbitration. Given the uncertainties resulting from these practical aspects, the phrase is understood to mean the seat of arbitration. See Wolff/*Wilske*/*Fox*, 2012, Art. V paras. 116 et seqq.

§ 3. Binding Effect of Article 1(1) in International Commercial Arbitration

the seat of arbitration in both of these aspects, the signatories of the New York Convention have enabled those States to make binding rules on the matters, in effect equipping them with legislative jurisdiction. This can be seen as an expression of *opinio iuris* of the signatory States of the New York Convention: The States involved believe that the competence to regulate these matters lies with the seat of arbitration. Many States around the world have followed suit by making arbitration statutes that are applicable to the arbitration agreement and procedure when they serve as the seats of arbitration. This can be seen as a corresponding State practice. Regarding the legislative jurisdiction for matters of arbitral procedure and the validity of arbitration agreements, it is possible to establish customary law in favor of the seat of arbitration.

However, this does not affect legislative jurisdiction regarding conflict of laws rules in international arbitration. The legislative jurisdiction to regulate the arbitration proceedings does not include the right to make conflict of laws rules, as these are not procedural in nature. Rather, they are part of substantive law, as they affect the outcome of the decision, albeit indirectly.[403] The fact that they are contained in the arbitration statutes of States along with procedural rules does not change this fact. While the notion of "procedure" in Article V(1)(d) of the New York Convention can be interpreted more broadly than encompassing only strictly procedural matters[404], it cannot be stretched to cover decisions – even indirect ones – on substantive matters.

Aside from the arbitration agreement and the arbitration procedure, the New York Convention makes no mention of any domestic law. There is no indication of which law is applicable to the merits of a dispute subject to international commercial arbitration, or what State is in charge of deciding this question. The only reference that it makes to substantive law is an indirect one, to the public policy – both procedural and substantive – of the State in which recognition and enforcement is sought, stipulating that its violation constitutes a ground for refusal of recognition and enforcement of the award.[405] This gives no insight into the source of the applicable substantive law.

---

403 See *infra*, p. 194, for further discussion of this aspect.
404 *Petrochilos*, Procedural Law, 2004, pp. 169 et seq. para. 5.06.
405 Art. V(2)(b) of the New York Convention: "Recognition and enforcement of an arbitral award may also be refused if the competent authority in the country where recognition and enforcement is sought finds that […] [*t*]he recognition or enforcement of the award would be contrary to the public policy of that country."

B. Competence to Make Conflict Rules Applicable

Thus, the New York Convention is not a source of *opinio iuris* for customary law on the legislative jurisdiction of a State to make conflict of laws rules for international arbitration.

b) *Travaux Préparatoires* of the UNCITRAL Model Law

The Model Law has led to the inclusion of a conflict of laws provision in a myriad of arbitration statutes around the world. The *travaux préparatoires* of the Model Law give some insight into the motivation behind this decision. The drafters of the Model Law utilized a strict territorial approach in determining its scope. This was done because an analysis of existing arbitration statutes had shown that most of these used the territoriality criterion to determine their scope, as well.[406] There was a lively discussion surrounding the issue of whether the application should hinge exclusively on the location of the arbitral seat, or whether there should additionally be an option for the parties to choose the applicable procedural law.[407] In the end, the Commission decided to retain only the territorial criterion. This confirms the principle set forth in Article V(1)(d) of the New York Convention that the State in which the seat of arbitration is located is competent to regulate the procedure. However, there is no clear evidence that the inclusion of conflict of laws rules in these rules of procedure is based on the belief that the State also necessarily has jurisdiction regarding private international law.

There is evidence to suggest that during the process of drafting Article 28 of the Model Law, the representatives of the States seemed to believe that conflict of laws rules would merely serve as a guideline.[408] It was also suggested that the provision should be taken out entirely when no consensus could be found, which would show that it was not deemed a crucial point. In this context it was noted that there was no sanction for a violation of the provision, and as such that it was no more than a guideline. The main reason it was kept in the Model Law was because it had already been discussed at length and a law on international commercial arbitration would be incomplete without a provision regarding the choice of law governing the dispute.[409]

---

406 *Hußlein-Stich*, Das UNCITRAL-Modellgesetz, 1990, pp. 19, 20.
407 Ibid.
408 UN doc. A/CN.9/RS. 327, p. 487, para. 16.
409 UN doc. A/CN.9/327, para. 17.

§ 3. Binding Effect of Article 1(1) in International Commercial Arbitration

Germany, in line with its tendency to restrict the arbitrators' leeway, initially proposed that the conflict of laws rules of the seat of arbitration should be applied by the arbitrator, but – crucially – only if the seat had been chosen by the parties.[410] Thus, even following this view the conflict of laws rules of the seat were not binding *per se*, but only due to a choice by the parties. In the absence of a party agreement on an arbitral seat, Germany proposed that the conflict of laws rules of the State most closely connected to the dispute should be applicable – a rule which would have given the arbitrator discretion in determining the closest connection. The delegation later withdrew its proposal as it was "now prepared to allow more discretion to the arbitrators than it had earlier thought desirable."[411] Similarly, Norway proposed that Article 28(2) be changed to stipulate that the conflict of laws rules of the "jurisdiction where the place is stipulated" be applied "provided that [the parties] have agreed on a place of arbitration".[412] It further clarified this stance by stating that even if the parties had not chosen a seat of arbitration but happen to have their seats of business in the same State, they would expect conflict rules of that State to be applied, even if the arbitral tribunal chose a different State in which to conduct the proceedings.[413] Thus, it can be said that the drafters were comfortable with binding arbitrators to the conflict rules of the State that the parties had chosen as their seat of arbitration.

In the end, most of the discussion did not revolve around whether a conflict of laws rule should be included in the Model Law, but rather around its content, specifically whether the arbitrators should not be allowed to determine the applicable substantive law directly. Argentina, Australia, Austria, Canada, Iraq, Sweden and the U.S. suggested that the reference to conflict of laws be deleted in order to give the arbitrator the option of choosing the applicable law without recourse to conflict of laws rules.[414] Reference to an existing trend in international arbitration law "towards a freer judgment of the question of choice of law" was made in written comments by Sweden[415] and the ICC[416]. Other States agreed, such

---

410 UN doc. A/CN.9/263, p. 41, para. 9.
411 UN doc. A/CN.9/SR.263, p. 485, para. 39.
412 UN doc. A/CN.9/263, p. 41, para. 10.
413 Ibid.
414 UN doc. A/CN.9/SR.263, p. 485, paras. 40, 41, 43, 46.
415 UN doc. A/CN.9/263, p. 40, para. 2.
416 UN doc. A/CN.9/263/Add.1 (article 28), p. 16, para. 1.

as the U.S.[417] and Hungary[418], and no State rejected the notion that such a trend exist. The argument brought in favor of the reference to conflict of laws rules was that it would enhance certainty and predictability for the parties,[419] although it is not clear in what way the application of conflict rules chosen by the arbitrator would provide more predictability, as was pointed out by the Austrian delegation.[420]

This whole discussion, however, shows that the delegations based their deliberations on the premise that arbitrators were not bound *a priori* by the conflict of laws rules of a particular State. However, it also shows that the drafting States were comfortable including a conflict rule into a set of procedural arbitration laws, and making the application of those laws contingent on the location of arbitral seat, so long as the arbitrators still had substantial freedom in selecting the applicable substantive law. This is not surprising, since even before the UNCITRAL Model Law came into existence, national arbitration statutes recognized – either expressly or by staying silent on the matter – that the arbitrators enjoyed vast discretion when determining the applicable substantive law.[421]

3. Conclusion

Due the nearly universal practice of arbitration statutes containing an arbitration-specific conflict rule and accompanying *opinio iuris*, it is possible to establish a rule of customary international law that the State in which the seat of arbitration is located has legislative jurisdiction to set forth (broad) conflict of laws rules for international arbitration.

V. Conclusion

There is no legal basis to bind arbitrators to the general rules of private international law that are designed to be applied in domestic court proceedings. Neither do international arbitral tribunals form part of the State'

---

417 UN doc. A/CN.9/SR.263, p. 485, para. 40.
418 UN doc. A/CN.9/SR.263, p. 485, para. 47.
419 UN doc. A/CN.9/SR.263, p. 486, para. 53.
420 UN doc. A/CN.9/SR.263, p. 486, para. 55.
421 *Derains*, Possible Conflict of Laws Rules and the Rules Applicable to the Substance of the Dispute, paras. 11 et seq.

domestic dispute resolution system to a degree as to be considered quasi-courts, nor does the seat constitute a genuine link to the dispute, be it territorial or through a hypothetical party choice. Due to a rule of customary public international law, States have legislative jurisdiction to set forth arbitration-specific conflict of law rules that give arbitrators a large amount of leeway.

C. Inapplicability of the Rome I Regulation in International Commercial Arbitration

Despite the established global practice of broadly-worded arbitration-specific conflict rules, the emergence of the Rome I Regulation[422] (the "Regulation") in 2008 triggered the discussion on the role of private international law in international commercial arbitration anew.[423] The rule of customary law described above, concerning a State's right to set forth broadly-worded arbitration-specific conflict rules, could easily disappear if enough States expressed the belief that international arbitrators are bound by the Regulation, and thus the general rules of private international law directed at State organs. Given these circumstances, its relationship to international commercial arbitration warrants a closer look.

As an EU regulation as set forth in Article 288 TFEU it is directly applicable in all EU Member States.[424] It contains rules of private international law concerning contractual obligations. The Regulation appears to offer relief from the cognitive dissonance between the freedom of international arbitration and the strictness of domestic legal systems: due to its inherently international and consensus-based nature it holds the promise of dissolving any concerns regarding its application as domestic private international law in the non-domestic realm of international arbitration. If the Regulation were applicable in international arbitration, it would open

---

422 Regulation (EC) No 593/2008 of the European Parliament and of the Council of 17 June 2008 on the law applicable to contractual obligations (Rome I).
423 *Gößling*, Europäisches Kollisionsrecht, 2019; *Babić*, Jour. P. I. L. 2017, 71; *Grimm*, SchiedsVZ 2012, 189; *Mankowski*, RIW 2011, 30; *McGuire*, SchiedsVZ 2011, 257; *Nueber*, ibid.2014, 186; *Schilf*, RIW 2013, 678; *Yüksel*, J. Priv. Int. 2011, 149.
424 With the exception of Denmark, which made a reservation. As a consequence, the predecessor of the Rome I Regulation, the Rome Convention, still applies in Denmark.

C. Inapplicability of the Rome I Regulation in International Commercial Arbitration

the door for the application of the CISG, including Article 1(1) of the CISG, via its Article 25, which stipulates that the Regulation

> *shall not prejudice the application of international conventions to which one or more Member States are parties at the time when this Regulation is adopted and which lay down conflict-of-law rules relating to contractual obligations.*

Thus, the applicability of the Regulation in international commercial arbitration would also lead to the applicability of the CISG's rules of application by international commercial arbitrators. If parties opted out of the application of the CISG,[425] their dispute would be governed by the provisions of the Regulation.

However, an analysis of the Rome I Regulation shows that it was not designed to apply in international arbitration (**I.**) and that its international genesis does not change the fact that it is just as ill-suited to govern disputes subject to international commercial arbitration as any body of traditional private international law (**II.**).

I. No Intention of Application by Drafters

1. Exception Regarding "Arbitration Agreements"

The Rome I Regulation defines its own applicability. Article 1(2)(f) stipulates that it does not apply to "arbitration agreements and agreements on the choice of court." This wording is rather narrow, both in the English and other language versions of the Regulation,[426] and conspicuously does not expressly exclude arbitration in its entirety from the scope of the Regulation. This is particularly noteworthy because the Brussels Ia Regulation[427], which regulates the jurisdiction of the national courts of the EU Member States and the recognition and enforcement of the courts' decisions, does contain an exception for "arbitration" (Article 1(2)(d) of

---

425 Regarding opt-out agreements, see *supra*, pp. 56 et seq.
426 *Gößling*, Europäisches Kollisionsrecht, 2019, p. 71.
427 Regulation (EU) No 1215/2012 of the European Parliament and of the Council of 12 December 2012 on jurisdiction and the recognition and enforcement of judgments in civil and commercial matters, http://eur-lex.europa.eu/legal-content/EN/ALL/?uri=celex%3A32012R1215.

§ 3. Binding Effect of Article 1(1) in International Commercial Arbitration

the Brussels Ia Regulation).[428] This regulation is considered a "sister regulation" to the Rome I Regulation,[429] and the substantive scope and the provisions of the latter are supposed to be consistent with those of the former, as Recital 7 of the Rome I Regulation stipulates.[430] This makes the disparate wording stand out all the more, leading some to the conclusion that the exception in the Rome I Regulation should be interpreted in the same way as the exception in the Brussels Ia Regulation, exempting the entirety of the arbitral process.[431] Others, however, have argued that the discrepancy in the wording of the Regulations can easily be explained by their different purposes and should thus be interpreted differently, as well, according to the clear meaning of the wording.[432]

The wording appears clear: the agreement to arbitrate is excluded from the scope of the Regulation – *argumentum e contrario*, the underlying dispute is not.[433] According to the doctrine of separability, the arbitration agreement's validity can and must be determined separately from the rest of the contract containing it.[434] The law applicable to the arbitration agreement is not necessarily the same as the law applicable to the merits of the case.[435] It is therefore plausible that the law applicable to each could be found via different conflict rules, namely by applying the Rome I Regulation to determine the substantive law and another set of private international law rules for the law governing the arbitration agreement. However, interpreting the exclusion as including the underlying dispute would necessarily entail that the exception pertaining to choice-of-court agreements would have to be interpreted in the same manner, with the

---

428 *Mankowski*, RIW 2011, 30, 38, referencing the Brussels I Regulation, which is the predecessor of the Brussels Ia Regulation and uses the same terminology; *McGuire*, SchiedsVZ 2011, 257, 262 et seq.
429 *Magnus/Mankowski*, Joint Response to the Green Paper, 2002, p. 29.
430 Recital 7 of the Rome I Regulation states: "The substantive scope and the provisions of this Regulation should be consistent with Council Regulation (EC) No 44/ 2001 of 22 December 2000 on jurisdiction and the recognition and enforcement of judgments in civil and commercial matters (Brussels I) and Regulation (EC) No 864/2007 of the European Parliament and of the Council of 11 July 2007 on the law applicable to non- contractual obligations (Rome II)."
431 See reference in *Gößling*, Europäisches Kollisionsrecht, 2019, fn. 323.
432 Ibid., pp. 80 et seq.
433 *Mankowski*, RIW 2011, 30, 31.
434 See generally *Born*, International Commercial Arbitration, ed. 2 2014, chapter 3 pp. 349 et seqq.
435 Ibid., p. 475.

C. Inapplicability of the Rome I Regulation in International Commercial Arbitration

strange consequence that the Regulation would not be applicable in judicial proceedings, either.[436]

There is a more plausible explanation for the exception being limited to arbitration agreements: domestic courts must regularly assess the validity of the arbitration agreement.[437] When one party attempts to initiate court proceedings, even though it initially agreed to arbitrate any future disputes, the court must determine whether the arbitration agreement is valid. If it is, the court has to stay the court proceedings and refer the parties to arbitration, as set forth in Article II(1) of the New York Convention.[438] Thus, a court attempting to assess whether it has jurisdiction over a dispute must first make sure that there is no arbitration agreement, just as it must ensure that the parties have not chosen a different court for litigation, which would also lead to a lack of jurisdiction. Consequently, the court faced with a contract containing an arbitration agreement will need information on what law to apply to the arbitration agreement.

In conclusion, the exception in Article 1(2)(f) of the Rome I Regulation only refers to arbitration agreements and gives no indication whether the Regulation should be applied to the merits of a dispute being arbitrated.

2. Reference to "Court or Tribunal"

An analysis of the textual references to the addressees of the Regulation is not helpful, either. The English text of the Regulation uses the word "court" most of the time, leaving little room for interpretation.[439] In two

---

[436] *Babić*, Jour. P. I. L. 2017, 71, 81; *Gößling*, Europäisches Kollisionsrecht, 2019, p. 74.
[437] *Gößling*, Europäisches Kollisionsrecht, 2019, p. 82.
[438] Art. II(1) of the New York Convention: "Each Contracting State shall recognize an agreement in writing under which the parties undertake to submit to arbitration all or any differences which have arisen or which may arise between them in respect of a de ned legal relationship, whether contractual or not, concerning a subject matter capable of settlement by arbitration."
[439] Recital 6: "[…] to designate the same national law irrespective of the country of the **court** in which an action is brought."
Recital 8: "[…] interpreted in accordance with the law of the Member State in which the **court** is seised."
Recital 16: "[…] The **courts** should, however, retain a degree of discretion to determine the law that is most closely connected to the situation."

§ 3. Binding Effect of Article 1(1) in International Commercial Arbitration

instances, "court" is supplemented by "or tribunal"[440], opening up the possibility that arbitral tribunals could also be intended targets of the Regulation. However, the Brussels Ia Regulation uses the same terms, but undoubtedly means only national courts, seeing as it excludes arbitration in its entirety, as just discussed. Given the parallels between the regulations, it seems likely that the terms would have to be interpreted in the same manner for both regulations. Further, the German version of the Rome I Regulation speaks only of *"Gericht"*, which translates to "court". Admittedly, the Romance language versions of the Regulation use far more inclusive terms such as *for, foro* and *forum*, which are broad enough to include arbitral tribunals.[441] However, the versions of the Regulation in those languages also use the terms *"giudice"*[442] and *"juez"*[443], which translate unambiguously to "judge" and leave no room for an inclusive interpretation that might include arbitrators.

If one were inclined to see the express language of the Regulation as restrictive, the terms used by the Regulation could still be considered stand-ins for any type of adjudicative body that is subject to private international law. The narrow vocabulary would then act as a *pars pro toto*,[444] and in and of itself have no limiting effect on who is bound by the text of the Regulation. The wording therefore lends itself to both interpretations and is not helpful.

Recital 37: "Considerations of public interest justify giving the **courts** of the Member States the possibility, in exceptional circumstances, of applying exceptions based on public policy and overriding mandatory provisions. [...]"
Article 12: The law applicable to a contract by virtue of this Regulation shall govern in particular: [...] (c) within the limits of the powers conferred on the **court** by its procedural law [...].
440 Recital 12: An agreement between the parties to confer on one or more **courts or tribunals** of a Member State exclusive jurisdiction [...].
Recital 15: [...] This rule should apply whether or not the choice of law was accompanied by a choice of **court or tribunal**.
441 *Mankowski*, RIW 2011, 30, 37.
442 Recital 16 of the Spanish version, http://eur-lex.europa.eu/legal-content/ES/TXT/HTML/?uri=CELEX:32008R0593&from=EN.
443 Recitals 6, 8, 16 and 37 as well as Articles 12 (1) lit. c and 18 (2) of the Italian version, http://eur-lex.europa.eu/legal-content/IT/TXT/HTML/?uri=CELEX:32008R0593&from=EN.
444 *Babić*, Jour. P. I. L. 2017, 71, 78.

3. *Travaux Préparatoires* of the Rome Convention

The Rome Convention was the predecessor of the Rome I Regulation. It contained the same wording as the Rome I Regulation does now, creating an exception for arbitration agreements.[445] While the much-cited Explanatory Report authored by Giuliano and Lagarde on the Rome Convention[446] dictates no specific interpretation of the exception, it does describe the controversy between the various delegations during the drafting process.[447] Several delegations, among them the English delegation, asked to have the exclusion for arbitration agreements taken out, stating that they were no different from other agreements in regard to contractual law aspects, and that the treaties dealing with arbitration either did not cover this aspect at all or not satisfactorily.[448] Other delegations, in particular from Germany and France, countered, among other things, that the arbitration agreement did not lend itself to the criterion of the closest connection that dominates the Rome I Regulation, and that it is difficult to separate the procedural and the substantive elements in such agreements, making it advisable to just take them out of the scope altogether.[449] What is notable is that these arguments very specifically address arbitration agreements in their limited function as such, not as a stand-in for arbitration as a whole.

However, although the issue was not uncontroversial, it was generally understood that the Rome Convention was not meant to be applied in international arbitration proceedings.[450] The drafters were convinced that arbitration had been dealt with to a satisfactory degree on an international level in the New York Convention[451] and the European Convention on

---

445 Art. 1(2): "[The rules of this Convention] shall not apply to [...] (d) arbitration agreements and agreements on the choice of court; [...]".
446 Report on the Convention on the law applicable to contractual obligations by Mario Giuliano, Professor, University of Milan, and Paul Lagarde, Professor, University of Paris I, Official Journal C 282, 31 October 1980 pp. 1–50 – Giuliano/Lagarde Report, https://eur-lex.europa.eu/LexUriServ/LexUriServ.do?uri= CELEX:31980Y1031(01):EN:HTML.
447 Giuliano/Lagarde Report (fn. 446), pp. 11 et seq.
448 BT Drucks. 10/503, 43.
449 BT Drucks. 10/503, 44.
450 *Nueber*, SchiedsVZ 2014, 186; *Martiny*, Anwendbares Sachrecht, pp. 532 et seq.
451 See fn. 202.

International Commercial Arbitration from 1961[452]; the latter containing a conflict rule of its own. The Rome I Regulation contains the same exact wording regarding the arbitration exception as the Rome Convention, and the EU legislature was aware of the issue.[453] Thus, if it had wanted to change the meaning or implications of the exceptions, a clarification in this regard would have been indispensable.[454] Seeing as no such clarification exists, one can expect that they wanted the legal situation to remain the same with the Rome I Regulation.

II. Incompatibility with International Arbitration

An argument in favor of applying the Regulation in international commercial arbitration proceedings is that the parties would benefit from it.[455] The Rome I Regulation as a modern, well-crafted legal instrument should be able to assist as many parties in dispute as possible. On its face, there is little to object regarding the notion that the Rome I Regulation might complement international commercial arbitration nicely: It originated from a neutral source, not from a State that could be suspected of trying to force the application of its domestic laws.[456] It also contains liberal, common-sense rules that grant party autonomy to a large extent, limiting it where weaker parties are in need of protection, and it ensures a minimum legal standard. Taking this argument further, if applying the Regulation led to any infringement of freedoms traditionally enjoyed in arbitration, this would simply have to be considered a worthy sacrifice, given the immense benefits gained.

---

452 2. European Convention on International Commercial Arbitration, Geneva, 21 April 1961, https://treaties.un.org/doc/Treaties/1964/01/19640107%2002-01%20 AM/Ch_XXII_02p.pdf.
453 In the Green Paper on the Conversion of the Rome Convention into EU law, the Commission states that it is advisable to consider permitting a party choice of "rules of law", a more lax term than "law of a State", as a practice before the court "as this is already admitted (in many countries) before arbitrators". This shows that the EU legislator was aware of the disparities between the choice of law mechanisms in front of courts and in front of arbitral tribunals. See also *Babić*, Jour. P. I. L. 2017, 71, 87.
454 *Schack*, FS Schütze, p. 515.
455 *Mankowski*, RIW 2011, 30, 39.
456 *Basedow*, RabelsZ 2009, 455, 458: "[...] since and to the extent that the Community is not a player in this field, it rather acts as a referee when legislating on private international law".

C. Inapplicability of the Rome I Regulation in International Commercial Arbitration

The first objection to this notion is that the European Union is not necessarily a neutral source. While it certainly cannot be considered a State in its own right (yet), it has become an important crafter of civil law instruments, which it has an interest in seeing applied. Furthermore, there is no such thing as one EU law-making body to begin with; instead, there is an amalgamation of various actors, such as the Council, the Commission and the Parliament. The Rome I Regulation as such is also not a neutral set of conflict rules, it is also a tool for advancing the objectives of the Union.[457] These goals are promoting the internal market, heightening legal certainty and protecting weaker parties in contractual relationships.[458] There is value to the argument that these objectives should be supported not only by national courts, but also in international arbitration.[459]

However, it is not as simple as applying the Rome I Regulation in international arbitration. Doing so would effectively limit the party autonomy of parties opting for arbitration while weaker parties being protected may be better served in the realm of dispute resolution through alternative mechanisms. Also, the provisions ensuring the application of mandatory rules and the protection of public policy actually complicate matters in an area that is already quite well covered by arbitration-specific rules. Finally, forum shopping is not a problem in international commercial arbitration.

1. Party Autonomy: Limitations to the Choice of Law

Recital 11 of the Rome I Regulation addresses the relevance that party autonomy has in the system of the Regulation:

> *The parties' freedom to choose the applicable law should be one of the cornerstones of the system of conflict-of-law rules in matters of contractual obligations.*

Party autonomy is crucial for the functioning of the internal market, since it is the private international law equivalent of the principle of economic efficiency.[460] Granting parties the right to select the law governing their

---

457 For a general discussion of how the Rome I Regulation furthers the objectives of the EU, see *Lehmann*, FS Spellenberg, pp. 425 et seqq; *Ungerer*, BTWR 2015, 5; *Weller*, IPRax 2011, 429.
458 *Weller*, IPRax 2011, 429, 433-435.
459 *Gößling*, Europäisches Kollisionsrecht, 2019, pp. 97-103.
460 MüKo-BGB/*von Hein*, ed. 7 2018, Einl IPR para. 37; *Arnold*, Parteiautonomie, p. 23; *Weller*, IPRax 2011, 429, p. 433.

contract reduces transactional costs because they can choose a law that is familiar to them (or their attorneys). They do not have to pay for expensive legal counsel specialized in foreign law and hire different counsel for every legal system in which their contract is litigated. Also, the contract does not have to be drafted with a myriad of potentially applicable laws in mind, which streamlines the process and lowers legal fees. Aside from the cost aspect, granting party autonomy furthers the internal market by lowering inhibitions to engage in cross-border transactions, because being able to choose the applicable law makes inner-European trade more predictable. A big factor of predictability is legal certainty. A main aim of the Rome I Regulation is attaining legal certainty, as set forth in recital 6, which states that the internal market creates a need for uniform conflict of laws rules "in order to improve [...] certainty as to the law applicable".[461] This goal is achieved through granting party autonomy, because it gives parties the ability to select the governing law and trust that no other law will be applied by a court at a later stage.[462] This is stipulated in Article 3 of the Regulation: "A contract shall be governed by the law chosen by the parties. [...]"

International arbitration is based on party autonomy, and giving effect to the will of the parties is the arbitrators' main priority. Following the logic of the drafters of the Rome I Regulation, the mere existence of international arbitration advances the internal market by giving the parties a mechanism of dispute resolution that is tailored to their needs. Parties may go beyond merely choosing the applicable law by completely opting out of proceedings before national courts in foreign States. Within international commercial arbitration, the parties are traditionally granted freedom to make choices of law that are not possible under rules of private international law such as the Rome I Regulation. This has been codified in institutional rules, domestic arbitration legislation and international treaties. These regulations express the notion that arbitration is a mechanism of dispute resolution tailored to the needs of the parties of an international transaction, and these needs may include a more innovative choice of law than would be permitted in court proceedings. In particular, this concerns choices of conflict rules, of non-State law and of decision *ex aequo et bono*.

---

461 *Weller*, IPRax 2011, 429, 434.
462 MüKo-BGB/*von Hein*, ed. 7 2018, Einl IPR para. 36.

C. Inapplicability of the Rome I Regulation in International Commercial Arbitration

a) Choice of Conflict Rule

An agreement on conflict rules is not possible under the Rome I Regulation. The parties are not able to incorporate or refer to a conflict rule, the application of which would lead the arbitrator to the substantive law.[463] The Rome I Regulation gives the parties the option to choose (State) law, but not to agree on their own conflict rule. If a choice of law by the parties does not meet the requirements of Article 3 of the Regulation, it is invalid and the provisions of the Regulation determining the applicable law in the absence of a choice of law take effect.

This is incompatible with the way arbitration proceedings are typically planned. Parties often select rules of arbitral institutions, such as the ICC Rules of Arbitration or the UNCITRAL Arbitration Rules, thereby incorporating them into their arbitration agreement. These rules always contain a provision instructing the arbitrator to honor the parties' choice of law and also specifying which law to apply in the absence of a party choice. This is a conflict of laws rule, and by incorporating the entirety of the institutional rules into their contract, the parties effectively agree on their own conflict of laws rule. This would not be possible under the Rome I Regulation, which if applicable would effectively override any conflict rule incorporated by the parties.

b) Choice of Non-State Law

As stated, according to the wording of the Rome I Regulation, parties can only make a choice of law in favor of State law. Thus, parties are not able to validly make a conflict of laws choice in favor of non-State law, such as general principles of law or the *lex mercatoria*.[464] A reference to general principles of law can be considered to incorporate these into the contract, but only if their precise content can be determined for the case at hand.[465] The same goes for international sets of rules such as the Incoterms, the UNIDROIT Principles of International Commercial Contracts (PICC) or the Principles of European Contract Law (PECL). While

---

463 *Schilf*, RIW 2013, 678, 681 et seq.
464 Staudinger-BGB/*Magnus*, 2016, Rom I-VO Art. 3, paras. 55 et seq; *Junker*, Internationales Privatrecht, ed. 2 2017, pp. 293 et seq; MüKo-BGB/*Martiny*, ed. 7 2018, Rom I-VO Art. 3 paras. 32-39.
465 Staudinger-BGB/*Magnus*, 2016, Rom I-VO Art. 3, paras. 56, 57.

§ 3. Binding Effect of Article 1(1) in International Commercial Arbitration

there can be no question that their content is specific and they are capable of governing contracts, a reference to them will always only have the effect of incorporating the rules into the contract. Finally, the same goes for the contentious *lex mercatoria*. While some deny its existence altogether, others believe that it is of such great influence that it should override any domestic law, or at least be treated as equal to it. However, before domestic courts, it suffers the same fate as the other forms of non-State law: it is merely incorporated into the contract. In all these cases, the governing law is the law determined by applying the objective conflict of laws rules.

It was discussed above that the possibility to choose non-State law is essential to international commercial arbitration.[466] It goes hand in hand with the freedom of the parties to avoid domestic court proceedings and meet in the middle, on neutral ground, by deciding on proceedings that both sides are willing to subject themselves to and choosing the judges. More often than not, contracts that are subjected to international commercial arbitration are densely detailed and address most issues that might present a cause for dispute. Preventing parties that want to submit their dispute to arbitration from selecting non-State laws as the *lex contractus* does not serve these parties. Domestic laws can be a poor match for international contracts, as such laws are primarily designed for domestic situations and are therefore rarely suited to govern complex international cases.[467] They can contain surprising and unusual rules that have an outsize influence on the outcome of the case and that the parties may not have considered when choosing it. This can affect deadlines that have to be observed, which will typically be ill-fitting for international transaction that take more time, or requirements of notifying the other party of defects or similar problems, which can be strict in domestic law to an unrealistic extent for international situations. Thus, the Rome I Regulation's traditional approach to selectable laws is an impediment to international commercial arbitration.

---

466 See pp. 99 et seq.
467 *Petsche*, J. Priv. Int. 2014, 489, pp. 505 et seqq; *Berger*, Creeping Codification, ed. 2 2010, pp. 14 et seqq.

C. Inapplicability of the Rome I Regulation in International Commercial Arbitration

c) Decisions *Ex Aequo et Bono*

Finally, the Rome I Regulation does not enable parties to request a decision without the application of any law.[468] This is considered a *contrat sans loi*, which the parties believe to be exhaustively regulated through the contractual text itself and thus does not require a *lex contractus*. Contracts without any governing law are not accepted under the Rome I Regulation, which always requires that a law be determined by the court deciding the case, against which the contract is measured and with which it is supplemented.

In contrast, international arbitral tribunals can be requested to decide a case *ex aequo et bono* or as *amiables compositeurs*.[469] While there is a debate surrounding the question of whether this excludes the application of any and all law, it does enable the tribunal to decide the dispute in line with its own notions of fairness and morality. This is comparable to the *contrat sans loi* in that the only written rules governing the actions of the parties can be found in the contract itself.[470] Under the application of the Rome I Regulation, parties would not be able to request a decision *ex aequo et bono* from the arbitrators deciding their case. Just as with the choice of conflict of laws rules and of non-State laws, the possibility to request a decision not based on law is a defining element of international commercial arbitration. To bind arbitrators to the Rome I Regulation would infringe upon the parties' right, recognized in Article 28(3) of the UNCTRAL Model Law – and thus in arbitration statutes around the world, as well as in treaties governing international commercial arbitration.

In making a choice of law, parties exercise party autonomy, accepting their autonomy's inherent limitations when domestic conflict rules are applied by national courts. In choosing to subject their dispute to arbitration, parties take advantage of a far greater amount of party autonomy, again accepting its limitations in the rules governing the annulment and enforcement of awards through national courts. If the arbitrators entrusted to resolve the dispute instead of national courts are bound by the same domestic conflict rules as courts, this has the effect of whittling down the amount of party autonomy granted to the parties to the standards applicable to a mere choice of law. This is not only the case in the exceptional provisions in private international law that either do not allow for a choice

---

468 See only Staudinger-BGB/*Magnus*, 2016, Rom I-VO Art. 3, para. 55.
469 This concept will be discussed in chapter § 4, in particular on pp. 170 et seqq.
470 MüKo-BGB/*Martiny*, ed. 7 2018, Rom I-VO Art. 3 para. 40.

§ 3. Binding Effect of Article 1(1) in International Commercial Arbitration

of law at all or that subject the choice of law to restrictions. Rather, even the more common liberal concept of party autonomy provided for by most legal systems' conflict of laws rules would have a constricting effect on international arbitration. Even if parties are free to make a choice of law, they will not be able to make the choices traditionally granted in international arbitration. Thus, even if traditional private international law grants party autonomy, it constitutes a severe limitation of the amount of party autonomy that they expect – and are generally granted – when opting for international arbitration.

2. Superfluous Protections for Weaker Parties

An objective of the EU is to establish a minimum legal standard for the Member States in specific areas of law. This is achieved both with primary EU law, i.e. the Treaty on European Union (TEU) and the Treaty on the Functioning of the European Union (TFEU)[471], and secondary EU law, i.e. regulations, directives and decisions as set forth in Article 288 of the TFEU. The protection of consumers is a prime example for the law-making activity of the European Union. The Rome I Regulation contains special protections for certain types of contracts that embody values that the EU has chosen to protect. While parties enjoy the freedom to choose the applicable law – which is already stunted for international arbitration standards, as just laid out – the effect of that choice is further substantially limited in certain cases, specifically, in employment and consumer contracts. In both types of contracts, the Regulation contains safeguards ensuring that consumers and employers cannot be deprived of certain substantive legal protections. It may seem desirable to ensure the application of these protections enshrined in the Rome I Regulation by demanding its application in international arbitration. However, the specified weaker parties can more effectively be protected through other measures.

a) Consumer Protection

Consumers receive preferential treatment in European law, which has created a myriad of provisions offering them expansive protection.[472] This

---

471   See fn. 311.
472   In general, see *Heiderhoff*, Europäisches Privatrecht, ed. 4 2016, pp. 88 et seq.

protection goes beyond substantive provisions regulating consumer rights: EU private international law is also favorable to consumers. Specifically, Article 6 of the Rome I Regulation stipulates that in principle any contract that a consumer, defined as "a natural person for a purpose which can be regarded as being outside his trade or profession", concludes with a professional "shall be governed by the law of the country where the consumer has his habitual residence".[473] If a law other than that of the consumer's residence is applied pursuant to a party choice of law, this may not deprive the consumer of the protection contained in mandatory rules of his domestic legal system (Article 6(2) of the Rome I Regulation). This provision ensures that the choice of law – on which a consumer will regularly have little influence – cannot lead to a circumvention of protection that the consumer would have enjoyed with no choice of law.

Applying the Rome I Regulation may seem like an effective way to protect consumers from being subjected to unfavorable laws in arbitral proceedings in which arbitrators are free to apply whatever law they see fit. The answer, however, lies not in binding all arbitrators to the rules of private international law, but in restricting access to international commercial arbitral proceedings for these weaker parties and instead providing for specialized arbitration proceedings.

aa) ECJ Decisions

The ECJ has decided two landmark cases concerning consumers and arbitration, both stemming from Spanish court cases. They give some insight into effective consumer protection in international arbitration.

---

[473] Art. 6(1) of the Rome I Regulation:
Without prejudice to Articles 5 and 7, a contract concluded by a natural person for a purpose which can be regarded as being outside his trade or profession (the consumer) with another person acting in the exercise of his trade or profession (the professional) shall be governed by the law of the country where the consumer has his habitual residence, provided that the professional:
(a) pursues his commercial or professional activities in the country where the consumer has his habitual residence, or
(b) by any means, directs such activities to that country or to several countries including that country, and the contract falls within the scope of such activities.

§ 3. Binding Effect of Article 1(1) in International Commercial Arbitration

In *Mostaza Claro*[474], a consumer had lost in arbitration proceedings brought against her by a mobile phone company. She brought an action to have the award annulled, arguing that the agreement to arbitrate was invalid because it did not comply with the requirements set forth in Directive 93/13 on unfair terms in consumer contracts[475] ("Directive 93/13"). Article 6 of Directive 93/13 obliges Member States to ensure that terms that are deemed unfair – that is, that cause a significant imbalance to the detriment of the consumer and contrary to the requirement of good faith – do not bind the consumer. It has an Annex with an indicative list of such terms, which includes

> *terms which have the object or effect of: [...]*
> *(q) excluding or **hindering the consumer's right to take legal action** or exercise any other legal remedy, particularly **by requiring the consumer to take disputes exclusively to arbitration** not covered by legal provisions [...]. [emphasis added]*

The court, noting that the consumer had not brought the invalidity of the arbitration agreement as an argument during the arbitration proceedings, stayed the annulment proceedings and requested a preliminary ruling from the ECJ. The ECJ decided that it was the annulment court's task to determine on its own volition whether the term was unfair in order to effectively protect the consumer in her weak position.[476] It stated that Article 6(1) of Directive 93/13 was a mandatory provision, indicating that the Directive's aim, namely strengthening consumer protection, was "essential to the accomplishment of the tasks entrusted to the Community" and "to raising the standard of living and the quality of life in its territory", as enshrined in Art. 3(1) lit. t of the Treaty Establishing the European Community.[477] The Court then made a reference to *Eco Swiss*, elevating consumer protection to public policy "by analogy".[478]

---

[474] ECJ, decision of 26 October 2006, case C-168/05, ECLI:EU:C:2006:675 – *Mostaza Claro*.
[475] Council Directive 93/13/EEC of 5 April 1993 on unfair terms in consumer contracts, available at http://eur-lex.europa.eu/LexUriServ/LexUriServ.do?uri=CELEX:31993L0013:en:HTML.
[476] *Piers*, J.I.D.S. 2011, 209.
[477] Ibid., 219. The treaty is the predecessor of the TFEU.
[478] *Mostaza Claro* (fn. 474), para. 37. The decision *Eco Swiss* – see *infra*, fn. 496 – declared EU competition law part of public policy in the sense of the New York Convention.

C. Inapplicability of the Rome I Regulation in International Commercial Arbitration

In the second case, *Asturcom*[479], the situation was similar except that the consumer did not participate in the arbitration proceedings at all, the award was made in his absence and the telecommunications company went to court to have the judgment enforced against him. Despite the award having become final, the ECJ found that the enforcement court should be able to reassess the validity of the arbitration agreement in light of a potential violation of public policy, of which Article 6 of Directive 93/13 constituted a part.[480]

With these decisions, the ECJ demonstrated that consumers must be protected from the binding effect of awards resulting from an arbitration agreement that they should not have been party to in the first place. The court took issue not with the law that was applied by the arbitral tribunals, but with the fact that the consumers were subjected to arbitration at all. It chose to do so by elevating the use of an arbitration clause in consumer contracts to a violation of public policy.

bb) Specialized Arbitration Procedures

The key to protecting weaker parties is therefore policing the agreement to arbitrate, not the applicable law in the arbitration proceedings. Effective consumer protection in international arbitration can be established by keeping unassuming consumers out of the arena of unregulated arbitration, in which they are unable to adequately defend themselves vis-à-vis powerful corporate adversaries. The issue is not that the arbitrators sitting on the tribunals deciding the case apply the friendliest law, but that the consumers should not be caught off guard by an arbitration agreement that they had no part in negotiating in the first place. Invalidating arbitration agreements that result from one party being at the mercy of a stronger contractual counterpart is an effective way to disincentivize companies from using such arbitration clauses.

While the ECJ decided to categorize consumer arbitration agreements as a violation of EU public policy, invalid arbitration agreements are in and of themselves a reason to set aside an award and to refuse its recognition and enforcement, regardless of whether it is deemed a violation of public policy. Article V (1) lit. a of the New York Convention stipulates that

---

479 ECJ, judgement of 6 October 2009, case C-40/08, ECLI:EU:C:2009:615 – *Asturcom*.
480 *Asturcom* (fn. 479), paras. 52 and 53.

if the arbitration agreement is not valid under the law that the parties subjected it to or else the law of the country where the award was made, then the enforcement court can refuse recognition and enforcement. The UNCITRAL Model Law contains the same ground for setting aside arbitral awards in Article 34 (1)(i).

That is not to say that there should be no arbitration options for consumers. The Directive 2013/11/EU on alternative dispute resolution for consumer disputes[481] (ADR-Directive) sets forth the legal groundwork for mechanisms that enable affordable and balanced consumer arbitration and other methods of alternative dispute resolution. This entails "the intervention of an ADR entity which proposes or imposes a solution or brings the parties together with the aim of facilitating an amicable solution"[482]. The ADR-Directive lays out a myriad of protective provisions, e.g. regarding consumer information and applicable law. Crucially, the ADR-Directive contains a requirement of specific acceptance,[483] which stipulates that the agreement to arbitrate with an ADR entity is not binding if it was concluded before the dispute had materialized, and that the consumers have to be informed of the binding nature of the solution and specifically accept this.[484] This enables consumers to participate in arbitration and benefit from its advantages without leaving behind the legal framework designed to protect them.

Beyond such highly regulated consumer-specific ADR, consumers can take part in regular international commercial arbitration proceedings without any of the protective measures designed by the EU, if they wish to do so. This corresponds with the ideal of the informed consumer who is able to willingly make decisions to his detriment *if only given the necessary information in a format that promotes a thoughtful decision process*.[485] Such a process could consist in an arbitration agreement that is either individually negotiated or is at least presented to the consumer in a sufficiently obvious manner, neither of which option is governed by the Directive 93/13, as they do not qualify as unfair terms in the sense

---

481 Directive 2013/11/EU of the European Parliament and of the Council of 21 May 2013 on alternative dispute resolution for consumer disputes and amending Regulation (EC) No 2006/2004 and Directive 2009/22/EC (Directive on consumer ADR), http://eur-lex.europa.eu/legal-content/EN/TXT/?uri=celex%3A32013L0011.
482 Art. 2(1) of the Directive 2013/11/EU.
483 *Reich*, ERCL 2014, 258, 272 et seq.
484 Art. 10(1) and (2) of the Directive 2013/11/EU.
485 *Heiderhoff*, Europäisches Privatrecht, ed. 4 2016, p. 93 para. 203.

C. Inapplicability of the Rome I Regulation in International Commercial Arbitration

of the Directive.[486] Details can vary in each legal system, but a valid arbitration agreement with a consumer typically requires that the consumer has received a separate document with the agreement to arbitrate, to be agreed to independently from the main contract.[487]

In essence, the road to successful consumer protection does not necessarily also lead to international commercial arbitrators being bound by the Rome I Regulation. Rather, successful consumer protection depends on consumers having access to arbitral proceedings that are highly regulated and tailored to their needs, and only enable them to enter into less regulated types of proceedings if they are in a position to make a well-informed decision to this effect. In that case, the application of a law other than their own or with a lower level of consumer protection is part of the risk consumers are taking.

b) Employee Protection

Employees are protected in a manner similar to consumers. According to Article 8 of the Rome I Regulation, individual employment contracts are subject to the law chosen by the parties – however, as with consumers, this law can be overridden by protections contained in other laws. According to Article 8(2) and (3), one of these other laws is the law under which the employee habitually performs the work contract, and the other is the law of the State in which the business is located through which the employee was engaged. The Regulation thereby ensures that a choice of law in the employment contract cannot circumvent labor law protections of States that have a close connection to the dispute.

Again, however, applying this rule in international arbitration is not necessary to effectively protect employees from arbitration. Rather, individual employment contracts should not be arbitrable from the outset. In Germany, the legal basis for this is section 4 of the German labor court law (*Arbeitsgerichtsgesetz*, ArbGG), which stipulates that the jurisdiction of the labor courts can only be excluded in certain exceptional cases, i.e. in civil

---

486 Art. 3(1) and (2) of the Directive 93/13.
487 See e.g. Sec. 1031(5) of the German Code of Civil Procedure, which states: "Arbitration agreements in which a consumer is involved must be contained in a record or document signed by the parties in their own hands. [...] The document shall not include other agreements than those pertaining to the arbitration agreement [...]."

cases arising from collective labor agreements and disputes regarding the existence of such agreements. An explanation for this is that in such cases there is a parity between the parties, and an agreement to arbitrate will result from negotiations between equal adversaries. Individual employment contracts can never exclude the courts' jurisdiction, including by means of arbitration agreements. Such agreements are therefore invalid, and awards resulting from them can be set aside or refused enforcement.

In summary, weaker parties are not protected in international arbitration by mandating the application of the Rome I Regulation, but by restricting their access to it as a mechanism of dispute resolution in the first place.

3. Incongruent System of Public Policy and Overriding Mandatory Rules

Private international law is based on great deference to foreign legal systems. To a large extent, the decisions embodied in the foreign law are applied to the facts without judging their value. However, there are mechanisms to ensure that courts are not forced to make decisions based on foreign law that are incompatible with the basic principles of their domestic legal system. Typically, courts can apply overriding mandatory rules of their forum and potentially of other States connected to the dispute, and they can refrain from applying foreign law if the effect of the application violates the public policy of their forum.[488]

The role of mandatory rules and public policy in international commercial arbitration is highly debated.[489] It is unclear whether arbitrators have to apply mandatory rules, and if so, of which State, and whether they should pay attention to potential domestic or international public policy considerations. An argument could be made that if arbitrators in international arbitral proceedings were obligated to apply traditional private international law, this would provide for clear and predictable guidelines on what mandatory rules should be applied and what role public policy can play in their decision-making. However, as desirable a transparent

---

[488] For EU Member States, this is set forth in Article 9(2) and (3) of the Rome I Regulation.
[489] In general see *Beulker*, Eingriffsnormenproblematik, 2005; *Donovan/Greenawalt*, Mandatory Rules, pp. 11 et seqq; *Kleinheisterkamp*, RabelsZ 2009, 818; *Kleinheisterkamp*, Int'l & Comp.L.Q. 2018, 903; *Sachs/Niedermaier*, FS Hoffmann, pp. 1051 et seq; *Waincymer*, Asian Int'l Arb. J. 2009, 1.

C. Inapplicability of the Rome I Regulation in International Commercial Arbitration

approach for international arbitration is, the rules in general private international law are not the solution.

a) Public Policy

Article 21 of the Rome I Regulation sets forth that

> [t]he application of a provision of the law of any country specified by this Regulation may be refused only if such application is manifestly incompatible with the public policy (ordre public) of the forum.

This is a universal principle of private international law. It stems from the notion that the public policy of a State is the sacrosanct core of its legal system, which it is unwilling to surrender to foreign law.[490] Enabling courts to protect it becomes necessary in international cases, seeing as private international law is a "leap in the dark"[491], into a foreign legal system that may differ greatly from the forum's legal system. Such differences are generally tolerated – unless they are incompatible with the forum's public policy.

The concept of public policy is also used in international arbitration, in regard to the award resulting from the arbitral process.[492] A violation of both substantive and procedural public policy through an international arbitration award is a ground for annulling an award at the seat of arbitration pursuant to Article 34 of the UNCITRAL Model Law and the national laws modeled after it, such as section 1059 of the ZPO in Germany. In this context, the law is interpreted as requiring a violation of domestic public policy,[493] just as under Article 21 of the Rome I Regulation. The court can raise the violation of public policy *ex officio*. Thus, the domestic public policy of the State in which the seat of arbitration is located is already protected by the possibility of an annulment of the award.

Public policy is further protected by Article V(2)(d) of the New York Convention, which stipulates that a violation of public policy is also a ground for the refusal of recognition and enforcement of foreign international arbitration awards. The wording of the provision indicates that a

---

490 *Kegel/Schurig*, Internationales Privatrecht, ed. 9 2004, p. 516.
491 Ibid.
492 This will be discussed below, see *infra*, pp. 174 et seqq. and 203 et seqq.
493 Saenger/*Saenger*, ed. 7 2017, ZPO § 1059 para. 23; Musielak/Voit/*Voit*, ed. 15 2018, ZPO § 1059 para. 25; MüKo-ZPO/*Münch*, ed. 5 2017, ZPO § 1059 para. 38.

violation of the domestic public policy of the enforcement State suffices to refuse an awards enforcement:

> Recognition and enforcement [...] may also be refused if the competent authority in the country where [it] is sought finds that [it] would be contrary to the public policy of **that** country. [emphasis added]

And yet, given the international nature of the convention and its pro-enforcement bias[494], it is understood that this must involve a violation of *international* public policy, which is the public policy shared by a majority of the legal systems.[495] Even though this interpretation is narrow, this does not endanger the public policy of the enforcement States in a way that could be avoided by applying the Rome I Regulation. The enforcement State in international arbitration is comparable to the State in which court decisions are enforced in litigation, and those States' public policy is protected by a separate legal regime, e.g. in the EU by the Brussels I Regulation.

In general, however, the public policy of EU Member States is safeguarded with instruments of international arbitration law. This also includes substantive EU law, a result of ECJ decisions declaring some areas of European Union law to be public policy in the context of the New York Convention, most notably in the *Eco Swiss* decision[496]. The decision dealt with Article 101 of the TFEU[497], a core provision of European competition law. The ECJ clarified that Article 101 of the TFEU "may be regarded as a matter of public policy within the meaning of the New York Convention"[498] and that any Member State that considers the violation national public policy a ground for the annulment of an award must also consider the violation of European public policy such a ground.[499] This is a consequence of the principle of equivalency, which "requires the same remedies and procedural rules to be available to claims based on European Union

---

494 Blackaby et al., International Commercial Arbitration, ed. 6 2015, p. 623.
495 Kröll et al., Comparative International Commercial Arbitration, 2003, p. 721; Blackaby et al., International Commercial Arbitration, ed. 6 2015, pp. 643 et seqq., discussing case law on the matter.
496 ECJ, decision of 1 June 1999, case C-126/97, ECLI:EU:C:1999:269 – *Eco Swiss*.
497 Art. 101 of the TFEU prohibits agreements and concerted practices between undertakings (or associations) which may affect trade between Member States, and prevent, restrict or distort competition within the internal market either by object or effect.
498 *Eco Swiss* (fn. 496), para. 39.
499 *Eco Swiss* (fn. 496), para. 37.

C. Inapplicability of the Rome I Regulation in International Commercial Arbitration

law as are extended to analogous claims of a purely domestic nature."[500] This synchronization of European public policy with the public policy set forth in the New York Convention and the arbitration statutes based on the UNCITRAL Model Law is an effective way to ensure that the most basic values of European Union law are not violated when tolerating international arbitration in EU Member States. It is not necessary to bind arbitrators to the Rome I Regulation in order to achieve this protection.

b) Overriding Mandatory Provisions

Overriding mandatory provisions (*Eingriffsnormen, lois de police*) are defined in Article 9(1) of the Rome I Regulation as

> *provisions the respect for which is regarded as crucial by a country for safeguarding its public interests, such as its political, social or economic organization, to such an extent that they are applicable to any situation falling within their scope, irrespective of the law otherwise applicable to the contract under this Regulation.*

Thus, they are imperative provisions that must be applied regardless of the law governing a legal relationship.[501] Overriding mandatory provisions have a purpose similar to that of public policy: to protect certain interests from being infringed upon by the application of foreign law. But while public policy has a passive effect, impeding the application of unfavorable foreign law, overriding mandatory rules actively impose themselves, regardless of the content of the otherwise applicable law.

---

500 Opinion of Advocate General Jääskinen of 7 February 2013 in Case C-536/11, ECLI:EU:C:2013:67 – *Donau Chemie*, para. 3.
501 *Waincymer*, Asian Int'l Arb. J. 2009, 1, 4. Although the terminology used is not always consistent, overriding mandatory rules have to be distinguished from mere mandatory rules (*zwingende Normen*). Mandatory rules are rules within a legal system that cannot be derogated from through contractual agreements. They can, however, be derogated from by selecting a different legal system, as they are only mandatory within their own legal system. Overriding mandatory rules, conversely, take effect regardless of the applicable legal system. They "override" the choice of law by the parties and impose themselves regardless. While ordinary mandatory rules typically relate to the equilibrium between contractual partners, ensuring that parties cannot disenfranchise themselves to too great an extent, overriding mandatory rules embody core values of a legal system that primarily concern communal, societal interests.

The role of overriding mandatory rules in international commercial arbitration is highly contentious.⁵⁰² The problem lies in the seeming incompatibility of their nature with transnational commercial contracts, and they have been described as "the flexed muscle of the long arm of interest-driven legislatures reaching beyond their jurisdictions' domestic realm"⁵⁰³. Historically, situations in which overriding mandatory rules would apply were simply not considered arbitrable. This changed with the *Mitsubishi* decision⁵⁰⁴ of the U.S. Supreme Court, and the potential applicability of such provisions is no longer considered an obstacle to arbitrability.⁵⁰⁵ The Supreme Court relegated any control by State courts to the enforcement stage, instituting what became known as the Second Look Doctrine:

> [T]he national courts of the United States will have the opportunity at the award-enforcement stage to ensure that the legitimate interest in the enforcement of the antitrust laws has been addressed. [...] [I]t would not require intrusive inquiry to ascertain that the tribunal took cognizance of the antitrust claims and actually decided them.⁵⁰⁶

Now that arbitrators are called upon to resolve disputes which affect the core interests of a State, the struggle has been to identify which rules arbitrators must take into consideration when deciding the case. One much-discussed issue is whether arbitrators are required to respect the choice of the parties if they expressly exclude the application of mandatory rules.

One could assume that if arbitrators were bound by the Rome I Regulation, they would have clear instructions regarding the applicability of overriding mandatory rules, which would solve the problem. They would

---

502 See fn. 489 for literature on this issue in general.
503 *Kleinheisterkamp*, Int'l & Comp.L.Q. 2018, 903, 906.
504 U.S. Supreme Court, decision of 2 July 1985, Mitsubishi Motors Corporation v. Soler Chrysler-Plymouth, Inc., 473 U.S. 614 (1985) – *Mitsubishi*.
505 This was expressly stated by the German legislature in its explanatory memorandum to the provision governing arbitrability of disputes, see BTDrucks. 13/5274, p. 34, right column, available at http://dipbt.bundestag.de/doc/btd/13/0 52/1305274.pdf.
506 *Mitsubishi* (fn. 504). In fn. 19 of the decision, the Supreme Court did, however, state that it felt comfortable enforcing the arbitration agreement precisely because counsel had conceded that U.S. law was applicable to the case and that "in the event the choice-of-forum and choice-of-law clauses operated in tandem as a prospective waiver of a party's right to pursue statutory remedies for antitrust violations, [it] would have little hesitation in condemning the agreement as against public policy."

C. Inapplicability of the Rome I Regulation in International Commercial Arbitration

know what legal systems to look to for overriding mandatory rules and they could be sure that parties could not opt out of their application. However, just because a rule is clear does not mean that it is appropriate.

Article 9 of the Rome I Regulation has a two-step approach that works well in a domestic court setting: It stipulates that the overriding mandatory rules of the forum must always be applied, regardless of the choice of law by the parties (Article 9(1)). Beyond that, it allows for the application of such rules of States in which contractual obligations should be or have been performed, but only insofar those rules render the performance of the contract unlawful (Article 9(2)). It is sensible that domestic courts should be required to apply the overriding mandatory provisions of their forum, seeing as they are bound by the law of their forum and cannot simply ignore its core provisions, while applying foreign law. However, this is not transferable to international arbitration tribunals and the seat of arbitration.

As was discussed at length above, tribunals are not comparable to courts of the State in which the seat is located and they are thus not responsible for ensuring that the interests of that State in regulating certain matters are met. While additional factors could of course contribute to the relevance of the legal system of that State, e.g. that the contract is performed in its territory, the location of the seat alone does not give the State any say over the merits of the dispute. Forcing arbitrators to apply the overriding mandatory provisions of the arbitral seat in cases where the seat is chosen out of convenience or due to its lack of a connection to the dispute would give the State influence over the outcome of the dispute, which it simply should not have.[507] That is not to say that the arbitrator will necessarily ignore the legal system at the arbitral seat completely – after all, a violation of the public policy of the seat can lead to an annulment of the arbitration award. Thus, careful arbitrators will pay attention to the core values and interests of the arbitral seat and ensure that the award does not violate them in order to shield the award from potential annulment.

The second case in which overriding mandatory provisions may be taken into account under the Rome I Regulation is if obligations arising out of the contract are performed in the territory of a State and the application of the provisions render the performance of the contract unlawful. This is certainly sensible. The State has an interest in its law governing the performance of the contract given that a genuine territorial link exists to it, and as such it is reasonable to enable the application of the rules which

---

507 *Mayer*, Arb. Int. 1986, 274, 282, 283.

§ 3. *Binding Effect of Article 1(1) in International Commercial Arbitration*

it considers indispensable, regardless of the choice of law by the parties. However, the Rome I Regulation makes their application optional, leaving it to the estimation of the courts of the Member States. Such a rule is not suited to reduce uncertainty in arbitration.

How the issue of overriding mandatory rules in international commercial arbitration is to be resolved cannot be satisfactorily tackled here. As it stands, a failure to apply them can be penalized by courts by nullifying the award or refusing its recognition and enforcement if it amounts to a violation of public policy courts, which is not typically the case.[508] The failure to apply mandatory rules as such is not reviewable. A radical approach has been chosen by German and Belgian courts, which have refused to refer parties to arbitration due to a suspicion that the parties' choice of a foreign law combined with an arbitration agreement amounted to a circumvention of mandatory law.[509] It has been argued that the denial to refer parties to arbitration can constitute a valid method to ensure the efficiency of EU law in EU Member States, as long as the courts are reasonably certain that mandatory EU law would not be applied in the arbitration proceedings.[510] While this seems like a regression to the times in which situations governed by overriding mandatory law were simply inarbitrable, it is understandable that an *ex post facto* review of the award, in which only public policy plays a role, seems insufficient to many. Either way, this tension between a State's right to regulate certain issues and parties' procedural autonomy cannot be solved by binding arbitrators to the Rome I Regulation.

---

508 *Beulker*, Eingriffsnormenproblematik, 2005, p. 56.
509 For Belgium, see Cour de Cassation, decision of 14 January 2010, Sebastian International Inc v Common Market Cosmetics NV, Rechtskundig Weekblad 2010–2011, 1087; Cour de Cassation, decision of 3 November 2011, Transat International AT Inc v Air Agencies Belgium, Pourvoi no C.10.0613.N; Cour de Cassation, decision of 16 November 2006, Van Hopplynus Instruments SA v Coherent Inc, Revue Belge de Droit Commercial 2007, 889, analysed in the context of similar older decisions in *Kleinheisterkamp*, WAMR 2009, 91. For Germany, see BGH, decision of 5 September 2012, VII ZR 25/12, Betriebsberater 2012, 3103, discussed by *Basedow*, FS Bogdan, pp. 16 et seqq. and Oberlandesgericht München, decision of 17 May 2006, IPRax 2007, 322, analyzed by *Kleinheisterkamp*, WAMR 2009, 91.
510 This is the stance of the Belgian courts.

4. Forum Shopping

Finally, one of the goals of the European Union is to decrease forum shopping, for which the development of uniform conflict rules is an important tool. This has been brought as an argument to champion the application of the Regulation and other EU instruments of private international law in international commercial arbitration, as well.[511] The premise is that fighting forum shopping is as important in international commercial arbitration as it is in national litigation. This is, however, not a necessity, but rather a self-fulfilling prophecy.

Forums become relevant when they have influence on the outcome of a case. International arbitration proceedings, as has been stated repeatedly, do not have a forum in the sense court proceedings do. The seat of arbitration delivers the rules of procedure, and this only to the extent that institutional rules do not already cover all relevant aspects. If anything, forum shopping in international commercial arbitration extends to selecting the place that is most convenient for all parties to reach and considering the aspects of potential court intervention and annulment proceedings in the local courts. In fact, in this regard, States implementing modern liberal arbitration laws, usually based on the UNICTRAL Model Law, have openly admitted doing so in order to become a more attractive host for international arbitration proceedings. In other words, because the seat has a far lesser impact on the procedure and the outcome of an arbitration case than the forum does in domestic litigation, forum shopping is not regarded as a problem. Financially, the State neither massively benefits nor is burdened by arbitration proceedings taking place in their territory.[512] It is inherent to any arbitration agreement – and part of what makes it attractive – to also select a convenient seat of arbitration. It is a feature, not a bug. Only if arbitrators are tethered more closely to the legal landscape of the seat of arbitration, such as its private international law, does this even become a relevant factor in the choice of the arbitral seat. Once this is the case, uniform conflict rules can be very valuable. In the case of the Rome I Regulation, it would equalize all (participating) Member States as potential seats of arbitration. In the end, however, forum shopping is a self-imposed problem that should not be touted in favor of binding arbitrators to private international law in the first place.

---

511 *Gößling*, Europäisches Kollisionsrecht, 2019, p. 103.
512 Ibid., pp. 102, 103.

III. Conclusion

The Rome I Regulation is not applicable in international commercial arbitration and neither is Article 1(1) of the CISG via Article 25 of the Rome I Regulation. The Rome I Regulation was not intended for application in international commercial arbitration, as an analysis of its wording and particularly its history shows. Furthermore, while it is a modern and fairly liberal instrument of private international law, it is ill-suited to govern the determination of the applicable substantive law in international arbitration proceedings. By reducing the possible choices of law by the parties it would reduce party autonomy, even though bolstering party autonomy is one of its declared goals. Effective protection of weaker parties is better attained by limiting these parties' access to barely regulated commercial arbitration, and while it promises clarity regarding the application of overriding mandatory rules, the rules reveal themselves as incompatible with arbitral reality. The Rome I Regulation thus delivers a strong argument against the application of the general rules of private international law in international arbitration.

D. Practical Freedom of Arbitrators to Determine Substantive Law

Under both arbitration-specific conflict rules and the conflict rules contained in institutional rules, arbitration tribunals enjoy leeway in determining the applicable substantive law. Arbitrators have developed methods for determining the applicable substantive law in arbitral practice (**I.**). The leeway granted to arbitrators is complemented by the fact that the resulting award cannot be reviewed regarding the application of conflict rules (**II.**).

I. Methods Applied in Arbitral Practice

Arbitrators have leeway in determining the applicable law under the arbitration-specific conflict of laws rules. This freedom has led to the development of a series of different methods for finding the applicable law that pay tribute to the expectations of the parties. These methods are often influenced by clauses contained in rules of arbitral institutions or international conventions. They can be divided into approaches that still utilize conflict rules, or a semblance thereof, known as *voie indirecte*, and the direct application of substantive law, ostensibly with no conflict of laws considerations, called *voie directe*.

1. Voie Indirecte

Often, arbitral tribunals do apply conflict of laws rules, albeit typically not those of the seat of arbitration. The rules applied can vary from national conflict of laws rules of one State, to a mixture of relevant rules, to international conflict of laws principles.

a) Choice of Conflict of Laws Rules of a State

One method is that arbitral tribunals simply select conflict of laws rules, for example the rules that they consider most appropriate or the rules of the State that has the closest connection to the dispute.[513] Those rules are then applied to determine the applicable law. The approach of selecting conflict rules deemed appropriate is enshrined in Article 28 of the UNCITRAL Model Law and has found its way into many national arbitration statutes.[514] As shown above, this rule is then binding on the arbitrators. In rare cases, the conflict rules of the seat may actually be the most appropriate, perhaps precisely because they are neutral. It is more likely, however, that the tribunal will select the rules of a State with which both parties have a connection, or with which the case has some connection. When applying the conflict of laws rules of the State with the closest connection with the dispute, the arbitral tribunal selects rules from the State where the parties are from or where key parts of the transaction take place. The arbitrators may find that the seat of arbitration constitutes a close enough connection to the dispute to justify applying the private international law of the State in which the arbitral seat is located.

These methods manage to solve the main problem of the *lex fori* approach, which is that a State with little or no connection with the dispute and chosen only as a legal home to a procedure should have any influence at all, direct or indirect, on the law applicable to the merits of the case

---

513 *Born*, International Commercial Arbitration, ed. 2 2014, pp. 2642 et seq. This approach is recommended by *Hayward*, Conflict of Laws and Arbitral Discretion, 2017, pp. 188 et seqq.
514 See *supra*, pp. 117 et seq.

and thereby on its outcome. When the arbitrator is free to choose conflict rules that are appropriate, for example because they are rooted in a legal system with a close link to the dispute, unlike the seat of the arbitration, their application is justified. One flaw remains: as long as one single system of private international law is selected, it can contain surprising provisions and lead to unexpected results.[515] The most important aspect in international arbitration is the parties' will. Unexpected results due to the application of unconventional provisions of a conflict of laws system that the parties could not have foreseen are not compatible with this. While these approaches are far better than the fixed rule of *lex fori*, they still leave much to be desired.

b) Cumulative Method

The cumulative method involves the application of conflict of laws rules that are common to all legal systems (the *tronc commun* of those legal systems[516]) with which the dispute has a meaningful connection.[517] The arbitrators must first identify all such legal systems, analyze their rules of private international law, eliminate any rules that are not shared by all of the legal systems and then find the applicable law with the help of the rules common to the legal systems. It does not matter if the rules are not identical, as long as they lead to the same result.[518]

This method involves the legal systems that are relevant to the dispute and thus have some justification in being consulted. Its strength is that it eliminates the issue raised above concerning unconventional conflict of laws rules: If only those conflict of laws rules are selected that are shared by relevant legal systems, this guarantees a selection of general rules that could have been expected by the parties. The downside to this method is that it is complicated. It requires time and dedication on behalf of the

---

515 If the private international law in question determines the applicable law to be that of the State where the contract was concluded, this is an atypical rule and can lead to strange and fortuitous results in international transactions. Parties from different parts of the world may well have concluded the contract in a convenient but entirely unrelated place, simply because there was an airport there with a comfortable meeting room.
516 *Rubino-Sammartano*, International Arbitration, ed. 3 2014, p. 673.
517 *Gaillard/Savage*, International Arbitration, 1999, p. 871.
518 *Born*, International Commercial Arbitration, ed. 2 2014, p. 431.

tribunal, perhaps more than should be necessary to find the applicable substantive law.

c) General Principles of Private International Law

Finally, a popular method is to apply common or widely accepted principles in different systems of private international law.[519] This method is similar to the cumulative method in that it looks at a number of different legal systems and selects principles shared by them. However, it does not limit its gaze to jurisdictions with a meaningful connection to the dispute. Such a common conflict of laws principle can be the selection of the law of the State with the closest connection to the dispute, leading to the same result as the first method above, just with a slightly more elaborate justification.

At times it has been used to explain why the parties' choice of law is applied, seeing as party autonomy is an internationally respected principle of private international law.[520] However, because the will of the party dominates everything in international arbitration, this is an unnecessary detour. If the parties have made a choice, no recourse to private international law is necessary. Their choice of law stands alone – the fact that they have an arbitration agreement justifies their being able to choose the applicable law. Private international law is only consulted in case there is no party choice.

2. Voie Directe

There is a clear trend toward arbitrators not applying any conflict rule, at least not expressly, but instead using the *voie directe*: substantive law is chosen directly and applied to the merits of the case.[521] Tribunals may determine the applicable law without stating what rule lead them to it, or they may also provide a justification, e.g. citing it as the most appropriate law. In reality, no choice of law is made without applying some criteria, even if such an analysis happens subconsciously. The *voie directe* is there-

---

519 Ibid., p. 432; *Gaillard/Savage*, International Arbitration, 1999, p. 872.
520 ICC Award No. 1512 (1971), cited by *Gaillard/Savage*, International Arbitration, 1999, pp. 872, 873.
521 *Hayward*, Conflict of Laws and Arbitral Discretion, 2017, p. 65.

fore sometimes declared as a "special conflict of laws rule [...] developed by arbitration practice"[522].

The *voie directe* is an approach utilized very often in modern institutional rules. The CIETAC arbitration rules merely state that the arbitrator shall determine the applicable law[523], but most rules specify that the arbitral tribunal should apply the law that it deems appropriate, such as the rules of the ICC[524], the LCIA[525], the SCC[526], the VIAC[527] and the SIAC[528], as well as the 2010 UNCITRAL Arbitration Rules[529]. By incorporating these institutional rules with that clause into their contract, parties make use of their party autonomy and give the arbitral tribunal a wide mandate.

This method gives a large amount of freedom to the arbitrators. Instead of relying on conflict rules that might lead to a surprising outcome, or going through the laborious process of comparing several different sets of private international law, or attempting to distill general rules of private international law, they can cut to the chase and serve the parties interests by applying laws that they deem appropriate. This can include the application of non-State laws, such as the UNIDROIT Principles,[530] where the tribunal believes that they adequately govern the contract.

---

522 *Kessedjan*, Determination and Application of Relevant National and International Law and Rules, p. 81.
523 Article 49 (2) CIETAC, available at http://www.cietac.org/index.php?m=Page&a=index&id=106&l=en (last accessed 8 February 2017).
524 Article 21(1) ICC Rules, available at https://iccwbo.org/dispute-resolution-services/arbitration/rules-of-arbitration/ (last accessed 15 September 2017).
525 Article 22.3 LCIA arbitration rules, available at http://www.lcia.org/dispute_resolution_services/lcia-arbitration-rules-2014.aspx (last accessed 15 September 2017).
526 Article 27(1) SCC arbitration rules, available at http://sccinstitute.com/media/169838/arbitration_rules_eng_17_web.pdf (last accessed 15 September 2017).
527 Article 27(2) VIAC arbitration rules, available at http://www.viac.eu/en/arbitration/arbitration-rules-vienna/93-schiedsverfahren/wiener-regeln/144-new-vienna-rules-2013 (last accessed 15 September 2017).
528 Article 31.1 SIAC arbitration rules, available at http://siac.org.sg/our-rules/rules/siac-rules-2016 (last accessed 15 September 2017).
529 Article 35(1) UNCITRAL arbitration rules 2010, available at http://www.uncitral.org/pdf/english/texts/arbitration/arb-rules-revised/arb-rules-revised-2010-e.pdf (last accessed 15 September 2017).
530 Case no 117/1999 of the Arbitration Institute of the Stockholm Chamber of Commerce, Stockholm Arbitration Report 2002, pp. 59–65, comment in *Mistelis*, Unif. Law Rev. 2003, 631.

D. Practical Freedom of Arbitrators to Determine Substantive Law

II. No Reviewability of Application of Private International Law

The leeway that arbitrators have in determining the applicable substantive law is accompanied by a lack of reviewability of this determination by the courts. Their legal freedom to select the law without resorting to a specific set of conflict of laws rules is thus supplemented by a practical freedom, because the application, lack of application or misapplication of any conflict of laws rules cannot be penalized.

1. Review of Arbitral Awards

Parties to an arbitration agree that the resulting award is final and binding on them. This is a cornerstone of international commercial arbitration. That does not mean, of course, that awards cannot be challenged under any circumstances. If recognition or enforcement of an award is sought abroad, i.e. in a State that is not the arbitral seat, the losing party may resist this motion pursuant to the provisions of the New York Convention.[531] An award can also be actively challenged by way of a request to set it aside at the seat of arbitration according to the national arbitration statute.[532] Since the New York Convention's grounds for refusing recognition and enforcement were copied by the drafters of the UNCITRAL Model Law, the grounds for setting aside an award at the seat of arbitration are the same in most national arbitration statutes as the grounds for refusing the recognition and enforcement of an award. Both an active and a passive attack on an international arbitral award can thus be based on nearly identical grounds.

The grounds for both annulment and refusal of enforcement are divided into two groups: the grounds that must be pled by the party making the "application" or "request" on the one hand – set forth in Article 34(2)(a) of the Model Law and Article V(1) of the New York Convention – and the grounds that the court must consider *ex officio* on the other hand – set forth in Article 34(2)(b) of the Model Law and Article V(2) of the New York Convention.[533] The first group of grounds include an invalid arbitration agreement, the fact that a party was unable to present its case, that

---

531 See already *supra*, p. 77.
532 This is the key competence within the otherwise limited jurisdiction of the courts at the seat of arbitration, see *supra* pp. 76 et seq.
533 Wolff/*Borris/Hennecke*, 2012, New York Convention Art. V para. 40.

the arbitral tribunal exceeded its authority, or that the arbitral tribunal was no composed correctly or procedure was not followed. All of these issues concern the parties' autonomy: Only if they validly opted for arbitration instead of litigation and got what they asked for do they have to submit to the award. These flaws all fall within the sphere of the parties, and as such, must be brought forward by them. The second group of grounds for annulment and refusal of recognition and enforcement, regarding which the court can act *sua sponte*, concerns matters of public interest. The court may set aside the award or refuse its enforcement if the subject matter is not arbitrable in its forum or if the award violates its forum's public policy. In such cases, the award's flaws touch upon issues of compatibility with a legal system. A court does not have to give effect to an award that violates the most basic principles of its legal system, and in such cases, it does not have to rely on any party to make a pleading in this regard.

While procedural aspects of arbitration proceedings are broadly reviewable, the contents of the decision are only subject to review only within the limits of substantive public policy.[534] This is called the prohibition of *révision au fond*, which is a characteristic aspect of international arbitration that ensures its efficiency.[535] Parties submitting their dispute to international arbitration assume the risk of an incorrect decision by the tribunal. If any misapplication of substantive law were reviewable by national courts, this would disrupt the nature of arbitration, effectively turning tribunals into a lower court at the seat of arbitration and in enforcement States.[536] The arbitral awards could no longer be considered truly binding, seeing as every aspect of the award and the proceedings would potentially be subject to review. The following will analyze whether an arbitral tribunal's decision on matters of private international law is shielded from review or whether a misapplication could potentially be the basis of an attack on the award on one of the grounds under the UNICTRAL Model Law or the New York Convention.

---

534 Kronke/Naciemiento/Otto/*Kronke*, 2010, Introduction, p. 11.
535 See only *Schütze*, Schiedsgericht und Schiedsverfahren, ed. 6 2016, paras. 680 et seq.
536 Kronke/Naciemiento/Otto/*Kronke*, 2010, Introduction, p. 9.

2. Individual Grounds for Annulment and Refusal of Recognition and Enforcement

The incorrect application of international private law by arbitrators is not expressly included in the reasons for which an award can be invalidated or refused recognition and enforcement. However, it could potentially be categorized as one of the following grounds: a violation of the procedure of either the arbitration agreement or the arbitral seat, an excess of authority exercised by the arbitral tribunal, or a violation of public policy. It will be shown that none of these grounds can serve as the basis of a valid attack on an award in the event that the tribunal failed to apply or misapplied private international law.

a) Excess of Authority

Article V(1)(c) of the New York Convention stipulates that the recognition and enforcement of an award may be refused if "[t]he award deals with a difference not contemplated by or not falling within the terms of the submission to arbitration [...]", i.e. the arbitrators act in excess of their authority. Article 34(2)(a)(iii) of the Model Law sets forth the same circumstances as a ground for annulment. The requirements for refusal are met when the contents of an award exceed the tribunal's jurisdiction, going beyond the issues that the arbitrators are authorized to consider.[537] Typically, this concerns cases in which the tribunal awarded damages that had not been claimed[538] or had been excluded[539]. Beyond the matter of jurisdiction, an excess of authority can manifest in an excess of competence, regarding the way in which the decision was reached.[540] This is the case when the parties have made an express choice of law and the arbitrators apply a different law, or when they make a decision *ex aequo et bono*[541] or on the basis of

---

537 Kronke/Nacimiento/Otto/*Port*, 2010, New York Convention Art. V(1)(c), p. 266; Musielak/Voit/*Voit*, ed. 15 2018, ZPO § 1061, para. 16; Saenger/*Saenger*, ed. 7 2017, ZPO § 1061 para. 11.
538 Decision of the Court of Appeal of Hamburg, 30 July 1998, YBCA 2000, 714.
539 Libyan American Oil Co. (Liamco) v Socialist People's Libyan Arab Yamahirya, formerly Libyan Arab Republic, VII YBCA 1982, p. 382.
540 Wolff/*Borris/Hennecke*, 2012, New York Convention Art. V paras. 234 et seqq; MüKo-ZPO/*Adolphsen*, ed. 5 2017, ZPO § 1061 Anhang UNÜ Art. V, para. 41.
541 This is discussed *infra*, pp. 183 et seqq.

lex mercatoria even though there is no mandate in this regard from the parties.[542]

As in these cases of an excess of competence, the misapplication of conflict of laws rules at least indirectly affects the outcome of the case. It does not, however, constitute an excess of authority in the sense of the New York Convention or the Model Law. There is a distinction between decision a based on a different law than the one chosen by the parties on the one hand and the application of "wrong" conflict rules on the other: Applying a different law than the one chosen by the parties is a violation of the party mandate, which is the source of the arbitrators' authority. The same goes for decisions that would necessitate a clear party mandate and are made despite the absence of such a mandate, such as a decision *ex aequo et bono* or based on non-State law.[543] If, however, the parties have not made a choice of law and have not given the arbitrators a clear mandate on which conflict of laws rules to apply, the authority of the tribunal is not limited in this regard and an application of conflict of laws rules cannot exceed its authority.

b) Procedure

Article V(1)(d) of the New York Convention stipulates that an award's enforcement can be denied because "arbitral procedure was not in accordance with the agreement of the parties, or, failing such agreement, was not in accordance with the law of the country where the arbitration took place". This is mirrored in Article 34(2)(a)(iv) of the Model Law as a ground for annulment of an award. As the clear wording indicates, the party's agreement, including any institutional rules incorporated into the agreement, is the primary source for the procedure, while *lex arbitri* takes effect where there is no party agreement.[544] Classic examples for procedural aberrations are that the proceedings were held in a language other than

---

542 MüKo-ZPO/*Adolphsen*, ed. 5 2017, ZPO § 1061 Anhang UNÜ Art. V, para. 40; *Gottwald*, FS Nagel, p. 63; Saenger/*Saenger*, ed. 7 2017, ZPO § 1061, para. 11; Musielak/Voit/*Voit*, ed. 15 2018, ZPO § 1061, para. 16; BeckOK ZPO/*Wilske/Markert*, ed. 30 2018, ZPO § 1061, para. 31.
543 As shown above, a mandate for decisions *ex aequo et bono* is not needed in some countries, see *supra*, pp. 104 et seq.
544 Saenger/*Saenger*, ed. 7 2017, ZPO § 1061, para. 12 ("in Ermangelung einer solchen Abrede"); BeckOK ZPO/*Wilske/Markert*, ed. 30 2018, ZPO § 1061, para. 35 ("subsidiär").

D. Practical Freedom of Arbitrators to Determine Substantive Law

the one agreed upon by the parties, or that they were held in several phases even though the institutional rules provide for only one phase.[545]

Conflict of laws rules directed specifically at arbitrators, as demonstrated, are typically embedded in institutional arbitration rules and in national arbitration legislation. One might be led to believe that their misapplication or misinterpretation could therefore constitute a procedural mistake. However, conflict of laws rules do not share the procedural nature of the bulk of the arbitration law and institutional rules. Arbitration procedure begins when a claim is filed and ends when the award is issued,[546] "with the exception of the decision-making process as such".[547] Private international law is substantive law; its application already constitutes part of the decision-making process.[548] Although it does not directly produce rights and obligations, it determines the law that is applicable to the facts at hand, which does have a direct effect on the outcome of the case. Put another way, conflict of laws rules are applied *in iudicando* and not *in procesando*.[549] Misapplication or misinterpretation of conflict rules can therefore does not violate the arbitration procedure.[550] The court's revision of the tribunal's application of substantive law through a court would amount to a prohibited *révision au fond*.[551] Recognition and enforcement of resulting awards can thus neither be refused under Article V(1)(d) of the New York Convention on the basis of a perceived misapplication of private international law, nor annulled pursuant to Article 34(2)(b)(iv) of the Model Law.[552]

---

545 Kronke/Nacimiento/Otto/*Nacimiento*, 2010, New York Convention Art. V(1)(d), pp. 294 et seq.
546 Nacimiento/Kröll/Böckstiegel/*Kröll*, ed. 2 2015, ZPO § 106 para. 117; Kronke/Nacimiento/Otto/*Nacimiento*, 2010, New York Convention Art. V(1)(d, pp. 293 et seq.
547 Nacimiento/Kröll/Böckstiegel/*Kröll*, ed. 2 2015, ZPO § 1061 para. 117.
548 See only *Kegel/Schurig*, Internationales Privatrecht, ed. 9 2004, p. 54.
549 Cf. *Sandrock*, JZ 1986, 370, 374. *Sandrock* uses this terminology to argue that whether an award is made *ex aequo et bono* or based on law is also a matter of substantive law, a decision made *in iudicando*, an issue which will be discussed further below, on pp. 179 et seq. This terms *in iudicando* and *in procesando* are seen critically by MüKo-ZPO/*Münch*, ed. 5 2017, § 1059 para. 28.
550 MüKo-ZPO/*Adolphsen*, ed. 5 2017, ZPO § 1061 Anhang UNÜ Art. V para. 41.
551 Wolff/*Borris*/Hennecke, 2012, Art. V para. 244.
552 MüKo-ZPO/*Adolphsen*, ed. 5 2017, ZPO § 1061 Anhang UNÜ Art. V para. 41; Musielak/Voit/*Voit*, ed. 15 2018, ZPO § 1059 para. 18; *Schlosser*, Anhang zu ZPO § 1061, para. 277, in regard to § 1059 of the German Code of Civil Procedure, which is a copy of Art. 34(2)(a)(iv) of the UNCITRAL Model Law.

c) Public Policy

One aspect that would justify a review of the application of substantive rules – and thus potentially also of private international law – is that of a potential violation of substantive public policy pursuant to Article V(2)(b) of the New York Convention. This provision gives a court the right to refuse the recognition and enforcement of a foreign arbitral award if it finds that "[t]he recognition or enforcement of the award would be contrary to the public policy of that country". This is also the wording used to justify an annulment under Article 34(2)(ii) of the UNCITRAL Model Law. Public policy was intentionally not defined in the Convention or the Model Law and its contents of it may vary from jurisdiction to jurisdiction.[553] In general, public policy is interpreted as pertaining to basic principles or values of societies in civil law countries, or broad, imprecisely defined values such as justice, fairness and morality in common law jurisdictions.[554] While each State can define its own national public policy standard,[555] a refusal to recognize and enforce foreign arbitration awards according to the New York Convention is generally believed to require a violation of international or even transnational public policy.[556] In regard

---

[553] International Bar Association Subcommittee on Recognition and Enforcement of Arbitral Awards, Report on the Public Policy Exception in the New York Convention, October 2015, p. 1. Only two jurisdiction have included definitions of public policy in their law, the UAE and Australia, as the Report lays out on pp. 3 and 4: "In the UAE, Article 3 of the Civil Transactions Law states in general (thus not limited to the context of arbitration) that public order 'include[s] matters relating to personal status such as marriage, inheritance, and lineage, and matters relating to systems of government, freedom of trade, the circulation of wealth, rules of individual ownership and the other rules and foundations upon which society is based, in such a manner as not to conflict with the definitive provisions and fundamental principles of the Islamic Sharia.' In Australia, Section 8(7A) of the 1974 International Arbitration Act provides that 'To avoid doubt and without limiting paragraph (7)(b) [which makes the violation of public policy a ground for refusing to enforce a foreign award], the enforcement of a foreign award would be contrary to public policy if: (a) the making of the award was induced or affected by fraud or corruption; or (b) a breach of the rules of natural justice occurred in connection with the making of the award.'".
[554] Ibid., p. 6.
[555] Wolff/*Wolff*, 2012, Art. V para. 402.
[556] *Lalive*, Transnational (or Truly International) Public Policy and International Arbitration; *Mayer*, International Public Policy; *Born*, International Commercial Arbitration, ed. 2 2014, pp. 3652 et seq. *Adolphsen* argues that the differentiation between national and international public policy is only necessary in legal

D. Practical Freedom of Arbitrators to Determine Substantive Law

to the annulment of arbitration awards, some national arbitration statutes explicitly require the violation of "international public policy"[557] or "principles of international public policy"[558]. An English court has described public policy as follows:

> *It has to be shown that there is some element of illegality or that the enforcement of the award would be clearly injurious to the public good or, possibly, that enforcement would be wholly offensive to the ordinary reasonable and fully informed member of the public on whose behalf the powers of the state are exercised.*[559]

Thus, the bar is set quite high. It can include both procedural and substantive aspects.[560] As was just shown, the application of conflict rules is a matter of substantive law. The enforcement of the award must be in some way untenable due to the effects it has on the legal system of the State in which it the enforcement takes place.[561] Similarly, a violation of German public policy (*"öffentliche Ordnung"* or *"ordre public"*) as set forth in section 1051(2) no. 2 lit. a of the ZPO (i.e. Article 34(2)(b)(ii) of the Model Law) can only manifest in the effect that the existence of the award has on the German legal system.[562] Typical cases of substantive public policy issues are the awarding of unlawful relief, aiding globally recognized criminal offenses such as terrorism or slavery, or the violation of mandatory commercial laws such as competition law.[563]

In order to constitute a violation of public policy, the application of certain conflict of laws rules would have to result in an award whose enforcement would constitute a violation of the public policy of the en-

---

systems that use a broad definition of public policy, MüKo-ZPO/*Adolphsen*, ed. 5 2017, ZPO § 1061 Anhang UNÜ Art. V, para. 69.
557 Art. 1520(5) of the French Code of Civil Procedure.
558 Art. 1096(f) of the Portuguese Code of Civil Procedure.
559 Deutsche Schachtbau- und Tiefbohrgesellschaft mbH v. Ras Al Khaimah National Oil Co., Shell Int'l Petroleum Co. Ltd., Court of Appeal, 24 March 1987, quoted by Maxi Scherer, Report, England, p. 6.
560 See e.g. MüKo-ZPO/*Münch*, ed. 5 2017, § 1059 paras. 45-48.
561 *Schütze*, Schiedsgericht und Schiedsverfahren, ed. 6 2016, para. 784.
562 BGH, decision of 6 October 2016 – I ZB 13/15, NJW-RR 2017, 313, 319 para. 55: "Die öffentliche Ordnung (ordre public) steht der Anerkennung und Vollstreckung eines Schiedsspruchs in Deutschland entgegen, wenn seine Anerkennung oder Vollstreckung zu einem **Ergebnis** führt, das mit wesentlichen Grundsätzen des deutschen Rechts offensichtlich unvereinbar ist." [emphasis added].
563 Wolff/*Wolff*, 2012, New York Convention Art. V paras. 566-573, 575 and 579.

forcement State. However, as a rule, conflict rules are inherently neutral. They do not have any direct effect on the facts; they merely lead the adjudicatory body to the appropriate law, which then contains substantive rules that directly affect the outcome of the case. Private international law only decides which law should most appropriately govern the case. As such, conflict rules could hardly contain a regulation that would be so devastating for the outcome of a case that it might justify refusing recognition of an award.

Conflict rules can admittedly take on less neutral elements when they explicitly aim to protect certain parties. As shown above, the Rome I Regulation for example calls for the application of the consumer's home country's law to consumer contracts, or the law of the country in which an employee habitually carries out his work to employment contracts.[564] If the parties have chosen a different law to govern the consumer or employment contracts, then the Regulation ensures that certain protections of the otherwise applicable law cannot be overridden. Such conflict rules are arguably no longer entirely neutral. They seek to protect one party over another. But this protection does not amount to explicit instructions on how that is to be done, substantively. It relies on the law that it determines to be applicable to contain the necessary safeguards. Thus, it is not the application of the conflict of laws rule favoring one law over another that would lead to the violation of public policy, but the application of the favored law itself.

The purpose of the public policy defense is to have a safety valve mechanism to protect a legal system from having to give effect to arbitral awards that are incompatible with its basic principles and values. Public policy primarily comes into play when the law that is actually applicable to the dispute according to private international law leads to untenable results in the enforcement State:

> *The paradigmatic case of a refusal of recognition on ordre public grounds is the use of a statute – typically even one belonging to a legal system that is applicable according to our notions of private international law – that goes against fundamental domestic notions of justice.*[565]

---

564 See *supra*, pp. 141 et seqq.
565 *Schlosser*, Anhang zu ZPO § 1061, Art. V(2)(b), para. 326.: „Der paradigmatische Fall einer Anerkennungsversagung aus ordre-public-Gründen ist die Anwendung einer Rechtsnorm – typischerweise sogar aus einer Rechtsordnung, die auch nach unseren kollisionsrechtlichen Vorstellungen anwendbar ist –, die fundamentalen inländischen Gerechtigkeitsvorstellungen zuwiderläuft."

E. Application of the CISG as Non-State Law

The fact that the application of the "correct" – that is, applicable – law can lead to results that violate ordre public shows that the underlying conflicts analysis is not what is being penalized. If the tribunal applies a different law and the resulting award violates the public policy of the enforcement State, the problem can therefore not lie in why the law was applied, but only in the fact that it leads to intolerable results. Misapplying or misinterpreting conflict of laws rules cannot justify the annulment of an award or a refusal of its recognition and enforcement due to a violation of public policy.

3. Conclusion

Arbitration awards cannot be reviewed regarding the application of conflict of laws rules by the arbitration tribunal, as this constitutes neither an excess of authority pursuant to Article 34(1)(a)(iii) of the UNCITRAL Model Law and Article V(1)(c) of the New York Convention, nor a procedural mistake pursuant to Article 34(1)(a)(iv) of the UNCITAL Model Law and Article V(1)(d) of the New York Convention, nor a violation of public policy under Article 34(2)(b)(ii) of the Model Law and Article V(2)(b) of the New York Convention. A review of the private international law applied by the tribunal would amount to a *révision au fond*, which is prohibited.

E. Application of the CISG as Non-State Law

As was demonstrated, arbitrators are bound by the arbitration-specific conflict rules of the arbitral seat. These are typically very broad and allow arbitrators to select either conflict rules or substantive laws of a State that they deem appropriate or applicable. Either of these can lead to the application of the CISG, either by virtue of its rules of application, which are conflict of laws rules, or directly as the body of international sales law of each and any of its Signatory States. However, these conflict rules usually also allow for the parties to choose non-State laws as their *lex causa*. To some, this is another gateway for the application of the CISG by arbitration tribunals. This would require categorizing the Convention as non-State law, despite it being designed to serve as part of the Contracting State's State law.

§ 3. Binding Effect of Article 1(1) in International Commercial Arbitration

One way to permit the application of the CISG as non-State law is to categorize it as part of the *lex mercatoria*. Also known under the moniker "law merchant", the exact content and even existence of the *lex mercatoria* is a matter of great debate.[566] An heir of the medieval *law merchant*, which was developed by "geographically dynamic" merchants as norms of commercial behavior tailored to interregional commerce untethered from static feudal society,[567] it was revived in the 1960s by the French scholar Goldman and his peers. They advocated a transnational legal system, independent of a national legislature, consisting of general legal principles and rules of international commercial law that takes into account the relevant trade usages and contractual stipulations of the parties.[568] The main criticism of this system is that it lacks the legitimacy necessary to bind any commercial actors.[569] It is decried as a "diffuse and fragmented body of law without much substance"[570] that is unable to give parties the guidance they need in international commerce. According to critics, it is wishful thinking to assume that the international commercial community had the authority to give itself rules, autonomously from existing national legal structures.[571]

However, especially in international arbitration, application of the *lex mercatoria* has become a matter of fact. Parties choose it to govern their dispute and arbitral tribunals apply it. Parties are traditionally free to select non-State laws to govern the merits of their dispute. This is reflected in rules of arbitral institutions and in arbitration statutes, in particular those based on the UNCITRAL Model Law ("Model Law"),[572] which directs arbitrators to apply the "rules of law" chosen by the parties, in contrast to simply "law" as a reference to State law.[573] As a consequence, parties are able to validly select set of rules that do not stem from a State legislature,

---

566 For an overview over the objections against the *lex mercatoria*, see *Berger*, Creeping Codification, ed. 2 2010, chapter 2, pp. 32 et seqq; *Lando*, Int'l & Comp.L.Q. 1985, 747.
567 *Cremades/Plehn*, B.U. Int'l L. 1984, 317, 319.
568 *Berger*, Law & Pol'y Int'l Bus. 1996-1997, 943, 950.
569 *Mankowski*, RIW 2011, 30, 41.
570 *Lando*, FS Kurt Siehr, p. 398.
571 *Mankowski*, RIW 2011, 30, 41.
572 UNCITRAL Model Law on International Commercial Arbitration of 1985, amended in 2016, to be found at http://www.uncitral.org/pdf/english/texts/arbitration/ml-arb/07-86998_Ebook.pdf (last accessed on 11 February 2019).
573 Article 28(1), first sentence of the UNCITRAL Model Law, see Explanatory Note by the UNCITRAL secretariat on the 1985 Model Law on International Commercial Arbitration as amended in 2006, para. 39, available at http://www.

E. Application of the CISG as Non-State Law

and arbitrators can apply those rules, unlike domestic courts would. Also outside of arbitration there is a trend towards legitimizing the practice of choosing laws that are not of national origin. Notably, a draft of the Rome I Regulation contained the possibility for parties to choose "the principles and rules of the substantive law of contract recognised internationally or in the Community"[574] as applicable law. The purpose of this rule was to "boost the impact of the parties' will", which was described as "a key principle of the Convention"[575] – a reference to the Rome Convention, the predecessor of the Rome I Regulation. While it excluded the possibility of a choice of *lex mercatoria* as such due to its unclear nature, existing sets of transnational rules, such as the UNIDROIT Principles[576] and the Principles of European Contract Law (PECL),[577] could be chosen by the parties.[578] The Rome I Regulation in its current form only permits the choice of national law,[579] but this was an early sign of a sea change in private international law. The *lex mercatoria* may – justifiably – still be considered too opaque a concept to be given free range in all types of dispute resolution, but certain reputable specimens of it can serve as a gateway to giving the parties broader discretion in their choice of law.

Outside of its scope of application, the CISG is categorized by some as *lex mercatoria*, as are the UNIDROIT Principles and the PECL.[580] There is an argument to be made that due to its unique nature, the CISG can serve

---

uncitral.org/uncitral/en/uncitral_texts/arbitration/1985Model_arbitration.html (last accessed on 11 February 2019).
574 Article 3(2) of the EU Commission Proposal COM(2005), 650 final of 15 December 2005, available at http://www.europarl.europa.eu/meetdocs/2004_20 09/documents/com/com_com(2005)0650_/com_com(2005)0650_en.pdf (last accessed on 11 February 2019). For more information on the UNCITRAL Model Law, see *infra*, pp. 78 et seq.
575 EU Commission Proposal COM(2005), 650 final of 15 December 2005 (fn. 573), p. 6.
576 Available at http://www.unidroit.org/english/principles/contracts/principles201 0/integralversionprinciples2010-e.pdf (last accessed on 11 February 2019).
577 Available at https://www.trans-lex.org/400200/_/pecl/ (last accessed on 11 February 2019).
578 EU Commission, Proposal COM(2005), 650 final of 15 December 2005 (fn. 573), p. 6; *Petsche*, J. Priv. Int. 2014, 489, 4; *Magnus/Mankowski*, Joint Response to the Green Paper, 2002, pp. 16 et seqq.
579 Art. 3(1) of the Rome I Regulation.
580 *Kappus*, Lex mercatoria und CISG, 1990, p. 133; *Cuniberti*, Colum. J. Transnat'l L. 2014, 369, 381; *Petsche*, J. Priv. Int. 2014, 489, 496; Internationales Vertragsrecht/*Ferrari*, ed. 3 2018, Rom I VO Art. 3, para. 19; *Kondring*, IPrax 2007, 241, 245.

as a kind of supercharged *lex mercatoria*. It is a worthy contender to govern even those international sales contracts that do not fall within its scope due to the high quality of the law as a self-sufficient body of law that is based on broad international consensus from representatives with different legal backgrounds. The vast amount of literature and court decisions that exist to help interpret it thwart the reservations that critics generally have towards the *lex mercatoria*. It constitutes truly international, comprehensive regulation for international sales contracts. Additionally, it has democratic legitimacy, seeing as over 90 States have ratified it.

However, the CISG does not fit the definition of *lex mercatoria*. The CISG was specifically not conceived as a *lex mercatoria*, but instead as part of the domestic law of the Signatory States. It is a treaty of international public law and not the product of a private organization. When the requirements of the rules of application are met, courts in Member States have to apply the CISG, while *lex mercatoria* does not have such power. The fact that conceiving of the CISG was such a long, arduous process belies the notion that it is simply a reflection of a shared vision of sales regulations. Instead, it is a hard-fought compromise, albeit one that has found broad acceptance.

Despite this, in the rare cases that parties actually choose *lex mercatoria* as the applicable substantive law, the CISG may well be exactly the kind of law they have in mind. If the arbitral tribunal wants to apply the CISG, there are good arguments in favor if this, but it would be advisable to consult the parties first.

F. Conclusion

Arbitrators in international commercial arbitration proceedings are not bound by Article 1(1) of the CISG. The Contracting States can set forth a broad arbitration-specific conflict rule as a part of their arbitration law, but they lack the competence to bind international commercial arbitrators to their general conflict of law rules, such as Article 1(1) of the CISG. These can merely serve as guidelines in arbitration proceedings.

Since arbitration tribunals are not State organs, traditional conflict of laws rules do not automatically apply to them the way they do to State organs. Arbitrators receive their jurisdiction purely from the arbitration agreement between the parties, they do not partake in the constitutional role of courts to shape and interpret law and their awards are not automatically enforceable. The arbitral seat does not grant the State in which it is located legislative competence to make conflict of laws because it does not create the necessary geographical connection to the seat to establish a genuine territorial link. The fact that the arbitral seat is purportedly chosen by the parties also does not create a genuine link like a choice of court does.

However, there is a rule of customary international rule endowing States with the competence to regulate arbitral procedure if the arbitral seat if located in their territory. This competence extends to conflict of laws rules. Virtually all arbitration statutes typically contain arbitration-specific conflict rules, following the UNCITRAL Model Law, and this practice is supported by *opinio iuris* regarding the legislative jurisdiction of States to dictate both procedural arbitration rules and broadly worded arbitration-specific conflict rules.

The Rome I Regulation, which has ignited a fresh debate regarding the effect of private international law in arbitration and whose applicability would entail the same forArticle 1(1) of the CISG, is not applicable in international commercial arbitration, as an analysis of its wording and history shows. In particular, however, a systematic analysis exposes that it is ill-suited to be applied by arbitrators, impeding the very objectives the Regulation is supposed to further.

This freedom of arbitrators to select the substantive law is buttressed by the fact that this decision cannot be reviewed by courts. As long as the arbitral tribunal does not go against an agreement by the parties to apply or not apply a specific law, the determination of the applicable law is not a ground for either annulment or for refusal of enforcement of the award abroad. Within the broad wording of the conflict rules in arbitration laws and institutional rules, arbitrators have evolved different methods to determine the substantive law.

The leeway given to arbitrators by the arbitration-specific conflict of law rules enables them to apply the CISG when they deem it appropriate, as long as they apply it as State law. If the parties select the application of non-State law, the application of the CISG as such must first be proposed to and discussed with them, since it does not clearly qualify as such.

§ 4. Application of Substantive Provisions of the CISG in International Commercial Arbitration

Once the claim has been made that international arbitrators are not bound by Article 1(1) of the CISG and other traditional rules of private international law, the following question poses itself: Are arbitrators bound by law at all? After all, private international law is domestic law just like substantive law is and if arbitrators are not bound to one type of law, they may well not be bound by any type of domestic law. In the context of this thesis, this issue can be narrowed down to whether arbitrators are bound by the "truly substantive" rules in the CISG, i.e. all the provisions that set forth rights and obligations of the contractual partners – the *Entscheidungsnormen* rather than the *Rechtsanwendungsnormen*. For example, if international arbitrators decide that the CISG is the most appropriate law to govern a dispute, do they have to apply it to the letter, or can they apply it flexibly, selecting provisions they find appropriate and disregarding others?

It has been demonstrated that arbitrators are not bound by the law of a specific State by virtue of "belonging" to that State like courts do.[581] Because they are not organs of any State, there is no constitutional mandate for them to apply the laws, including the substantive laws, of any State.[582] Instead, a customary rule of international public law has been established that grants States legislative jurisdiction to set forth conflict of laws rules for international arbitration proceedings that have the seat of arbitration is their territory.[583] As such, while States can set forth broad arbitration-specific conflict rules, arbitrator have the discretion to definitively select the governing law. Thus, no State's substantive law binds the arbitrator *per se*. It would be incorrect, however, to deduce from this that arbitrators are not bound by substantive law.

Whether arbitrators are bound by substantive law depends entirely on the parties' mandate. International commercial arbitration is a method of dispute resolution in which substantive law plays a different, less rigid role than in court proceedings, and the parties' mandate is key. If the parties want a decision based on law, the arbitrators are bound by law –

---

581 See *supra*, pp. 93 et seqq.
582 See *supra*, pp. 108 et seqq.
583 See *supra*, pp. 131 et seqq.

regardless of whether the parties have chosen it or the arbitrators did so in the absence of a party choice (**A.**). However, the application of substantive law is subject to extremely limited review, in effect giving arbitrators some leeway in applying the law, as long as the decision can still be considered as being based on law (**B.**).

A. Binding Effect of Substantive Law Dependent on Party Choice

International commercial arbitration is defined by its less rigid relationship to law in contract to domestic court proceedings. This is a main feature for parties who are skeptical of foreign legal systems and their unexpected intricacies which may have an outsize impact on the outcome of the case. Parties that select international arbitration have a choice: they can have arbitrators decide *ex aequo et bono* or as *amiable compositeurs*, or they can mandate a decision based on law.[584] This distinction is rooted in the history of international arbitration. Today, the unique role of law in arbitration is reflected in different arbitration-specific modes of decision-making, which are codified in domestic and international arbitration law.

I. Historical Application of Law in Arbitration

Historically, arbitrators were no always expected to apply the law strictly, or even any law at all. The distinction that is made today between an arbitral decision based on law on the one hand and a decision by an *amiable compositeur* on the other hand that originates from canon law.[585] It is based on a misinterpretation of Roman law, under which arbitrators were actually not bound to apply the law, in two aspects: the weakness of the arbitration agreement, and the distinction between different types arbitration.

Under Roman law, the arbitration agreement – or *compromissum* – was a *pactum nudum*, a contract that was easily rescinded because there was no penalty for non-compliance.[586] This limited binding effect of the arbitration agreement warranted giving the arbitrator far-reaching powers, since the parties were free to opt out of arbitration and into court proceedings

---

584 See also *supra*, pp. 99 et seqq.
585 *Cohn*, U. Toronto L.J. 1941, 1, 13.
586 Ibid.

until a late stage. However, by the middle ages, municipal laws precluded parties to an arbitration agreement from going to court and called for the possibility of immediate execution of arbitral awards.[587] The broad powers that arbitrators had under Roman law, combined with the binding effect that the arbitration agreement was later endowed with, led to the conclusion that arbitrators must have been bound to apply law. This overlooked the fact that because the parties had been free to back out of the *compromissum* unchallenged originally, it had not been crucial to bind the arbitrator to law.[588]

The other misinterpretation resulted from the distinction in original Roman texts between proper arbitration and the "determination of an obligation of uncertain extent by a third party, who had already been appointed for this purpose by the parties in the original contract".[589] Regarding the latter, the judgment could be revised through a *iudicium bonae fidei* in case of a *manifesta iniquitas*[590], while a judgement resulting from proper arbitration had to be accepted whether it was right or wrong. Scholars later extrapolated from this distinction in the treatment of the resulting awards that the role of substantive law must be different in each case. The resulting misconception was that there is one kind of arbitrator that is bound by law and one that is not – a distinction ostensibly based on Roman law, but in reality completely new.[591]

These misinterpretations of Roman law persisted up to modern times. The new *Code de procédure civile* of France contained the distinction between arbitrators bound by law and *amiables compositeurs*.[592] A break came in the second half of the 19th century when the German code of civil procedure of 1877 stipulated: "In the absence of a party agreement

---

587 This switch was due to the influence of Germanic ideas. Under Germanic law, arbitration agreements precluded the parties from submitting to ordinary court proceedings and resulting awards were enforced in the same manner as court judgments. In regard to law versus equity, the parties could decided on what basis the arbitrator was to come to a decision. See ibid.
588 Paulus was often quoted in this regard: *compromissum ad similitudinem iudiciorum redigitur*, Dig. 4.8.1. This quote, however, was taken out of context.
589 *Cohn*, U. Toronto L.J. 1941, 1, p. 13. This type of arrangement still exists today in continental law, such as in Germany in the form of the *Schiedsgutachter*.
590 Dig. 17.2.76.: "arbitrorum enim genera sunt duo, unum eiusmodi, ut sive aequum sit sive iniquum, parere debeamus (...), alterum eiusmodi, ut ad boni viri arbitrium redigi debeat".
591 *Ziegler*, ZRG 1967, 239, p. 376.
592 *Cohn*, U. Toronto L.J. 1941, 1. This was certainly not universally well received, see *Oertmann*, Schiedsrichter und staatliches Recht, p. 115.

A. Binding Effect of Substantive Law Dependent on Party Choice

regarding the proceedings these will be decided by the arbitrators at their discretion".[593] The motives for the draft state that parties who agree to arbitrate want to escape the difficulties that result from the application of positive law; instead, they want justice to be what the arbitrator decides *ex aequo et bono*.[594] The purpose of an arbitration agreement, according to the motives, can only be reached if the arbitrators decide the case *"comme amiables compositeurs"*.[595] The notion that arbitrators were first and foremost supposed to decide based on commercial considerations or *ex aequo et bono*, not on the basis of law, can be found in German court decisions in the early 20th century.[596]

This brief respite from the shackles of substantive law ended mid 20th century. The European Treaty of 1961[597] stated: "The arbitrators shall act as amiables compositeurs if the parties so decide and if they may do so under the law applicable to the arbitration." Today, virtually all arbitration statutes contain a similar provision, also due to Article 28(3) of the UNCITRAL Model Law: "The arbitral tribunal shall decide *ex aequo et bono* or as *amiable compositeur* only if the parties have expressly authorized it to do so."

II. Arbitration-Specific Modes of Decision

The difference between law in international arbitration and law in court proceedings manifests in three aspects: the possibility of decisions *ex aequo et bono*, the applicability of non-State law, and the role of trade usages. The parties have the option of choosing "rules of law" – a term that includes both national laws and non-State law – to apply to the merits of their case. They can go further and ask the arbitral tribunal to decide *ex aequo et bono*

---

[593] § 860 (1) Civilprozessordnung: "In Ermangelung einer Vereinbarung der Parteien über das Verfahren wird dasselbe von den Schiedsrichtern nach freiem Ermessen bestimmt."
[594] *Hahn*, Zivilprozeßordnung, ed. 2 1881, p. 449.
[595] Ibid.
[596] RG SeuffA 80 (1926) Nr. 189, S. 348 (349) („weniger vom Standpunkt des strengen Rechts, als aus dem Gesichtspunkte der Wirtschaft zu entscheiden in der Lage"); BayObLG JW 1929, 866 left column („den Streit der Parteien schiedlich – ex aequo et bono – nicht nach den Buchstaben des Gesetzes zu entscheiden"), as quoted by MüKo-ZPO/*Münch*, ed. 5 2017, § 1051 fn. 87.
[597] See fn. 452.

or as *amiables compositeurs*. Arbitration laws also regularly stipulate that arbitrators must take trade usages into consideration.

1. *Ex Aequo et Bono* and *Amiables Compositeurs*

International arbitrators can decide cases on a non-legal basis. According to Article 28(3) of the Model Law, the "arbitral tribunal shall decide *ex aequo et bono* or as *amiable compositeur*", but "only if the parties have expressly authorized it to do so".

Arbitrators deciding *ex aequo et bono* or as *amiables compositeurs* should decide according to what is "fair" and "in good conscience" under the circumstances.[598] What exactly this means is not clear. Some believe that arbitrators should apply some sort of substantive law and in cases in which the strict application of law leads to unjust outcomes should adjust the outcome according to fairness.[599] More often, however, a decision *ex aequo et bono* is interpreted to mean that arbitrators should decide unrestrained by any legal basis.[600] The decision is imputed to an "extra-legal realm".[601] Arbitrators are allowed to ignore any substantial law (but not the contract) and decide solely based on fairness and common-sense principles.[602] As an outer limit to such discretion, mandatory rules are sometimes invoked[603]; other times, no such limits are imposed.[604] However, in order to ensure

---

598 *Trakman*, Chi. J. Int'l L. 2008, 621, 623.
599 *Rubino-Sammartano*, J. Int'l Arb. 1992, 5, 12; *Hußlein-Stich*, Das UNCITRAL-Modellgesetz, 1990, p. 149.
600 *Gaillard/Savage*, International Arbitration, 1999, p. 837; *Born*, International Commercial Arbitration, ed. 2 2014, p. 2770.
601 *Trakman*, Chi. J. Int'l L. 2008, 621, 627. Sometimes a distinction is made between *ex aequo et bono* and *amiables compositeurs* is made, with one method freeing arbitrators from the constraints of any law and the other enabling them to adjust aspects of an applicable law. However, even among scholars that differentiate, there is no consensus on which nomenclature should be equated with which method. *Rubino-Sammartano*, J. Int'l Arb. 1992, 5, attributing more leeway to arbitrators acting as amiables compositeurs.
602 *Kröll et al.*, Comparative International Commercial Arbitration, 2003, p. 470.
603 Ibid.
604 The role of mandatory rules in international commercial arbitration has already been discussed above, pp. 143 et seqq.. If the parties ask the arbitrators to decide *ex aequo et bono*, it is unclear which mandatory rules the arbitrators would have to apply.

the enforceability of the award, the arbitrators should ensure that it does not violate the public policy of potential enforcement states.

In virtually all national arbitration statutes, the option of having the arbitrator decide in such a manner is tied to an agreement by the parties in this regard, as suggested by the Model Law. One exception is Ecuador, where the default is an arbitral award based on the tribunal's sense of fairness, and arbitrators are to apply a legal system only if so directed.[605]

2. Application of Non-State Law

If the decision is not to be made *ex aequo et bono* or as *amiables compositeurs*, the arbitrators must base the decision on law. In such cases, which are the most typical, arbitrators act in a manner similar to that of judges. However, the latter apply the legal system of their forum, and apply it strictly. In contrast, Article 28(1) of the UNCITRAL Model Law sets forth that arbitrators "shall decide the dispute in accordance with such **rules of law** as are chosen by the parties as applicable to the substance of the dispute" [emphasis added]. Use of the term "rules of law", in contrast to simply "law" or "system of law", is interpreted as going beyond established and autonomous systems of law to include legal rules that do not emanate from domestic legal systems.[606] As has been laid out above in connection with qualifying the CISG as transnational law, this enables parties to choose the *lex mercatoria* or general principles of law,[607] or more specifically such sets of rules such as the UNIDROIT Principles or the CISG.

Currently, this is not possible in national court proceedings. If a contract in which parties have chosen non-State law as applicable were to come before a national court in the European Union, for example, such a choice of law clause would be regarded as invalid. Article 3(1) of the Rome I Regulation only allows for the choice of a "law", which replaced a more liberal draft that would have enabled parties to choose certain well-developed bodies of non-State law such as the UNIDROIT Principles.[608] A court confronted with such a choice of law clause would therefore treat the

---

605 See *supra*, pp. 104 et seq.
606 See only *Blackaby et al.*, International Commercial Arbitration, ed. 6 2015, p. 215.
607 See *supra*, pp. 159 et seq.
608 See *supra*, p. 175.

contract as if no choice had been made, apply the provisions of the Rome I Regulation and find the applicable law through a conflict of laws analysis. An arbitral tribunal, untethered from such restrictive private international law, would be able to apply the rules as desired by the parties.

3. Influence of Trade Usages

Finally, arbitrators "shall take into account the usages of the trade applicable to the transaction" in all cases, whether they are deciding on the basis of law or not, as Article 28(4) of the UNICTRAL Model Law stipulates. This was already set forth in Art. VII(1) of the European Treaty of 1961. Most institutional rules contain such a provision, as well.[609] Trade usages have been described as follows:

> *A usage grows up because everybody in the market, knowing the usages, tacitly assumes that the contract he is making, whether as a buyer or seller, is subject to the usage. The binding character of a usage is born of innumerable individual transactions entered into by the parties to them in the knowledge that certain usages are in practice habitually followed in that market. For a practice to amount to a recognized usage, it must be certain, in the sense that it is so well known in the market in which it is alleged to exist, that those who conduct business in the market contract with the usage as an implied term; and it must be reasonable.*[610]

The relevance of trade usages to international commercial arbitration is due to its roots as medieval merchant courts that settled disputes not according to the local monarch's laws, but according to what the merchants expected given the typical usages of their trade.[611]

Article 28 of the Model Law stipulates that arbitrators should take trade usages into account "in all cases". This obligation is set out in the last paragraph of the provision and makes no distinction between decisions based on law and decisions *ex aequo et bono* or as *amiables compositeurs*.

---

609 A notable exception is the English Arbitration Act of 1996, which makes no reference to trade usages, because the drafters considered developed legal systems to take such usages into account in fashioning and applying rules of commercial law, *Born*, International Commercial Arbitration, ed. 2 2014, p. 2664.

610 Ibid., p. 2665, quoting K. Lewison, The Interpretation of Contracts 311 (5th ed. 2011) (quoting Cunliffe-Owen v. Teather & Greenwood [1967] 1 WLR 1421 (Ch.D.)).

611 *Macassey*, ABA J. 1938, 518, 519.

A. Binding Effect of Substantive Law Dependent on Party Choice

It therefore appears that trade usages take precedence in both cases. This would mean that even if a national legal system is applicable, trade usages that deviate from the substantive trade law would override the legal provisions.[612] This interpretation has been followed by arbitral tribunals in a few cases.[613] However, most commentators believe that if a legal system is applicable because of a choice of law by the parties or due to a lack of agreement regarding a non-legal decision, that the law takes precedence over trade usages.[614] Trade usages merely aid in interpreting statements and actions taken by the parties and ambiguous terms in the contract.[615] Article 28(4) of the Model Law would have to be interpreted to only reference decisions *ex aequo et bono* or as *amiables compositeur*, set out in Article 28(3). Only if the arbitrator is not bound by law, rather is tasked with deciding according to his own notions of fairness, is he bound by trade usages above all else.[616]

III. Decisions Based on Law

Although these arbitration-specific modes of decision exist, the default in almost all existing arbitration statutes and institutional rules today is a decision based on law. In international arbitration, a decision based on law can be a decision based on domestic law, non-State law or general principles of law and is the opposite of a decision *ex aequo et bono*. The duty of arbitrators to decide on the basis of law results from the party mandate. The parties can express their preference for a decision based on law by choosing a law to govern their dispute, by expressly asking for a decision based on law or by selecting institutional rules in which a decision based on law is the default and making no choice to the contrary. If the parties have not followed any of these paths the arbitrators must apply the arbitration statute of the seat of arbitration. Most arbitration

---

612 *Gaillard/Savage*, International Arbitration, 1999, p. 844.
613 See ibid., p. 844, fn. 323 for examples.
614 *Born*, International Commercial Arbitration, ed. 2 2014, p. 2666 (referencing Final Award in ICC Case No. 13954, XXXV Y. B. Comm. Arb. 218, 234 (2010)); *Hußlein-Stich*, Das UNCITRAL-Modellgesetz, 1990, p. 154.
615 *Gaillard/Savage*, International Arbitration, 1999, p. 845.
616 Regarding the identical provision in German law, Sec 1051 (3) and (4) of the ZPO, Musielak/Voit/*Voit*, ed. 15 2018, ZPO § 1051 para. 8, referencing the explanatory memorandum given by the legislature.

statutes state that unless the parties expressly agree on a decision *ex aequo et bono* the arbitral award has to be based on law.

A decision based on law is made within a certain framework of rules. Even if no law was chosen and the arbitrators must select the applicable law, it is no less important that the arbitrators adhere to the law they end up determining to be applicable. In contrast to a decision *ex aequo et bono*, a law-based decision does not rest on the arbitrators' notions of fairness and morality. Sets of rules such as bodies of law are expected to follow a certain logic, i.e. one rule that may disadvantage one party is counterbalanced by another rule that goes in the other direction. As such, a decision based on a law, even on a law that the parties have not chosen, is more predictable and objective and less prone to subjective errors of judgement than a decision that rests entirely on the personal sense of fairness of an arbitrator or tribunal.

In order to give effect to the underlying system, however, the rules must be applied exactly and entirely. If arbitrators were free to disregard single provisions or entire portions of a law chosen by the parties or determined to be applicable by the arbitrators themselves the decision would no longer be based on that law. Rather, it would be one based on the arbitrators' own sense of fairness. There would be no discernable difference from a decision *ex aequo et bono* of which some parts are inspired by a law. Thus, a decision based on law must be faithful to the law that has been determined to be applicable to the dispute.

B. *Reviewability*

As discussed above in the context of private international law, the review of arbitral awards is extremely limited.[617] The application of substantive law is subject to almost no review. The systems of the UNCITRAL Model Law regarding annulment of awards and the New York Convention regarding refusal of recognition and enforcement of foreign arbitration awards are nearly identical. In principle, parties are bound by the contents of the award resulting from the arbitration proceedings. They may only attack the award on the basis that, broadly speaking, the process leading up to it was in some way flawed, or that the award is not compatible with the public policy of the arbitral seat or of a potential enforcement State. Below

---

617 See *supra*, pp. 165 et seqq.

the public policy threshold, the actual decision on the merits is final and binding and is not subject to review. A *révision au fond* is prohibited.

Thus, if the arbitrators were mandated to deliver a decision based on law but in deciding the case strayed from the law determined to be applicable, the application of substantive law in the resulting award can only be reviewed under two aspects. The first aspect is whether the award violated the substantive public policy of the arbitral seat or an enforcement State (**I.**). Second, if the liberties taken by the arbitrators in applying the law are too great, the decision can no longer be considered as based on law but may in actuality qualify as a decision *ex aequo et bono* (**II.**).

I. Reviewability of Substantive Law Application

Application of substantive law by an arbitral tribunal is generally not reviewable due to the prohibition of *révision au fond*. The only exception is a violation of substantive public policy. Another potential exception is a review of the merits to ensure the effectiveness of EU law, which ultimately has to be rejected.

1. Public Policy Violation

Only if the award violates the substantive public policy of the court's forum can the merits of the case be reviewed at all. This includes the application of mandatory rules of any legal system. The parties can ask that an award be set aside or its recognition and enforcement refused on the grounds of substantive law issues if the award violates public policy, either in the forum of the annulment court at the seat of arbitration (Article 34(b)(ii) of the Model Law), or in the forum of a potential enforcement court (Article V(2)(b) of the New York Convention). It is accepted in most jurisdictions that the award must be a violation of international public policy, not merely the internal public policy of the court's forum.[618] A misapplication of substantive law can thus only be penalized if it amounts to violation of international public policy.

The debate on what mandatory rules must be applied by international commercial arbitrators also finds its limits here. Courts apply mandatory rules of their forum or other legal systems that their private international

---

618 See fn. 494.

law deems relevant. As laid out above, Article 9 of the Rome I Regulation sets forth that courts must apply such rules when they are anchored in their forum legal system, and that they may apply them if they are rules of the State in which obligations from the contract in question are performed.[619] In international arbitration, the tribunal has no forum; the seat is no equivalent to a court's forum despite its undeniable significance.[620] The seat, chosen for its neutrality and lack of connection to the dispute, should not be able to impose its mandatory law on the merits of that dispute. Which other legal system's mandatory rules the arbitrators want to give effect to is up to them. If they fail to consider mandatory rules that the parties believed they should have observed, the parties can only ask for the annulment of the award on the basis that it violates public policy. Thus, in international arbitration, only the application of mandatory rules that reach the level of international public policy can be controlled. If the arbitrators apply, misapply or fail to apply any other rules, be they mandatory by some measure or not, this is beyond the scope of any potential court review.

This system pays tribute to the very nature of arbitration: parties are free to agree to settle their disputes outside of a national court system, but legal systems have the right to reject resulting awards that are incompatible with their basic notions. National courts asked to review an award can therefore annul it or refuse its enforcement on the grounds that the process, including the arbitration agreement itself and the constitution of the deciding tribunal, was defective, or because the award violates the public policy of their forum.

The contents of the decision itself are shielded from review to a large extent. The process must conform to the party agreement or some national standard, and the award cannot violate public policy, but below the public policy threshold, the tribunal's decision on the merits cannot be attacked.

2. *Effet Utile* of European Law

Although substantive law is not reviewable below the threshold of public policy, the laws of the EU may be able to overcome this obstacle. EU law is idiosyncratic in how it ensures its application. It can only have its desired effect if it is applied in the Member States. Of course, it can rise

---

619 See *supra*, pp. 152 et seq.
620 See *supra*, pp. 104 et seq.

to the level of *ordre public*. The ECJ has found that this is the case for EU competition law, which is regulated in Article 101 of the TFEU, in the *Eco Swiss* decision.[621] In *Mostaza Claro*, consumer protection law was qualified as *ordre public*, as well.[622] As long as EU law can be classified as public policy, a failure to apply it correctly or even at all can be dealt with within the existing international framework of recognition and enforcement.

However, it has been discussed that EU law may be reviewable below the threshold of public policy, as well.[623] This is owed to the principle of effectiveness, or *effet utile*, under which Member States have to ensure that claims based on EU law are not rendered impossible in practice or excessively difficult to enforce due to national procedural rules and remedies.[624] This principle has been introduced as a possible tool to ensure that when an arbitral award contains claims based on European law, that award can be reviewed in case errors are believed to have been made in the application of the law.[625] If a failure to apply EU law correctly or at all leads to an award that is still compatible with public policy and therefore enforceable, then this might be considered as making it impossible for the parties to enforce their EU law-based claims due to domestic procedural law, i.e. the arbitration statute and the New York Convention.

A parallel can be drawn to the Brussels Ia Regulation[626], which deals with the recognition and enforcement of court decisions within the EU and is not applicable to arbitral awards.[627] This Regulation has a standard regarding the review of the merits in judgements issued by courts in other Member States of the EU that is similar to the standard that the New

---

621 See *supra*, p. 139 et seq. and in particular fn. 495.
622 See *supra*, pp. 143 et seq.
623 See *Penades Fons*, AEDIP 2016, 249, 254 et seqq.
624 Opinion of Mr Advocate General Jääskinen in Donau Chemie (see fn. 500). The other important principle that ensures the enforcement of claims based on EU law is principle of equivalence, which sets forth that Member States must make the same procedural rules and remedies available for claims based on European law as they do for those based on domestic law. However, the New York Convention and domestic arbitration statutes do not treat awards differently depending on whether EU law is involved. Therefore, this principle cannot help enforce EU law in arbitration proceedings.
625 *Penades Fons*, AEDIP 2016, 249, 261 et seq.
626 See fn. 337.
627 *Penades Fons*, AEDIP 2016, 249, 262 et seq. See Art. 1(2)(d) of the Brussels I bis Regulation. In contrast to the Rome I Regulation, this is not a matter of debate.The New York Convention is the only international instrument applicable to the recognition and enforecement of foreign arbitral awards.

§ 4. Application of Substantive Provisions of the Cisg

York Convention has for foreign arbitral awards: court decisions can only be reviewed on the merits if they manifestly violate the public policy of the recognition and enforcement State.[628] *Effet utile* does not change this standard for court decisions – why then should it have an effect on the review of arbitral awards? It could be argued that, since arbitration tribunals do not take part in the relationship of mutual trust that Member States share, their awards need to be subjected to more scrutiny.[629] In general, courts in Member States are entrusted with the application of EU law, while the responsibility for review in international arbitration is shifted downstream, to the annulment and enforcement courts.[630] Arbitral awards are not subject to appeal and arbitral tribunals cannot request preliminary ruling from the ECJ.[631] Thus, it is feasible that the principle of effectiveness requires a more thorough review of foreign arbitral awards than of court decisions from other EU Member States.

However, this is a false equivalency: arbitral awards cannot be compared to court decisions from other Member States. Rather, they must be equated to court decisions from States outside of the EU. Even if the arbitral process has its seat in a Member State, the tribunal is still not an organ of that State, as has been demonstrated above.[632] The review of court decisions from outside of the EU is subject to the domestic law of each Member State, and this standard can vary. German law, for instance, stipulates that "foreign" court decisions – i.e. those from outside of the EU – can only be reviewed if they manifestly violate public policy. German law thus uses the same criterion as the Brussels Ia Regulation.[633] This standard remains unaffected by substantive EU law. International arbitration tribunals should not be reviewed more thoroughly than courts outside of the EU, seeing as they are just as likely to be required to apply EU law and just as likely to do so well – neither can make requests for preliminary rulings to the ECJ. There is no good reason to treat arbitral awards any differently in regard to the *effet utile* of EU law than court decisions from Non-Member States of the EU.

---

628 Art. 45(1)(a) of the Brussels Ia Regulation.
629 *Penades Fons*, AEDIP 2016, 249, 265.
630 Opinion of Advocate General *Wathelet* of 17 March 2016 in case C-567/14, ECLI:EU:C:2016:177 – Genentech, para. 60.
631 See *supra*, pp. 154 et seqq.
632 See *supra*, pp. 92 et seqq.
633 Sec. 328 (1) No. 4 of the ZPO.

II. Reviewability of Type of Decision

If arbitrators are tasked with making a decision based on law, then they must apply law. If they take too much liberty in doing so, to the extent that their decision can no longer be considered as being based on law, it must be seen as a decision *ex aequo et bono*. This can constitute a reason for setting an award aside or refusing its enforcement.[634]

1. Procedural Mistake

As opposed to a mere misapplication of substantive provisions, a decision that is not based on law could potentially be considered a violation of the arbitral procedure – a stance taken by several commentators[635] and courts.[636] Following Article V(1)(d) of the New York Convention and Article 34(2)(a)(ii) of the Model Law, a violation of the procedure is measured first by the party agreement, and by the arbitration law of the seat of arbitration if there is no party agreement on the issue. The obligation to make a decision based on law and not merely on notions of fairness can thus result from a choice of a particular law by the parties, and in the absence of such a choice, from an interpretation of other contractual clauses, or finally from the *lex loci arbitri*.

This requires that the mode of decision, i.e. based on law or *ex aequo et bono*, is a procedural matter to begin with. There is reason to doubt this because much like the decision regarding the applicable law – which has been identified as a substantive and not a procedural matter[637] – the decision whether or not to base a decision on law is one that indirectly affects the outcome of the case. Much as when parties choose a particular substantive law to govern their dispute, to request that arbitrators should not apply strict legal provisions, but rather base the decision on notions of fairness and morality, is an exercise of party autonomy.[638]

However, it is more convincing that an award based on notions of morality and fairness is the product of an entirely different type of process

---

634 Regarding the review of arbitration awards, see *supra*, pp. 163 et seq.
635 *Schlosser*, RIW 1982, 857, 866 et seq; Wolff/*Borris/Hennecke*, 2012, Art. V para. 338.
636 BGH, decision of 16 September 1985, III ZR 16/84, NJW 1986, 1436, 1437.
637 See *supra*, pp. ## et seq.
638 *Sandrock*, BB 2001, 2173.

§ 4. Application of Substantive Provisions of the Cisg

than one based on the application of laws. It is true that the mode of decision has an impact on the outcome of the case: whatever the arbitral tribunal would find to be the solution under the law it deems applicable to the merits of the dispute, it may well decide differently if given the option to follow only its notions of fairness. However, most procedural choices have some impact on the outcome of the case. An arbitrator may have decided the case differently if he had been appointed sole arbitrator instead of part of a tribunal, but while the composition of the tribunal has an impact on the outcome of the case, it is still certainly a procedural matter. Another example is rules on evidence: the final decision can turn on what type of evidence is allowed and to what extend and in what regard the tribunal takes it into account. Nevertheless, evidence is a procedural matter. Whether a decision is generally based on law or not is more comparable to such technical aspects than to the finer point of which out of several substantive laws will govern the dispute.

Following these arguments, the choice between a decision based on law and a decision *ex aequo et bono* is a procedural choice. Thus, if the parties have not made a discernable choice in this regard, the tribunal must look to the procedural law of the seat of arbitration, or risk annulment or a refusal of recognition of the award due to a procedural mistake – Article V(1)(d) of the New York Convention. In most arbitration statutes, a decision based on law is the default.[639] If the arbitrator, contrary to what the *lex arbitri* of the arbitral seat stipulates, acts as *amiable compositeur* despite not having the parties' permission to do so, this is a violation of the procedure set forth by the parties or of the *lex arbitri*. The award can be set aside pursuant to Article 34(2)(a)(ii) of the Model Law and refused recognition and enforcement according to Article V(1)(d) of the New York Convention.

Of course, a court review of an award in this regard has to be conservative. How can the court discern whether the tribunal strayed too far from the law as to have landed in *ex aequo et bono* territory without reviewing the tribunal's decision in depth? First of all, pursuant to Article V(1)(d) of the New York Convention and Article 34(2)(1)(iv) of the UNCITRAL Model Law, this is a claim that the parties have to raise, not a ground for annulment or refusal of enforcement that the court can take into consideration *sua sponte*. Unless one party invokes such a procedural mistake, this aspect is not reviewable to begin with. Further, one has to keep in mind that a decision can only be considered to have been made *ex aequo to bono*

---

639 See *supra*, pp. 102 et seqq.

if it is not based on law at all.⁶⁴⁰ Thus, the disregard for the law must be so egregious as to lack any basis in the law that is supposedly applicable according to the determination of the tribunal. Such a disregard for the law must be plausibly claimed by the parties, and the court should be able to verify it without a complete review of the decision on the merits, thus without violating the prohibition of a *révision au fond*.

2. Excess of Authority

A different aspect under which a decision *ex aequo et bono* can be reviewed by courts is that of an excess of authority under Article 34(2)(a)(iii) of the Model Law and Article V(1)(c) of the New York Convention, respectively. As explained before, an excess of authority means that the arbitrator has overstepped the boundaries set for him by the parties, while a mere violation of the *lex loci arbitri* does not suffice.⁶⁴¹ Thus, as long as the parties agree explicitly or implicitly that the tribunal should decide their dispute based on law, a decision *ex aequo et bono* constitutes a violation of the arbitration agreement itself. For example, if an arbitration agreement contains a choice of law clause, the parties are thereby excluding the possibility of the tribunal deciding on the basis of notions of fairness and morality. While a misapplication of the chosen law is not a violation of the choice of the law by the parties, the complete disregard of the chosen law is.

A reference to institutional rules also shapes the party mandate. Such rules typically require a party agreement for an *ex aequo et bono* decision, such as Article 21(3) of the ICC Arbitration Rules 2017. If the parties incorporate the rules into their agreement, they make the requirement part of their party mandate. In this case, a decision *ex aequo et bono* without an explicit mandate by the parties would also constitute a violation of the arbitration agreement. Only if the parties have not agreed on a law, have not incorporated institutional rules such as the ICC rules into their agreement and if there is no indication of an implicit agreement in favor of a decision based on law, a decision *ex aequo et bono* does not constitute an excess of authority.

---

640 See *supra*, pp. 183 et seqq.
641 See *supra*, pp. 196 et seq.

3. Public Policy

The one aspect under which the tribunal's decision on the merits of the dispute can be reviewed is to discern whether the award violates the public policy of the annulment State, as set forth in Article 34(2)(b)(ii) of the Model Law, or of the enforcement State, as stipulated in Article V(2)(b) of the New York Convention. A decision in which arbitrators fail to apply laws and instead decided *ex aequo et bono* without being mandated to do so by the parties could constitute a violation of public policy. Public policy can be divided into either procedural or substantive public policy.

A decision *ex aequo et bono* cannot lead to a violation of substantive public policy simply because the tribunal did not base its decision on law. As mentioned above, an award is subject to an annulment or refusal of enforcement only if its effect in the legal system of the annulment or enforcement State constitutes a violation of public policy.[642] It is feasible that the tribunal follows its notions of fairness and morality and ends up making an award that violates the public policy of the seat of arbitration, for example, because the solution it has deemed fair is incompatible with some basic tenet of substantive justice in that State. However, the problem then does not lie in the fact that the arbitrators did not base the award on any particular law, but that its effect violates one specific legal system. Thus, the mere fact that a tribunal decided *ex aequo et bono* instead of based on law cannot constitute a violation of substantive public policy.

It is possible that an unsolicited decision *ex aequo et bono* itself constitutes a violation of procedural public policy, however. A court may find that the domestic public policy of its forum requires a tribunal to always base its decisions on law unless mandated otherwise by the parties. It could then annul such an award upon request, even if the party does not raise a public policy violation.[643] In some States, such as Germany, the annulment of an award requires a violation of *international* public policy, as does the refusal of recognition and enforcement of an award under the New York Convention.[644] Not all legal systems require a party mandate for a decision *ex aequo et bono* – instead, it is the default for international arbitration proceedings in some States, with a decision based on law requiring a mandate.[645] However, these States are already the absolute exception, and their

---

642 See *supra*, p. 170.
643 See *supra*, p. 164.
644 See *supra*, p. 170.
645 See *supra*, p. 104.

numbers are dwindling. With Argentina changing its law in 2018, one of the more prominent members has left their ranks.[646] Thus, the rule that arbitrators may decide purely based on their notions of fairness and morality only if the parties have asked them to do so is a rule that almost all States share. It is also a matter of public policy, because it is tied to the very basic expectations of parties seeking justice. While arbitration does allow the parties to deviate from this basic expectation and ask for a decision based purely on the tribunal's understanding of fairness, this should only be the case if the parties have explicitly asked them to do so, specifically because the review of the resulting award is so limited. Otherwise, a decision *ex aequo et bono* constitutes a violation of the parties' wishes to an extent that it would be incompatible with international public policy.

III. Conclusion

The application of substantive law, including the substantive rules of the CISG, is only reviewable if the award violates public policy. This gives the arbitral tribunal some flexibility in applying the law. It does not, however, give the tribunal *carte blanche*: the decision must still be based on law. If the tribunal strays so far from the law that the decision no longer is based on the applicable substantive law, the decision must be considered as having been made *ex aequo et bono*, which may be a ground for annulment and for refusal of recognition and enforcement of the arbitral award. Such disregard for the law can constitute a violation of the arbitral procedure, an excess of authority or a violation of procedural public policy under Article 34(2)(a)(iv), (iii) and (b)(ii) of the Model Law and Article V(1)(d), (c) and (2)(b) of the New York Convention respectively.

C. Consequences for the Application of the CISG

If the CISG is applicable, either because the parties chose it as *lex causae* or in the absence of a party choice because the tribunal chose it, then the tribunal must apply it entirely and to the letter. The fact that arbitrators are not bound by Article 1(1) of the CISG does not absolve them from applying the substantive rules of the Convention once its application to a dispute has been determined.

---

646 See *supra*, fn. 323.

§ 4. Application of Substantive Provisions of the Cisg

If the tribunal does not apply the Convention despite a choice of law by the parties in its favor, or applies it in a manner that is so liberal that the award is effectively no longer based on the CISG, then the award may be annulled or its recognition and enforcement refused on the basis of an excess of authority on behalf of the tribunal, or due to a violation of procedure. If the tribunal does apply the CISG in accordance with the choice of law by the parties and does not exceed the limits of what can be considered a decision based on the law, then the application of the law cannot be reviewed under the threshold of substantive public policy. As such, the tribunal is free in its application of the law, as long the resulting award still can still be considered a decision based on the CISG. The perhaps more potent deterrence for arbitrators to not misapply the law is that such behavior may damage their reputation. However, no legal remedy exists for this, and such is the risk inherent to submitting one's dispute to binding private arbitration.

If the party agreement does not contain a mandate for a decision based on law, including through potentially incorporated institutional rules, the outcome depends on the arbitration statute of the reviewing court's forum. If the arbitration statute generally requires a mandate by the parties for a decision *ex aequo et bono*, a *de facto* lawless decision by the arbitrators constitutes a violation of procedure. It can also be considered a violation of public policy, even international public policy, seeing as the vast majority of States with arbitration statutes require an agreement by the parties in order for tribunal decisions *ex aequo et bono*.

Conclusion

In conclusion, Article 1(1) of the CISG is not binding on international commercial arbitrators. Arbitrators can apply the Convention even if the requirements of these provisions are not met and conversely are free to not apply it even if the requirements are met. They must honor a choice by the parties in favor of the CISG. This result rests on the following theses:
1. The rule of application of the CISG, i.e. Article 1(1)(a) and (b), constitutes a unilateral conflict of laws rule that effects the direct applicability of the Convention. It contains operative facts – the international sale of goods – and two alternatively applicable connecting factors – both parties having their seats of business in Contracting States (lit. a), or the rules of private international law leading to the law of a Contracting State (lit. b).
2. Article 1(1) of the CISG is not binding in international commercial arbitration because general private international law is not binding on international arbitrators. States have the power to make international private law binding on their own organs, and to make laws governing subjects to which they have a significant link. International arbitrators are neither inherently subject to the sovereignty of the State as domestic courts are, due to a lack of comparability, nor does the arbitral seat constitute a genuine territorial link to the State in which it is located. However, a rule of customary law grants that State the competence to regulate the arbitration procedure, including the competence to make arbitration-specific conflict of laws rules. These are broadly worded and grant arbitrators leeway in selecting the applicable substantive law.
3. The Rome I Regulation does not apply in international commercial arbitration. The drafters did not intend for it to govern arbitration proceedings. It would furthermore be ill-suited to do so, as its application would restrict party autonomy while burdening the process with ineffective protections of weaker parties and unsuitable rules on mandatory overriding rules and public policy.
4. Given the leeway granted to international commercial arbitrators, methods have been developed for determining the applicable law in arbitral practice. The application of private international law by arbitrators is not reviewable by annulment or enforcement courts. It is neither

Conclusion

    a matter of procedure, not of the arbitrator's mandate, nor of public policy.
5. Arbitrators that are mandated to base their decision on law by party agreement or statute must apply the law they determine to be applicable strictly. The application of the substantive law is not reviewable by the annulment or the enforcement courts under the threshold of a violation of substantive public policy. Only if the tribunal takes such liberties in applying the law that the decision is no longer based on law and qualifies instead as a decision *ex aequo et bono* can the award be annulled or refused enforcement due to an excess of authority by the tribunal, an infringement of procedural law or a violation of international public policy.

Bibliography

All links to websites contained in this thesis were last accessed on 1 November 2021.

Arnold, Stefan, Gründe und Grenzen der Parteiautonomie im Europäischen Kollisionsrecht, in: Arnold, Stefan (ed.), Grundfragen des Europäischen Kollisionsrechts, 2016, pp. 26 (cited Parteiautonomie)

Aust, Anthony, Modern Treaty Law and Practice, 3rd ed., Cambridge 2013

Babić, Davor, Rome I Regulation: binding authority for arbitral tribunals in the European Union?, Jour. P. I. L. 2017, pp. 71–90

Bajons, Ena-Marlis, Zur Nationalität internationaler Schiedssachen, in: Rechberger, Walter and Welser, Rudolf (ed.), Festschrift für Winfried Kralik zum 65. Geburtstag: Verfahrensrecht – Privatrecht, Wien 1986, pp. 3–35 (cited FS Kralik)

Bamberger, Karl Heinz et al. (Eds.), Beck'scher Online-Kommentar, 43rd ed. 2018 (cited BeckOK/*author*)

v. Bar, Christian, Typen des internationalen Einheitsrechts und das Internationale Privatrecht, in: Recht und Wirtschaft, Ringvorlesung im Fachbereich Rechtswissenschaften der Universität Osnabrück 1984/85, Köln, Berlin, Bonn, München 1984, pp. 19–36 (cited Typen des Einheitsrechts)

v. Bar, Christian/Mankowski, Peter, Internationales Privatrecht, 2nd ed., München 2003 (cited IPR I).

Basedow, Jürgen, The Communitarisation of Private International Law, RabelsZ 2009, pp. 455–460.

Basedow, Jürgen, Theorie der Rechtswahl oder Parteiautonomie als Grundlage des Internationalen Privatrechts, RabelsZ 2011, pp. 32–59

Batiffol, Henri, Aspects philosophiques du droit international privé, Paris 1956 (cited Aspects)

Benda, Ernst/Klein, Eckart/Klein, Oliver, Verfassungsprozessrecht, 3rd ed., Heidelberg et al. 2012

Berger, Klaus Peter, The Creeping Codification of the New Lex Mercatoria, 2 ed., Alphen an den Rijn 2010 (cited Creeping Codification)

Berger, Klaus Peter, The Lex Mercatoria Doctrine and the UNIDROIT Principles of International Commercial Contracts, Law & Pol'y Int'l Bus. 1996–1997, pp. 943–990

Beulker, Jette, Die Eingriffsnormenproblematik im internationalen Schiedsverfahren, Tübingen 2005 (cited Eingriffsnormenproblematik)

Bianca, Cesare Massimo/ Bonell, Michael Joachim (eds.), Commentary on the International Sales Law – The 1980 Vienna Sales Convention, Milan 1987, (cited Bianca/Bonell/*author*)

Bibliography

Blackaby, Nigel/ Partasides, Constantine/ Redfern, Alan/ Hunter, Martin, Redfern and Hunter on International Commercial Arbitration, 6th ed., New York 2015 (cited International Commercial Arbitration)

Bleckmann, Albert, Die völkerrechtlichen Grundlagen des internationalen Kollisionsrechts, Köln 1991 (cited Völkerrechtliche Grundlagen)

Born, Gary B., International Commercial Arbitration, 2nd ed., Alphen aan den Rijn 2014

Calavros, Constantin, Das UNCITRAL-Modellgesetz über die internationale Handelsschiedsgerichtsbarkeit, Bielefeld 1988 (cited Das UNCITRAL-Modellgesetz)

Cassese, Antonio, International Law, 2nd ed., Oxford 2005

Cohn, E. J., Commercial Arbitration and the Rules of Law: a Comparative Study, U. Toronto L.J. 1941, pp. 1–32

Colombi Ciacchi, Aurelia, Party autonomy as a fundamental right in the European Union, ERCL 2010, pp. 303–318

Crawford, James, Brownlie's Principles of Public International Law, 8th ed., Oxford 2012

Cremades, Bernardo/ Plehn, Steven, The New Lex Mercatoria and the Harmonization of the Laws of International Commercial Transactions, B.U. Int'l L. 1984, pp. 317–348

Cuniberti, Gilles, Three Theories of Lex Mercatoria, Colum. J. Transnat'l L. 2014, pp. 369–434

Czerwenka, Beate, Rechtsanwendungsprobleme im internationalen Kaufrecht, Berlin 1988 (cited Rechtsanwendungsprobleme)

Derains, Yves, Possible Conflict of Laws Rules and the Rules Applicable to the Substance of the Dispute, in: Sanders, Pieter (ed.), UNCITRAL's Project for a Model Law on International Commercial Arbitration, 1984, pp. 169–195

Donovan, Donald Francis/Greenawalt, Alexander K.A., Mitsubishi After Twenty Years: Mandatory Rules Before Courts and International Arbitrators, in: Mistelis, Loukas A./Lew, Julian D. (eds.), Pervasive Problems in International Arbitration, 2006, pp. 11–60 (cited Mandatory Rules)

Drobnig, Ulrich, Anwendungsnormen in Übereinkommen zur Vereinheitlichung des Privatrechts, in: Stoffel, Walter A./Volken, Paul (eds.), Conflits e harmonisation: Mélanges en l'honneur d' Alfred E. von Overbeck à l'occasion de son 65ème anniversaire, Fribourg 1990, pp. 15–30 (cited FS Overbeck)

Ferrari, Franco et al. (eds.), Internationales Vertragsrecht, 3rd ed., Munich 2018 (cited Internationales Vertragsrecht/*author*)

Fountoulakis, Christiana, The Parties' Choice of Neutral Law in International Sales Contracts, Eur. J. L. Reform 2005, pp. 303–329

Friedrich, Fabian (ed.), Das UNCITRAL-Modellgesetz über die internationale Handelsschlichtung: ein Kommentar, Maastricht 2006, (cited UNCITRAL-Modellgesetz/*author*)

Gaillard, Emmanuel, Legal Theory of International Arbitration, Leiden 2010

Gaillard, Emmanuel, Transcending National Legal Orders for International Arbitration, in: Berg, Jan van den (ed.), International Arbitration: The Coming of a New Age?, Alphen aan den Rijn 2013, pp. 371–377

Gaillard, Emmanuel/ Savage, John, Fouchard Gaillard Goldman on International Commercial Arbitration, The Hague, Boston 1999 (cited "International Arbitration")

Geimer, Reinhold, Internationales Zivilprozessrecht, 7th ed., Köln 2015

Goldman,, Les conflits de lois dans l'arbitrage international de droit privé, RdC 109, 1963-I, pp. 347–485

Gottwald, Peter, Die sachliche Kontrolle internationaler Schiedssprüche durch staatliche Gerichte, in: Habscheid, Walther and Schwab, Karl Heinz (ed.), Beiträge zum internationalen Verfahrensrecht und zur Schiedsgerichtsbarkeit: Festschrift für Heinrich Nagel zum 75. Geburtstag, 1987, pp. 54–69 (cited FS Nagel)

Grimm, Alexander, Applicability of the Rome I and II Regulations to International Arbitration, SchiedsVZ 2012, pp. 189–200

Gößling, Sebastian, Europäisches Kollisionsrecht und internationale Schiedsgerichts-barkeit, Tübingen 2019

Habscheid, Walther, Das neue Recht der Schiedsgerichtsbarkeit, JZ 1998, pp. 445–450

Hachem, Pascal, Applicability of the CISG – Articles 1 and 6, in: Schwenzer, Ingeborg (ed.), Current Issues in the CISG and Arbitration, Munich 2013

Hahn, Carl, Materialien zur Zivilprozeßordnung, 2nd ed., Aalen 1881 (cited Zivilprozeßordnung)

Handeyside, Hugh, The Lotus Principle in ICJ Jurisprudence: Was the Ship Ever Afloat?, Mich. J. Int'l L. 2007, pp. 71–93

Hayward, Benjamin, Conflict of Laws and Arbitral Discretion, Oxford 2017

Herdegen, Matthias, Völkerrecht, 17th ed., München 2018

v. Hoffmann, Bernd, Internationale Handelsschiedsgerichtsbarkeit: Die Bestimmung des maßgeblichen Rechts, Frankfurt a.M. 1970 (cited Internationale Handelsschiedsgerichtsbarkeit)

Honsell, Heinrich (ed.), Kommentar zum UN-Kaufrecht, 2nd ed., Heidelberg 2010, (cited Honsell/ *author*)

Horspool, Margot/ Humphreys, Matthew/ Wells-Greco, Michael, European Union Law, 10th ed., Oxford 2008

Hotz, Kaspar, Richterrecht zwischen methodischer Bindung und Beliebigkeit?: Plädoyer für eine offene Anerkennung richterlicher Rechtsmitgestaltungspflicht und eine verstärkte öffentliche Begleitung richterlicher Rechtsgewinnung, Zürich/St. Gallen 2008

Huber, Peter Michael/ Voßkuhle, Andreas (eds.), v. Mangoldt/Klein/Starck – Kommentar zum Grundgesetz: GG, Volume 2: Art. 20–82, Volume 3: Art. 83–146, 7th ed., 2018, (cited v. Mangoldt/Klein/Starck/*author*)

Bibliography

Hußlein-Stich, Gabriele, Das UNCITRAL-Modellgesetz über die internationale Handelsschiedsgerichtsbarkeit, Köln 1990 (cited Das UNCITRAL-Modellgesetz)

Iturralde, Victoria, Precedent as subject of interpretation, in: Bustamente, Thomas/ Bernal Pulido, Carlos (eds.), On the Philosophy of Precedent, Beijing 2012

Janssen, André/Spilker, Matthias, The Application of the CISG in the World of International Commercial Arbitration, RabelsZ 2013, pp. 131–157

Jayme, Erik, L'autonomie de la volonté des parties dans les contrats internationaux entre personnes privées, Annuaire de l'Institut de Droit International, 64-I (Session de Bâle 1991), Paris 1991, pp. 14–23

Junker, Abbo, Internationales Privatrecht, 2nd ed., München 2017

Kappus, Andreas, "Lex mercatoria" in Europa und Wiener UN-Kaufrechtskonvention 1980, Frankfurt a.M. 1990 (cited Lex mercatoria und CISG)

Kegel, Gerhard/ Schurig, Klaus, Internationales Privatrecht, 9th ed., München 2004

Kessedjan, Catherine, Determination and Application of Relevant National and International Law and Rules, in: Mistelis, Loukas A./Lew, Julian D. (eds.), Pervasive Problems in International Arbitration, 2006, pp. 71–88

Kleinheisterkamp, Jan, Eingriffsnormen und Schiedsgerichtsbarkeit – Ein praktischer Versuch, RabelsZ 2009, pp. 818–841

Kleinheisterkamp, Jan, Overriding Mandatory Rules in International Arbitration, Int'l & Comp.L.Q. 2018, pp. 903–930

Kondring, Jörg, Nichtstaatliches Recht als Vertragsstatut vor staatlichen Gerichten – oder: Privatkodifikation in der Abseitsfalle?, IPRax 2007, pp. 241–245

Kröll, Stefan/Lew, Julian D. M./Mistelis, Loukas A., Comparative International Commercial Arbitration, Alphen van den Rijn 2003

Kröll, Stefan/Mistelis, Loukas A./Perales Viscasillas, Pilar (eds.), UN Convention on the International Sales of Goods Commentary, 2nd ed., München 2018, (cited Kröll/Mistelis/Perales Viscasillas/*author*)

Kronke, Herbert et al. (eds.), Recognition and Enforcement of Foreign Arbitral Awards: A Global Commentary on the New York Convention, Alphen van den Rijn 2010, (cited Kronke/Naciemiento/Otto/*author*)

Kropholler, Jan, Der "Ausschluss" des internationales Privatrechts im einheitlichen Kaufgesetz, RabelsZ 1974, pp. 372–387

Kropholler, Jan, Internationales Einheitsrecht, Tübingen 1975

Kropholler, Jan, Internationales Privatrecht, 6th ed., München 2006

Lalive, Pierre, Problèmes relatifs à l'arbitrage international commercial, RdC 120, 1967-I, pp. 569–725

Lalive, Pierre, Transnational (or Truly International) Public Policy and International Arbitration, in: Sanders, Pieter (ed.), Comparative Arbitration Practice and Public Policy in Arbitration, 1987, pp. 258–318

Lando, Ole, The Lex Mercatoria in International Commercial Arbitration, Int'l & Comp.L.Q. 1985, pp. 747–768

Lando, Ole, The Principles of European Contract Law and the lex mercatoria, in: Basedow, Jürgen (ed.), The Hague, Zürich 2001 (cited FS Kurt Siehr)

Lehmann, Matthias, Savigny und die Rom I-Verordnung, in: Bernreuther, Jörn et al. (eds.), Festschrift für Ulrich Spellenberg, München 2010, pp. 245–260 (cited FS Spellenberg)

Leible, Stefan, Parteiautonomie im IPR – Allgemeines Anknüpfungsprinzip oder Verlegenheitslösung?, in: Mansel, Heinz et al. (eds.), Festschrift für Erik Jayme, 2004, pp. 485–503 (cited FS Jayme)

Lipstein, Kurt, Principles of the Conflict of Laws, National and International, The Hague, Boston, London 1981

Lohmann, Arnd, Parteiautonomie und UN-Kaufrecht, Tübingen 2005

Lord Collins of Mapesbury/Harris, Jonathan (eds.), Dicey, Morris and Collins on The Conflict of Laws, 15th ed., London 2012

Macassey, Lynden, International Commercial Arbitration, -its Origin, Development and Practice, ABA J. 1938, pp. 518–524, 581–582.

Magnus, Ulrich/ Mankowski, Peter, Joint Response to the Green Paper on the Conversion of the Rome Convention of 1980 on the Law Applicable to Contractual Obligations into a Community Instrument and Its Modernisation COM(2002) 654 final, 2002 (cited Joint Response to the Green Paper)

Mankowski, Peter, Interessenpolitik und europäisches Kollisionsrecht, Baden-Baden 2011

Mankowski, Peter, Rom I-VO und Schiedsverfahren, RIW 2011, pp. 30–44

Mann, F.A., The doctrine of international jurisdiction revisited after twenty years, RdC 186, 1984, pp. 9–116

Mann, F.A., Lex Facit Arbitrum, in: Sanders, Pieter (ed.), International Arbitration. Liber Amicorum for Martin Domke, The Hague 1967; reprinted in Arbitration International 1986, pp. 241–261 (cited␣Lex Facit Arbitrum)

Mäsch, Gerald, Rechtswahlfreiheit und Verbraucherschutz, Berlin 1993

Maultzsch, Felix, Die Rechtsnatur des Art. 1 Abs. 1 lit. b CISG zwischen internationaler Abgrenzungsnorm und interner Verteilungsnorm, in: Büchler, Andrea/ Müller-Chen, Markus (eds.), Festschrift für Ingeborg Schwenzer zum 60. Geburtstag, 2011, pp. 1213–1227 (cited FS Schwenzer)

Mayer, Pierre, Effect of International Public Policy in International Arbitration, in: Mistelis, Loukas A./Lew, Julian D. (eds.), Pervasive Problems in International Arbitration, 2006, pp. 61–69 (cited International Public Policy)

Mayer, Pierre, Mandatory Rules of Law in International Arbitration, Arb. Int. 1986, pp. 274–293

McGuire, Mary-Rose, Grenzen der Rechtswahlfreiheit im Schiedsverfahrensrecht? Über das Verhältnis zwischen der Rom-I-VO und § 1051 ZPO, SchiedsVZ 2011, pp. 257–267

Meyer-Sparenberg, Wolfgang, Staatsvertragliche Kollisionsnormen, Berlin 1990

Mills, Alex, The Confluence of Public and Private International Law, Oxford 2009 (cited Confluence)

Mistelis, Loukas A., CISG and Arbitration, in: Janssen, André/Meyer, Olaf (eds.), CISG Methodology, 2009, pp. 375–395

Mistelis, Loukas A., The UNIDROIT Principles Applied as Most Appropriate Rules of Law in a Swedish Arbitral Award, Unif. L. Rev. 2003, pp. 631–640

MüKo-BGB/*author*, Münchener Kommentar zum BGB, Schuldrecht Besonderer Teil I, §§ 433–534, Finanzierungsleasing, CISG, 8th ed., 2019; Internationales Privatrecht I, Europäisches Kollisionsrecht, Einführungsgesetz zum Bürgerlichen Gesetzbuche (Art. 1–24), 7th ed., 2018

MüKo-HGB/*author*, Münchener Kommentar zum HGB, 4th ed., Munich 2018

MüKo-ZPO/*author*, Münchener Kommentar zur ZPO, Zivilprozessordnung, 5th ed., Munich 2017

Nacimiento, Patricia/ Kröll, Stefan/ Böckstiegel, Karl-Heinz (eds.), Arbitration in Germany: The Model Law in Practice, 2nd ed., Alphen an den Rijn 2015 (cited Nacimiento/Kröll/Böckstiegel/*author*)

Nadelmann, Kurt H., The Uniform Law on the International Sale of Goods: A Conflict of Laws Imbroglio, Yale L.J. 1964, pp. 449–464

Neumayer, Karl H., Anwendung des UN-Abkommens über den internationalen Warenkauf, RIW 1994, pp. 99–109

Nueber, Michael, Nochmals: Schiedsgerichtsbarkeit ist vom Anwendungsbereich der Rom I-VO nicht erfasst, SchiedsVZ 2014, pp. 186–190

Oertmann, Paul, Schiedsrichter und staatliches Recht, Zeitschrift für deutschen Zivilprozess und das Verfahren in Angelegenheiten der freiwilligen Gerichtsbarkeit, 1918, pp. 105–149

Paulsson, Jan, Arbitration in Three Dimensions, LSE Law, Society and Economy Working Papers 2/2010, pp.

Paulsson, Jan, Arbitration Unbound: Award Detached from the Law of its Country of Origin, Int'l & Comp.L.Q. 1981, pp. 358–387

Paulsson, Jan, The Idea of Arbitration, Oxford 2013

Penades Fons, Manuel Alejandro, El effet utile del Derecho de la Unión Europea y la prohibición de revision au fond en el arbitraje internacional, AEDIP 2016, pp. 249–278

Petrochilos, Georgios, Arbitration Conflict-of-Laws Rules and the 1989 International Sales Convention, RHDI 1999, pp. 191–218

Petrochilos, Georgios, Procedural Law in International Arbitration, Oxford 2004 (cited Procedural Law)

Petsche, Markus, The Application of Transational Law (Lex Mercatoria) by Domestic Courts, Jour. P. I. L. 2014, pp. 489–515

Piers, Maud, Consumer Arbitration in the EU: A Forced Marriage with Incompatible Expectations, J.I.D.S. 2011, pp. 209–230

Piltz, Burghard, Internationales Kaufrecht, 2nd ed., München 2008

Pünder, Hermann, Das Einheitliche UN-Kaufrecht – Anwendung kraft kollisionsrechtlicher Verweisung nach Art. 1 Abs. 1 lit. b UN-Kaufrecht, RIW 1990, pp. 869–873

Randelzhofer, Albrecht, Staatsgewalt und Souveränität, in: Isensee, Josef and Kirchhof, Paul (ed.), Handbuch des Staatsrechts, 2004, pp. 143–161 (cited HBdSR)

Rauscher, Thomas, Internationales Privatrecht, 5th ed., München 2017

Reich, Norbert, A 'Trojan Horse' in the Access to Justice – Party Autonomy and Consumer Arbitration in conflict in the ADR-Directive 2013/11/EU?, ERCL 2014, pp. 258–280

Reinhardt, Michael, Konsistente Jurisdiktion: Grundlegung einer verfassungsrechtlichen Theorie der rechtsgestaltenden Rechtsprechung, Tübingen 1997

Renner, Moritz, Zwingendes transnationales Recht, Baden-Baden 2010

Roth, Wulf-Henning, Zur Wählbarkeit nichtstaatlichen Rechts, in: Mansel, Heinz, et al. (eds.), Festschrift für Erik Jayme, 2004, (cited FS Jayme)

Rubino-Sammartano, Mauro, Amiable Compositeur (Joint Mandate to Settle) and Ex Bono et Aequo, J. Int'l Arb. 1992, pp. 5–16

Rubino-Sammartano, Mauro, International and Foreign Arbitration, J. Int'l Arb. 1988, pp. 85–96

Rubino-Sammartano, Mauro, International Arbitration – Law and Practice, 3rd ed., The Hague, Boston 2014 (cited International Arbitration)

Ryngaert, Cedric, Jurisdiction in International Law, 2nd ed., Oxford 2015 (cited Jurisdiction)

Sabater, Aníbal, When Arbitration Begins Without a Seat, J. Int'l Arb. 2010, pp. 443–472

Sachs, Klaus/ Niedermaier, Tilman, Overriding Mandatory Provisions Before Arbitral Tribunals – Some Observations, in: (ed.), Liber Amicorum Bernd von Hoffmann, 2012, pp. 1051–1065 (cited FS Hoffmann)

Sachs, Michael (ed.), Grundgesetz Kommentar, 8th ed., München 2018, (cited Sachs/ author)

Saenger, Ingo (ed.), Zivilprozessordnung, 7th ed., Baden-Baden 2017, (cited Saenger/ author)

Samuel, Adam, Jurisdictional Problems in International Commercial Arbitration. A Study of Belgian, Dutch, English, French, Swedish, USA and West German Law, Zürich 1989 (cited Jurisdictional Problems)

Sandrock, Otto, "Gewöhnliche" Fehler in Schiedssprüchen: Wann können sie zur Aufhebung des Schiedsspruches führen?, BB 2001, pp. 2173–2180

Sandrock, Otto, Neue Lehren zur internationalen Schiedsgerichtsbarkeit und das klassische Internationale Privat- und Prozessrecht, in: *Hohloch, Gerhard* et al. (eds.), Festschrift für Hans Stoll zum 75. Geburtstag, Heidelberg 2001, pp. 661–690 (cited FS Stoll)

Sandrock, Otto, Zügigkeit und Leichtigkeit versus Gründlichkeit, JZ 1986, pp. 370–378

Schack, Haimo, Sonderkollisionsrecht für private Schiedsgerichte?, in: (ed.), Festschrift für Rolf A. Schütze zum 80. Geburtstag, 2015, pp. 511–518 (cited FS Schütze)

Schilf, Sven, Römische IPR-Verordnungen – kein Korsett für internationale Schiedsgerichte, RIW 2013, pp. 678–692

Schlechtriem, Peter, Internationales UN-Kaufrecht, 4th ed., Tübingen 2007

Schlechtriem, Peter/Schroeter, Ulrich G., Internationales UN-Kaufrecht, 6th ed., Tübingen 2016

Schlosser, Peter, Das Recht der internationalen privaten Schiedsgerichtsbarkeit, 2nd ed., Tübingen 1989 (cited Schiedsgerichtsbarkeit)

Schroeder, Hand-Patrick, Die lex mercatoria arbitralis – Strukturelle Transnationalität und transnationale Rechtsstrukturen im Recht der internationalen Schiedsgerichtsbarkeit, Frankfurt a.M, München 2007 (cited Die lex mercatoria arbitralis)

Schroeter, Ulrich, The CISG's Final Provisions, in: Andersen, Camilla; Schroeter, Ulrich (eds.), Sharing International Commercial Law across National Boundaries – Festschrift for Albert H Kritzer on the Occasion of his Eightieth Birthday, London 2008, pp. 425–455 (cited FS Kritzer)

Schultz, Thomas, The Concept of Law in Transnational Arbitral Legal Orders and some of its Consequences, J.I.D.S. 2011, pp. 59–85

Schurig, Klaus, Kollisionsnorm und Sachrecht, Berlin 1981

Schütze, Rolf A., Die Bestimmung des anwendbaren Rechts im Schiedsverfahren und die Feststellung seines Inhalts in: Briner, Robert et al. (eds.), Law of International Business and Dispute Settlement in the 21st Century – Liber Amicorum Karl-Heinz Böckstiegel, pp. 715–725 (cited FS Böckstiegel)

Schütze, Rolf A., Schiedsgericht und Schiedsverfahren, 6th ed., München 2016

Schwab, Karl-Heinz/ Walter, Gerhard, Schiedsgerichtsbarkeit, 7th ed., München 2005

Schwenzer, Ingeborg (ed.), Schlechtriem & Schwenzer: Commentary on the UN Convention on the International Sale of Goods (CISG), 4th ed., Munich, New York 2016 (cited Schlechtriem/Schwenzer/*author*)

Schwenzer, Ingeborg/ Schroeter, Ulrich (eds.), Schlechtriem/Schwenzer/Schroeter: Kommentar zum Einheitlichen UN-Kaufrecht – CISG, 7th ed., Basel and Munich 2019, (cited Schlechtriem/ Schwenzer/Schroeter/*author*)

Schwenzer, Ingeborg/ Hachem, Pascal, The CISG – Successes and Pitfalls, Am. J. Comp. L. 2009, pp. 457–478

Siehr, Kurt, Der Internationale Anwendungsbereich des UN-Kaufrechts, RabelsZ 1988, pp. 587–616

Siehr, Kurt, „False Conflicts", „lois d'application immédiate" und andere „Neuentdeckungen" im IPR, in: Basedow, Jürgen, et al. (ed.), Festschrift für Ulrich Drobning zum siebzigsten Geburtstag, 1998, pp. 443–454 (cited FS Drobning)

Solomon, Dennis, Die Verbindlichkeit von Schiedssprüchen in der internationalen privaten Schiedsgerichtsbarkeit, Köln 2007 (cited Verbindlichkeit von Schiedssprüchen)

Sono, Kazuaki, The Vienna Sales Convention: History and Perspective, in: Sarcevic, Petar/Volken, Paul (eds.), International Sale of Goods: Dubrovnik Lectures, 1986, pp. 1–17

Spickhoff, Andreas, Internationales Handelsrecht vor Schiedsgerichten und staatlichen Gerichten, RabelsZ 1992, pp. 116–140

Starck, Christian, Der Gesetzesbegriff des Grundgesetzes, Baden-Baden 1970 (cited Gesetzesbegriff)

Staudinger-BGB/*author*, Kommentar zum Bügerlichen Gesetzbuch mit Einführungsgesetz und Nebengesetzen, Wiener UN-Kaufrecht (CISG), 2018; Einleitung zur Rom I-VO, Art 1–10 Rom I-VO, 2016; Einleitung zum IPR, 2012

Stein Friedrich/Jonas Martin (eds.), Kommentar zur Zivilprozessordnung, Volume 10: §§ 1023–1051, 23rd ed., Tübingen 2014 (cited Stein/Jonas/*author*)

The Max Planck Encyclopedia of Public International Law, Wolfrum, Rüdiger (ed.), The Max Planck Encyclopedia of Public International Law, Oxford 2012 (cited author, title of entry in The Max Planck Encyclopedia of Public International Law)

Thirlway, Hugh, Sources of International Law, in: Evans, Malcolm (*ed.*), International Law, 2003, pp. 117–144

Trakman, Leon, Ex Aequo et Bono: Demystifying an Ancient Concept, Chi. J. Int'l L. 2008, pp. 621–642

Trautmann, Clemens, Ermittlung ausländischen Rechts, in: Jürgen, Basedow et al. (eds.), Handwörterbuch des Europäischen Privatrechts, Volume I, Tübingen 2009

Ungerer, Johannes, Das europäische IPR auf dem Weg zum Einheitsrecht – Ausgewählte Fragen und Probleme, BTWR 2015, pp. 5–26

Vékás, Lajos, Zum persönlichen und räumlichen Anwendungsbereich des UN-Einheitskaufrechts, IPRax 1987, pp. 342–346

Vorwerk, Volkert/ Wolf, Christian (eds.), Beck'scher Online-Kommentar Zivilprozessordnung, 30 ed., 2018, (cited BeckOK ZPO/author)

Voßkuhle, Andreas, Rechtsschutz gegen den Richter: zur Integration der Dritten Gewalt in das verfassungsrechtliche Kontrollsystem vor dem Hintergrund des Art. 19 Abs. 4 GG, München 1993 (cited Rechtsschutz gegen den Richter)

Waincymer, Jeff, International Commercial Arbitration and the Application of Mandatory Rules of Law, Asian Int'l Arb. J. 2009, pp. 1–45

Weller, Marc-Phillipe, Anknüpfungsprinzipien im Europäischen Kollisionsrecht: Abschied von der "klassischen" IPR-Dogmatik?, IPRax 2011, pp. 429–437

Winship, Peter, Private International Law and the U.N. Sales Convention, Cornell Int'l L.J. 1988, pp. 487–533

Wolff, Reinmar (ed.), New York Convention – Commentary, München 2012, (cited Wolff/*author*)

Wolff, Reinmar (ed.), New York Convention on the Recognition and Enforcement of Foreign Arbitral Awards of 10 June 1958 – Commentary, München 2012, (cited Wolff/*author*)

Yüksel, Burcu, The Relevance of the Rome I Regulation to International Commercial Arbitration in the European Union, Jour. P. I. L. 2011, pp. 149–178

Ziegler, Karl-Heinz, Arbiter, arbitrator und amicabilis compositor, Savigny-Zeitschrift 1967, pp. 239–276

Bibliography

Zweigert, Konrad/ Drobning, Ulrich, Einheitliches Kaufgesetz und internationales Privatrecht, RabelsZ 1965, pp. 146–165